NIETZSCHE and OTHER BUDDHAS

WORLD PHILOSOPHIES

Bret W. Davis, D. A. Masolo, and Alejandro Vallega, editors

NIETZSCHE AND OTHER BUDDHAS

Philosophy after Comparative Philosophy

Jason M. Wirth

INDIANA UNIVERSITY PRESS

This book is a publication of

Indiana University Press
Office of Scholarly Publishing
Herman B Wells Library 350
1320 East 10th Street
Bloomington, Indiana 47405 USA

iupress.indiana.edu

© 2019 by Jason M. Wirth

All rights reserved

No part of this book may be reproduced or utilized in any form or by any means, electronic or mechanical, including photocopying and recording, or by any information storage and retrieval system, without permission in writing from the publisher. The paper used in this publication meets the minimum requirements of the American National Standard for Information Sciences—Permanence of Paper for Printed Library Materials, ANSI Z39.48-1992.

Manufactured in the United States of America

Cataloging information is available from the Library of Congress.

ISBN 978-0-253-03970-5 (hdbk.)
ISBN 978-0-253-03971-2 (pbk.)
ISBN 978-0-253-03972-9 (web PDF)

1 2 3 4 5   24 23 22 21 20 19

For Elizabeth Myōen Sikes,
Impish Bodhisattva

CONTENTS

Acknowledgments ix
List of Abbreviations xi
Introduction: Philosophy after Comparative Philosophy xv

1 Thinking about Nietzsche and Zen   1
2 Strange Saints: Schopenhauer, Nietzsche, Hakuin   13
3 Convalescence: Nietzsche, James, Hakuin   35
4 Nietzsche in the Pure Land: Nietzsche, Shinran, Tanabe   55
5 Planomenal Nourishment: Nietzsche, Deleuze, Dōgen   75
   Concluding Thoughts: Pure Experience and Philosophy after Comparative Philosophy   100

Bibliography 113
Index 127

ACKNOWLEDGMENTS

THIS BOOK IS BORN OF YEARS OF BOTH Sōtō Zen practice and valuable philosophical engagement with good books and, more important, my colleagues and students. I have learned more than I can calculate or thank. I would at least like to extend my wholehearted gratitude to my Sōtō Zen teacher, Kōshō Itagaki, abbot of the Eishoji Zen training and practice facility in south Seattle; to my brother Nathan and his amazing artwork; to my beloved Dharma sisters and brothers of CoZen, especially Brian Shūdō Schroeder, Bret Kanpū Davis, and Erin Jien McCarthy; to my companions at PACT (Pacific Association for the Continental Tradition), especially Gerard Kuperus, Marjolein Oele, Tim Freeman, Chris Lauer, Josh Hayes, Jason Winfree, and Brian Treanor; to my cherished interlocutors in Sweden, Marcia Sá Cavalcante Schuback and Hans Ruin; to my many companions at the CCPC (Comparative and Continental Philosophy Circle), especially David Jones and Michael Schwartz, with whom I have enjoyed spirited discussions regarding the materials and insights in this book for over two decades; to Graham Parkes whose pioneering work on both Nietzsche and comparative thinking is a sine qua non; to the poet, philosopher, and activist Gary Snyder who inadvertently inspired some of these thoughts; to Don Castro and Mark Unno, great teachers in word and deed of the Pure Land; to Sean McGrath of Memorial University in Newfoundland who pushes me hard and compassionately on these issues; and to the many members of the Seattle University EcoSangha, all of whom inspire me with the depth of their practice. Most significantly, I would like to express my gratitude to Elizabeth Myōen Sikes, who exemplifies the ordinary profundity of the everyday in all that she does.

May all beings flourish.

A very different version of some parts of the fourth chapter appeared as "Death and Resurrection as the Eternal Return of the Pure Land: Tanabe Hajime's Metanoetic Reading of Nietzsche," in *The Past's Presence: Essays on the Historicity of Philosophical Thought* (Södertörn Philosophical Studies 3), edited by Marcia Sá Cavalcante Schuback and Hans Ruin, 185–201 (Stockholm, Sweden: Södertörns Högskola, 2006).

Partial material from the fifth chapter appeared in a different form as "When Washing Rice, Know that the Water Is Your Own Life: An Essay on Dōgen in the Age of Fast Food," in *Ontologies of Nature: Continental Perspectives and Environmental Reorientations*, edited by Gerard Kuperus and Marjolein Oele, 235–244 (Cham, Switzerland: Springer International, 2017).

LIST OF ABBREVIATIONS

BHL   Hermann Oldenberg, *Buddha: His Life, His Doctrine, His Order*, trans. William Hoey (London: Williams and Norgate, 1882).

BM   Arthur Schopenhauer, "On the Basis of Morals," *The Two Fundamental Problems of Ethics*, trans. David E. Cartwright and Edward E. Erdmann (Oxford: Oxford University Press, 2010).

C1   Gilles Deleuze, *Cinema 1: The Movement-Image*, trans. Hugh Tomlinson and Barbara Habberjam (Minneapolis: University of Minnesota Press, 1986).

C2   Gilles Deleuze, *Cinéma 2: L'image-temps* (Paris: Les éditions de minuit, 1985); *Cinema 2: The Time Image*, trans. Hugh Tomlinson and Robert Galeta (Minneapolis: University of Minnesota Press, 1989). French citation is followed by the English citation.

CN   Roger-Pol Droit, *The Cult of Nothingness: The Philosophers and the Buddha*, trans. David Streight and Pamela Vohnson (Chapel Hill: University of North Carolina Press, 2003).

CP   Hakamaya Noriaki, "Critical Philosophy versus Topical Philosophy," *Pruning the Buddha Tree: The Storm over Critical Buddhism*, ed. Jamie Hubbard and Paul Swanson (Honolulu: University Press of Hawai'i, 1997), 56–80.

DPS   Eihei Dōgen, *Dōgen's Pure Standards for the Zen Community: A Translation of Eihei Shingi*, trans. Taigen Daniel Leighton and Shōhaku Okumura, ed. Taigen Daniel Leighton (Albany: State University of New York Press, 1996).

DR   Gilles Deleuze, *Difference and Repetition*, trans. Paul Patton (New York: Columbia University Press, 1994).

EN   Michel Mohr, "Emerging from Nonduality: Kōan Practice in the Rinzai Tradition since Hakuin," *The Kōan: Texts and Contexts in Zen Buddhism*, ed. Steven Heine and Dale S. Wright (Oxford: Oxford University Press, 2000), 244–279.

ERN   Graham Parkes, "The Early Reception of Nietzsche's Philosophy in Japan," in *Nietzsche and Asian Thought*, ed. Graham Parkes (Chicago: University of Chicago Press, 1991), 177–199.

ES	Arthur Schopenhauer, *The Essential Schopenhauer*, ed. Wolfgang Schirmacher (New York: Harper, 2010).
G	Friedrich Nietzsche, *On the Genealogy of Morality* (1887), trans. Maudemarie Clark and Alan J. Swensen (Indianapolis: Hackett, 1998).
GM	Arthur Schopenhauer, *Grundlage der Moral*, *Arthur Schopenhauers Sämmtliche Werke*, six volumes, 2nd edition, ed. Julius Frauenstädt (Leipzig: Brockhaus, 1891), volume 4.
HC	Hakuin Ekaku, *Zen Words for the Heart: Hakuin's Commentary on the Heart Sūtra*, trans. Norman Waddell (Boston: Shambhala, 1996).
HDS	Eihei Dōgen, *The Heart of Dōgen's Shōbōgenzō*, trans. Norman Waddell and Abe Masao (Albany: State University of New York Press, 2002).
HP	Hakuin Ekaku, *Hakuin's Precious Mirror Cave: A Zen Miscellany*, ed. and trans. Norman Waddell (Berkeley: Counterpoint, 2009).
IG	Nishida Kitarō, *An Inquiry into the Good* (1911), trans. Abe Masao and Christopher Ives (New Haven, CT: Yale University Press, 1990).
KSA	Friedrich Nietzsche, *Kritische Studienausgabe*, ed. Giorgio Colli and Mazzino Montinari (Munich: Deutscher Taschenbuch and Walter de Gruyter, 1980). Cited by volume number and then page number.
LS	*Scripture of the Lotus Blossom of the Fine Dharma*, trans. Leon Hurvitz (New York: Columbia University Press, 1976).
N	Nāgārjuna, *Nāgārjuna's Middle Way* (*Mūlamadhyamakakārikā*), trans. and ed. Mark Siderits and Shōryū Katsura (Boston: Wisdom Publications, 2013).
NAP	Arthur C. Danto, *Nietzsche as Philosopher* (New York: Macmillan, 1965).
NH	Graham Parkes, "Nietzsche and Zen Master Hakuin on the Roles of Emotion and Passion," *Nietzsche and the Gods*, ed. Weaver Santaniello (Albany: State University of New York Press, 2001), 115–134.
NIH	*Nothing Is Hidden: Essays on Zen Master Dōgen's Instructions for the Cook*, ed. Jisho Warner, Shōhaku Okumura, John McRae, and Taigen Daniel Leighton (New York: Weatherhill, 2001).
NP	Gilles Deleuze, *Nietzsche and Philosophy* (1962), trans. Hugh Tomlinson (New York: Columbia University Press, 1983).
OA	Yoshida Kiju, *Ozu's Anti-Cinema*, trans. Daisuke Miyao and Kyoko Hirano (Ann Arbor: University of Michigan Press, 2003).

PM	Tanabe Hajime, *Philosophy as Metanoetics*, trans. Takeuchi Yoshinori, Valdo Viglielmo, and James W. Heisig (Berkeley: University of California Press, 1987).
PS	Bryan Magee, *The Philosophy of Schopenhauer*, rev. ed. (Clarendon: Oxford University Press, 1998).
RE	Robert H. Sharf, "The Rhetoric of Experience and the Study of Religion," *Journal of Consciousness Studies* 7.11–12 (2000).
RL	*The Record of Linji*, trans. Ruth Fuller Sasaki, ed. Thomas Yūhō Kirchner (Honolulu: University Press of Hawai'i, 2009).
RVE	Eihei Dōgen, *Shōbōgenzō: La réserve visuelle des événements dans leur justesse*, ed. and trans. Nakamura Ryōji and René de Ceccatty (Paris: Éditions de la différence, 1980).
S	Eihei Dōgen, *Shōbōgenzō (Treasury of the True Dharma Eye)*, ed. Kazuaki Tanahashi (Boston: Shambhala, 2010).
SON	Nishitani Keiji, *The Self-Overcoming of Nihilism*, trans. Graham Parkes and Aihara Setsuko (Albany: State University of New York Press, 1990).
T	Shinran, *Tannishō (A Record in Lament of Divergences)*, *The Collected Works of Shinran*, trans. Dennis Hirota, Hisao Inagaki, Michio Tokunaga, and Ryushin Uryuzu (Kyoto: Jōdo Shinshū Hongwanji-ha, 1997), 659–682.
TB	Milan Kundera, *Testaments Betrayed: An Essay in Nine Parts*, trans. Linda Asher (New York: HarperCollins, 1995).
TNAP	Georges Canguilhem, *The Normal and the Pathological*, trans. Carolyn Fawcett and Robert Cohen (New York: Zone Books, 1989).
TP	Gilles Deleuze and Félix Guattari, *A Thousand Plateaus*, trans. Brian Masumi (Minneapolis: University of Minnesota Press, 1987).
VLW	Arthur Schopenhauer, "Nachträge zur Lehre vom Leiden der Welt," *Arthur Schopenhauers Sämmtliche Werke*, six volumes, 2nd edition, ed. Julius Frauenstädt (Leipzig: Brockhaus, 1891), volume 6.
VR	William James, *The Varieties of Religious Experience* (New York: Modern Library, 2002).
WI	Hakuin Ekaku, *Wild Ivy: The Spiritual Autobiography of Zen Master Hakuin*, trans. Norman Waddell (Boston: Shambhala, 1999).
WP	Gilles Deleuze and Félix Guattari, *What Is Philosophy?*, trans. Hugh Tomlinson and Graham Burchell (New York: Columbia University Press, 1994).

WWE   Peter Singer and Jim Mason, *The Way We Eat: Why Our Food Choices Matter* (Emmaus, PA: Rodale, 2006).
WWR   Arthur Schopenhauer, *The World as Will and Representation*, 2 vols., trans. E. F. J. Payne (Indian Hills, CO: Falcon's Wing, 1958).
WWV   Arthur Schopenhauer, *Die Welt als Wille und Vorstellung, Arthur Schopenhauers Sämmtliche Werke*, 2nd edition, ed. Julius Frauenstädt (Leipzig: Brockhaus, 1891), volumes 2 and 3.
ZMH   Hakuin Ekaku *The Zen Master Hakuin: Selected Writings*, trans. Philip B. Yampolsky (New York: Columbia University Press, 1971).
ZSZM Steven Heine, *Zen Skin, Zen Marrow: Will the Real Zen Buddhism Please Stand Up?* (Oxford: Oxford University Press, 2008).
ZT   Linji Yixuan, *The Zen Teachings of Master Lin-Chi*, trans. Burton Watson (New York: Columbia University Press, 1999).
ZZ   Bret W. Davis, "Zen After Zarathustra: The Problem of the Will in the Confrontation Between Nietzsche and Buddhism," *Journal of Nietzsche Studies* 28 (2004), 89–138.

INTRODUCTION
Philosophy after Comparative Philosophy

I. Other Buddhas

Nietzsche and other Buddhas?

By what right could one call Nietzsche a Buddha? He certainly did not consider himself one and, as we see in this study, he opposed his thinking to the impending catastrophe of what he called the "deification of nothingness" that is "European Buddhism."[1] To speak therefore of Nietzsche as a Buddha is not to speak of him as a philosopher who understood himself in this way. That Nietzsche in some way could be called a Buddha does not stem from his study of or personal engagement with Buddha Dharma.[2]

If one's image of the history of philosophy is the passing of the baton in a great relay race—ideas are passed from one thinker to another—then one ignores the creativity and genesis at the heart of the philosophical enterprise. Even what matters *as* philosophy has historically been subject to genesis. Despite occasional and sometimes acrimonious academic protests to the contrary, the nature of philosophical activity remains one of philosophy's most vexing questions. Nietzsche, whose creativity transformed the experience of philosophy as the European philosophical tradition recognized it, neither received the baton from the Mahāyāna nor passed it to them.

There are further considerations. (1) Although, as we see in the fourth chapter, the great Kyoto School philosopher Nishitani Keiji[3] rediscovered Japan's Zen tradition through the gate of his youthful infatuation with Nietzsche, it does not follow that one needs Nietzsche in order to appreciate Zen. (2) As several philosophers have already convincingly demonstrated, Nietzsche's philosophical creativity resonates in new ways with some ancient strands of Mahāyāna practice. However, the identification of coincidences or affinities does not ipso facto recommend them. (3) Finally, both the affinities and the differences are co-illuminating, transforming some of the ways that we can appreciate the accomplishments and resources of both. This confrontation is mutually transformative.

This co-illuminating confrontation, however, does not first transpire by lining up each thinker's array of concepts and comparing and contrasting them. Jumping to this task assumes that we know what we mean by philosophy, that what matters as philosophy is somehow self-evident or otherwise settled. By some conventional measures of what counts as philosophy, we cannot count Zen and other strands of Mahāyāna *as* philosophy, even if they are of interest to some philosophers as food for thought. Moreover, as I discuss in more detail shortly, it is important to concede from the outset that it would also be unwieldy at best and incoherent at worst to imagine that one can confront a single European philosopher with all or even a lot of Mahāyāna. The requisite generalizations necessary to consider the latter as a unified perspective would be untenable. This book therefore concentrates on a handful of singular and strikingly original East Asian Mahāyāna thinker-practitioners.

How then does this co-illuminating confrontation transpire if it is not first and foremost a sorting of concepts? Nietzsche's contribution to philosophy was not just a toolkit of new concepts—although this too is a formidable inheritance—but rather an expansion of the *experience of what matters as philosophy*. Nietzsche did not just transform the stock of philosophical concepts. He transformed both what could count as a philosophical concept and the manner in which concepts matter. Nietzsche challenged the conventions that govern how issues come to have philosophical value as well as the values by which we patrol the borders of philosophy. Given that Nietzsche's experience of philosophy is a non sequitur from the prevailing practices of philosophy, one could not say that he derived his sense of philosophy (in both senses of sense) from the status quo. Where then did it originate?

Zen practice also does not originate from or primarily conduct itself in discursive activity. Zen is not first and foremost a philosophical argument, although it has and does give rise to a proud philosophical tradition (despite the stereotype to the contrary). Dōgen's *Shōbōgenzō* or Hakuin's reformation of Rinzai practice, to cite two prominent examples germane to this book, are philosophically staggering works, although they do not originate in discursive gestures. They emerge, as Dōgen maintains, from the opening of the true Dharma eye.

The co-illuminating confrontation that is the concern of this book, therefore, is not a horizontal sorting but rather a *vertical* encounter. All is lost, however, when this gesture toward the vertical is a dishonest act of willful obscurantism. There is nothing mysterious or supernatural about this vertical dimension, although it is a question of finding a way to make the darkness shine and the silence ring forth. Rather it is our prevailing habits of philosophy that risk obscurantism in assuming that they are self-evident. There is nothing obvious about philosophy; its genesis and creativity do not reduce to its prevailing consensuses. In gesturing toward the vertical, whatever the limits of the metaphor of *depth*, we are not comparing "Western" and "East Asian" philosophies but rather inquiring into the prephilosophical ground of philosophy. Philosophy does not originate in itself, creating itself out of itself.

This vertical dimension is what the early Nishida Kitarō called *junsui keiken*, pure experience. This is not the experience of something but rather experience before it divides into an experiencing subject and an experienced object. It is to "see" (beyond seer and seen) the formless form and to "hear" (beyond auditor and audited) the soundless sound. Nishida would later come to regard the language of experience as too psychological, and that remains a risk in using such language. However we articulate it, we follow Nishida in trying to "give a philosophical foundation to this demand."[4] Yet can philosophy provide a philosophical foundation to its outside? No doubt this is problematic and to some extent doomed to fail, but it is the task of this study to somehow show that it is there and that it is a matter of great consequence to philosophy. In the co-illuminating confrontation in which Nietzsche emerges as a kind of Buddha, he and the other Buddhas do so by simultaneously revealing the prephilosophical ground of any possible philosophy.

II. Zen and the Experience of Philosophy

Since Zen, and Buddha Dharma more broadly, do not insist on the existence or relevance of God, some people wonder if Zen is less a religion and more a philosophy. Yet it would be hard to reconcile what we currently recognize as philosophy—the art of thinking and interlocution—with the following bold words of Sengcan Jianzhi (Jp. Sōzan Kanchi, d. 606)[5] in the *Xinxin Ming*:

> The more you think and talk,
> The more you lose the Way.
> Cut of all thinking
> And pass freely anywhere.

Return to the root and understand,
Chase outcomes and lose the source.
One clear moment within
Illumines the emptiness before you.

Emptiness changing into things
Is only our deluded view.
Do not seek the truth,
Only let go of your opinions.[6]

Although Sinologists and Buddhologists debate whether Sengcan, the legendary Third Patriarch of Chan Buddhism, wrote these words, the counsel remains provocative: cut off all thinking and return to the root and do this by abandoning all views and opinions. The more one thinks and talks, the part and parcel of philosophy, the more one loses the Way. Since this is a book about the confrontation between certain strains of East Asian Mahāyāna Buddha Dharma and Friedrich Nietzsche (and others), the problem is immediately evident: is not philosophy about the production, refinement, and critique of views? How can this dialogue transpire when one of the interlocutors speaks and writes endlessly and the other grows silent?

This is not to say that we cannot or should not write about Zen philosophically—one can and by all means should—but it in so doing, one should remember that Zen, despite its own claims to the contrary, is not a unified field and history and, more important, it is not in itself primarily discursive. In *Bendōwa* (1231),[7] an early writing by the great Kamakura period Zen Master Eihei Dōgen (1200–1253), we are admonished that "in studying sūtras you should not expend thoughts in the vain hope that they will be helpful for attaining realization" (S, 8). Purely academic practice realizes nothing. It is just words. Access to Dōgen's writings requires something more than discursive athleticism and scholarly diligence. The title of Dōgen's magnum opus, the *Shōbōgenzō* or *Treasury of the True Dharma Eye*, refers to the legend of the Buddha's first transmission. Holding up a flower, the Buddha blinked and Mahākāśyapa smiled. The Buddha responded, "I possess the true Dharma eye, the marvelous mind of Nirvana, the true form of the formless, the subtle dharma gate that does not rest on words or letters but is a special transmission outside of the scriptures. This I entrust to Mahākāśyapa."[8] The transmission outside sūtras is also outside philosophical argumentation and discursive demonstration.

Dōgen's insistence (found in most all Zen practice) on *transmission outside of the sūtras* does not mean, however, that one should not read sūtras and engage in the practice both of study and philosophical reflection. As Dōgen's Chinese teacher Rujing (Jp. Nyōjō) pressed him, "Why should the great Way of the buddhas and patriarchs concern inside or outside?"[9] It is a question rather of finding and practicing the most helpful and mindful relationship between thinking and Zen practice. The *Shōbōgenzō* is full of stories about the relationship between thinking and practice gone awry. In a particularly pointed example from *Keisei Sanshoku* (*Valley Sounds, Mountains Colors*, 1240), Dōgen recounts the celebrated awakening story of the Tang dynasty Chan Master, Xiangyan Zhixian (Jp. Kyōgen Chikan, d. 898). Students of the Zen record know that Xiangyan had been a student, along with Guishan Lingyou (Jp. Isan Reiyū), on Mount Gui (in contemporary Hunan province). He prided himself in his study of the Chinese classics and the great Mahāyāna sutras. When their teacher died, Guishan, later known as Zen Master Dayuan, cofounder of the Guiyang School, was installed as the abbot, and the confident scholar Xiangyan applied to become his student. Dōgen picks the story up at this point, beginning with Guishan's famous challenge to Xiangyan: "You are bright and knowledgeable. Say something about yourself before your parents were born, but don't use words learned from the commentaries" (S, 87). Guishan did not ask Xiangyan scholarly questions about Zen practice but rather to show his "original face (Jp. *honrai no menmoku*)," a traditional Zen phrase for one's Buddha nature or original Buddha mind. He was not asked to say what others in the sutras and commentaries had argued about the original face or to speak of it in general philosophical terms.

Alas, Xiangyan, unable to say something that he had not learned from the commentaries, did what many academics today still do: he furiously took to his books in order to find something that was not in his books. He vainly searched all night before realizing that he was on a fool's errand. "Deeply ashamed, he burned his books and said, 'A painting of a rice cake does not satisfy hunger. I will be just a cooking monk, not expecting to understand Buddha Dharma in this lifetime'" (S, 87). Xiangyan became a monk who helped prepare the morning and midday meals. One day, as he was doing his chores, his broom swept a small object (a tile or a pebble) into some bamboo. Surprised by the sound, he suddenly awoke. Xiangyan's original folly would be an example of what Dōgen strikingly dubs "bondage to Buddha," namely, "being bound by the view that our perception and cognition of enlightenment is actually enlightenment" (*Gyōbutsu Iigi*, 1241) (S, 261). Brain Zen, that is, confusing ideas about Zen with Zen experience, is not the practice of what Dōgen repeatedly called "the oneness of practice-realization [*shushō-ittō*]."

In the *Shin Fukatoku* (*Ungraspable Mind*, first version, 1241), Dōgen tells the *kōan*, which he took from the famous *Blue Cliff Record*, of another renowned Tang Dynasty master, Monk Deshan Xuanjian (Jp. Tokusan Senkan), who was known as Diamond King Chou because there was no part of the *Diamond Sūtra* that he had not mastered and commented on with scholarly prowess. Yet when asked about the ungraspable mind of the past, present, and future by an old woman selling rice cakes—with which of these minds will you satisfy your hunger?—he could not answer. "How regrettable," laments Dōgen. "The king of commentators, who wrote commentaries on hundreds of scrolls, a lecturer for decades, was so easily defeated by a humble old woman with a single question!" (S, 192). Diamond King Chou's failure spurred him to take up Zen practice and he eventually became the great Zen teacher known as Great Master Jianxing (Jp. Kenshō Daishi).

What does it then mean to speak of Zen philosophically if Zen practice is not fundamentally about generating a philosophical account? Moreover, what does it even mean to speak of Zen at all? What gets to count as Zen and who gets to speak on behalf of it? Surely this must minimally include the great Zen masters and the great Zen canons and records of recorded sayings of the most accomplished practitioners, although one rightly wonders why these sources included so few women. This assumption, however, can no longer automatically be taken for granted as various academics, East Asian as well as Western, have in recent decades raised many serious critical questions about and objections to the Zen tradition's apocryphal account of itself. Stephen Heine, in his important book, *Zen Skin, Zen Marrow: Will the Real Zen Buddhism Please Stand Up?*,[10] memorably characterizes the current reception of Zen as a battle between TZN, or the traditional Zen narrative, and HCC, or historical and cultural criticism. The former includes the uncritical practices of the true believers and committed practitioners, who, as we shall see, adhere strongly to Zen's "special transmission outside the scriptures [*kyōge betsuden*]."

Critical Buddhists in Japan, however, excoriate the generations of social and political passivity that the obsession with original enlightenment (Jp. *hongaku*) has wrought in Japanese Buddha Dharma. They contend that the emphasis on original enlightenment relegates equality and inclusivity to an ontologically pure dimension while justifying and enervating social critique of the inequities of everyday life. Buddha Dharma becomes reactionary, quietist, other-worldly, its own kind of opiate of the people. This may not be the last word on Zen, however, as one of its major proponents, Hakamaya Noriaki, recognizes that this position is a betrayal of Dōgen. "Is it not ironic that this idea, criticized by Dōgen, has from his time up to the present been accepted as the mainstream of Japanese Buddhism, even among Sōtō believers who revere Dōgen as their founder?"[11] Be that as it may be, Dōgen and his legacy are left to preside over centuries of Zen ruins and missteps. As the mounting critique of Zen gathers steam in the academic world, HCC argues, as Heine tells us, that Zen "apologists deliberately cloak Zen in a shield of opaqueness. This is done to avoid or to claim immunity from the careful scrutiny of historical examination, which would disclose inconsistencies, contradictions, and even basic flaws in the character of Zen as a social institution conditioned by the flux of everyday events and the turmoil of worldly affairs" (ZSZM, 8).

We can immediately cede much to the HCC position simply by remembering that some of Zen's most extraordinary teachers like Dōgen, Hakuin, and Ikkyū had ferocious critiques of the institutions of Zen and Buddha Dharma more broadly. Nonetheless, the HCC charges, however sobering and important, are in themselves intellectual assessments and cannot address the problem of Xiangyan's and Deshan's respective cerebral follies. To insist on this point, as we again do in the book's conclusion, is not to cloak Zen in a so-called rhetoric of immediacy that shrouds it in mystery and immunizes it from critique. Two of the most consequential and influential Japanese Zen Masters, Dōgen and Hakuin, the former credited with what came to be known as Sōtō Zen and the latter credited with the radical overhaul and renovation of Rinzai Zen, are both profoundly philosophical and devastatingly critical without either mystifying Zen or reducing it to an academic position.

Moreover, it is critical to develop a sensibility for the language of figures like Dōgen and Hakuin, respectively. Zen teaching is, after all, part of the *practice* of Zen, and teachings are as effective as their capacity to open the true dharma eye. The value of Zen doctrines is medicinal, and the best teachings are strong medicine that liberates thinking and living from the turmoil (*duḥkha*) of stupidity, ideological fixations, stinginess, greed, aggression, self-obsessiveness, and servility to the status quo. In this way it affirms what Manu Bazzano extols about Nietzsche's and Schopenhauer's respective refusals of servility to the status quo. "A philosophy laborer, far from being a seeker after truth—or truths—far from asking blunt, unsettling, untimely questions, will go a long way by using fashionable, obscure jargon, to present infinite variations on the party line."[12]

Moreover, Zen relies on *upāya* or "skillful means" (J. *hōben*), which is the capacity to translate something true into the terms and conventions of the prevailing mindset. As John Schroeder succinctly describes it: "Very generally, *upāya* refers to the different pedagogical styles, meditation techniques, and religious practices that help people overcome attachments, and to the ways in which Buddhism is communicated to others. . . . '[S]killful means' arises from the idea that wisdom is embodied in how one responds to others rather than an abstract conception of the world, and reflects an ongoing concern with the soteriological effectiveness of the Buddhist teachings."[13]

At its best, Zen discourses practice a subtle art of truth. Just as one would not fault literature for somehow being false because its narratives did not factually transpire, reading Zen texts at their best demands that readers alter not what they think but how they think. In *Kankin* (*Reading a Sūtra*, 1241) Dōgen was quite clear about this: "To read a sūtra is to take up and assemble all Buddha ancestors, turn them into an eyeball, and read it" (S, 229). Indeed, those who "expound discourses of teaching outside the way for the sake of seeking fame cannot practice the Buddha sūtras" (S, 222–223). One must learn to read with the Dharma eye so that one can see in the manner that the sūtra is seeing.

How does this relate to what is sometimes called comparative philosophy or intercultural philosophy? Does it make sense to speak of Dōgen or Hakuin as philosophers, given their fundamental refusal of the preeminence of discursive reflection? We could note that they do not refuse discursive acumen. They rely upon it. They deny that Zen is *fundamentally* discursive while simultaneously using the discursive to occasion the opening of the Dharma eye and employing discursive insights within the purview of the Dharma eye. Philosophy cannot in itself directly open the Dharma eye, but one can do philosophy with a Dharma eye as well as use philosophy to complement and refine the practices that directly seek to open the Dharma eye.

More to the point: *What does the opening of the true Dharma eye, the special transmission outside of the scriptures that does not rest on words or letters, to turn a sutra into a Dharma eyeball, have to do with comparative philosophy?* This is the question that ultimately guides this book.

The standpoint of the true Dharma eye is not in itself philosophical, but it is the possibility of philosophy as such. This question of philosophy's relationship to nonphilosophy demands, in turn, that one philosophize about the nature of what it is we do when we philosophize. In their remarkable work, *What Is Philosophy?*, Deleuze and Guattari argue: "The plane of philosophy is prephilosophical insofar as we consider it in itself independently of the concepts that come to occupy it, but nonphilosophy is found where the plane confronts chaos. *Philosophy needs a nonphilosophy that comprehends it; it needs a nonphilosopical comprehension just as art needs nonart and science needs nonscience.* They do not need the No as beginning, or as the end in which they would be called upon to disappear by being realized, but at every moment of their becoming or their development."[14]

Although I will return to Deleuze and this problem in chapter 5, suffice it to say right now that the relationship of philosophizing about Zen and the ground of the practice of Zen resonates with the problem of the nonphilosophical ground of philosophy. That there is philosophy at all allows us to do philosophy. We tend, however, to take the existence and procedures of philosophy for granted. We do what philosophers have already done or are already doing. Even if we resist traditional or contemporary practices of philosophy, we assume them in order to resist them. All of this, however, does not mean that philosophical activity originated in some a priori philosophical reality. Philosophy is not originally self-originating nor was it lying about, waiting to be discovered; philosophy is created out of nonphilosophy.

Philosophy therefore does not and cannot own its origin and consequently it cannot orient itself to any final sense of its ultimate purpose. Simply put: the origin and nature of philosophical activity are two of philosophy's most recalcitrant and profound questions. What is it that we do when we philosophize is a very philosophical question and the power of this question keeps philosophy from ever settling into itself and accounts for philosophy's extraordinary creativity; its inexhaustible elasticity is its paradoxical durability.

III. Scope of the Book

This book concerns the gap between the fact of philosophy—any kind of philosophy—and the ultimate inexplicability of that fact. It takes up the problem of the nonobviousness of what philosophy ultimately is and of what finally gets to matter or count as philosophy. It does so by considering Zen practice, and to a lesser extent, the True Pure Land sect (*Jōdo Shinshū*), primarily in relationship to Friedrich Nietzsche (1844–1900), although it will also briefly extend the analysis to other philosophers, including Gilles Deleuze (1925–1995) and William James (1842–1910). Both Nietzsche and Deleuze are already on the edge of what is recognizably philosophical.

Given my comments in the second section, it is neither prudent nor wise to speak in overly general terms of Zen, let alone Buddha Dharma. Just as it would be absurd to read Thomas of Aquinas or Meister Eckhart as if this were the key to figuring out the essence of Christianity, this book avoids methodologically the assumption that there is a determinate and unchanging essence of either Zen or Mahāyāna more broadly. It gives ample consideration to the great Rinzai reformer, Hakuin Ekaku (1686–1769), as well as to Dōgen, who, despite his aversion to "schools" or "sects" of Zen, inadvertently gave rise to what is now called the Sōtō School. It also engages other thinkers from Chinese and Japanese Zen as well as Dōgen's non-Zen contemporary, Shinran, the great spirit at the heart of the True Pure Land sect.

The book seeks to avoid from the outset some of the classical pitfalls that plague interpretations of Buddha Dharma writings. Sometimes Asian traditions are seen as inscrutably other, or uninterested in rational pursuits like argumentation and logic. Such "Orientalism" or stereotyping at least implicitly serves to shore up the superiority and presumed universality of one's own culture. (The initial response to Buddha Dharma in the nineteenth century, as we shall see in chapter 2, was horror at its purported nihilism and atheism.) It eschews characterizing the "Asian mind" and other uncharitable abstractions while at the same time endeavors to be acutely sensitive to the important differences in context and values that such an encounter presents. The Buddha Dharma is also sometimes subject to the wild New Age projections that uncritically fantasize that it is the panacea for the failures of the "Western mind." This book avoids this disposition like the plague.

At the same time, there is no one thing that is Zen or Buddha Dharma. Although the tradition speaks of attaining the "pith" or "marrow" of practice, this is not the same thing as saying that it attains the essence of anything. As we shall see in the opening chapter, in attaining the pith, one realizes that there is no freestanding self-same being—no *svabhāva* ("own-being"). When one speaks of Buddha Dharma, one has to speak of its immense variegation without assuming that there is some universal and transhistorical essence holding this variegation together.

In avoiding the Scylla and Charybdis of infantilizing projections and New Age delusions of grandeur while also rejecting monolithic accounts of Zen or Mahāyāna, the book nonetheless allows some classical Buddha Dharma writers to radicalize and renew our sense of the possibilities of philosophy and the philosophical life. Maybe, as Heidegger argued, we should abandon "philosophy" and turn to "thinking" or, in this case, as Steven Burik argues, move from "comparative philosophy" to "comparative thinking."[15] I do not reject such strategies, but call it what you will, there is something more creative, expansive, and inclusive repressed within the traditional habits of philosophy.

This challenge is more complex than the complaint, lamentably true, that the alleged "best practices" of some of our contemporary academic institutions tend to prefer parochially only "Western" thought or to assume that Western philosophy is a pleonasm. The dominant (and dominating) forms of official philosophy generally have too little curiosity about radically different experiences of philosophy. There are important and precious exceptions to this and they call for celebration, but too often they are the exceptions that prove the rule.

This is therefore an opportunity to take up the question of the powers and possibilities of "philosophy" as liberating both thinking and ways of living. Dōgen, for example, is an incomparable "philosopher" who also wrote just as incomparably of the precious quotidian aspects of living and practice. In the *Shōbōgenzō*, the Dōgen who could write breathlessly about the inseparability of being and time (*uji*) was the same Dōgen who could in the next moment write about the proper manner of cleaning your body (*Senjō*), including how to wipe your ass after defecating in the woods after practicing zazen (sitting meditation) outdoors,[16] or washing your face (*Semmen*).[17] "It is not only cleansing the body and mind, but also cleansing the entire land" (S, 49). Dōgen gave equal attention to the great and small. Everything mattered. This book takes to heart interrelated philosophical problems like health, poison, nutrition, rumination, digestion, and walking, hardly canonical concerns.

The opening chapter explores the stakes and challenges of bringing the Zen tradition, or at least distinctive voices from within this tradition (Linji, Dōgen, Hakuin), into dialogue with Friedrich Nietzsche. The second chapter builds on the first by tracing the development of Schopenhauer's self-proclaimed Buddhism—he eventually came to be known as the Buddha of Frankfurt—as well as Nietzsche's critique of both Schopenhauer and Buddhism. According to Nietzsche, Schopenhauer unleashed a passive and self-enervating nihilism upon Europe just as the Buddha had done upon India. Although Nietzsche's conflation of Buddhism with Schopenhauer prevented him from fully grasping Buddha Dharma, Nietzsche's own philosophy inadvertently resonates with some powerful strains of it. More specifically, Hakuin's critique of the sickness of an attachment to *śūnyatā* (or emptiness) reverberates with Nietzsche's critique of Schopenhauer and the spiritually pestilent outbreak of European Buddhism.

The third chapter picks up the theme of physical and spiritual sickness by bringing Nietzsche into dialogue with William James and Hakuin in order to articulate in a transcultural manner what Nietzsche called the Great Health. The fourth chapter brings Nietzsche into dialogue with a different aspect of Japanese Mahāyāna, namely, Shinran and the True Pure Land sect. The key interlocutor is Tanabe Hajime (1885–1962) who found in Nietzsche the most unexpected demonstration of Shinran's account of *metanoēsis* (*zangedō*) and the dynamic nonduality of repentance and conversion. This confluence of voices provides important clues toward articulating how *philosophy after comparative philosophy* can reverberate today.

The final chapter engages Dōgen and Dōgen Zen by taking up the question of a philosophy and practice of food and nourishment. It does so amid the prevailing ecological crisis, including the industrial degradation of our relationship to food (what it is and where it comes from). The analysis benefits from Nietzsche's engagement with "nourishment" as a worthy philosophical problem and from Deleuze's contention that Dōgen was a "planomenal" thinker.

The book concludes by turning full circle and again taking up the problem of Zen experience and its relevance for *philosophy after comparative philosophy*.

IV. "After" Comparison

The subtitle of this book speaks of *philosophy after comparative philosophy*. This "after" can be read in two ways: (1) *after* comparative philosophy in the sense that this book *pursues* comparative philosophy (it is after it, on the hunt for it, trying to elucidate its space and its possibilities); (2) *after* comparative philosophy in the sense that it seeks what is subsequent to this enterprise, what comes when we are done with it. This book is trying to get beyond comparing apples and oranges.

The book intends "after" in both senses and cultivates their ambiguity.

As philosophy, amid a well-deserved crisis of confidence and relevance, ponders and reevaluates who its audience is and to what extent the traditions that it honors are merely Occidental traditions, it is well worth our time to take a breath and ask ourselves, After all is said done, *what is comparative philosophy*? Is it merely lining things up and sorting them out?

This is a deceptively innocent question. Prima facie, its innocence derives from the simple assumption that we are asking what type of the genus philosophy is indicated by its specification as *comparative*. This assumes that we already know about philosophy in general and that we consequently seek to know or debate something new about it in particular. This is at best a false composite, that is, it generalizes about experiences of thinking that are irreconcilably different in kind. To ask about comparative philosophy is first to ask more fundamentally about the *nature* of philosophy itself.

How does philosophical thinking decide what rightfully belongs to it? What is it entitled to call its own? When it comes to the intelligibility of comparative philosophy, we must begin at this level. If one is "comparing" works from two vastly different historical times and/or geographically remote cultures, to what does one appeal to mediate the materials at hand? Moreover, what gets to be compared? What gets to count as philosophy such that it can transgress historical and cultural boundaries? The term *comparison* is itself already loaded and as such relies on certain unstated assumptions about philosophy. Comparison is literally to couple together, to form in pairs, to bring together, to collect [from *com*, "with" + *parare*, "to make, provide, get, prepare"]. One can see this in the German verb *vergleichen*—bringing together what has *die gleiche Gestalt*, that which has the same (homogeneous) form or figure. In contrast, contrast itself speaks not of *com*, being with or together, but *contra*, standing against each other, resisting coming together.

Let us say we ask ourselves, *Is Confucius the Aristotle of China*? What would bring them together, or in failing to do so, keep them apart? In a classical model, the *tertium comparationis*, the shared term or a quality of a comparison, is a third thing, the shared feature that both thinkers have in common. We recognize something the same in both, or something similar, something distributed to some extent in both. If Confucius is indeed the Aristotle of China, we are saying that the two thought alike, or thought from the same place, or one thought as the other thought, or one is an example of the other, or that they shared some critical doctrines or were concerned with similar problems. Or one could say that Confucius was uniquely Chinese. Or perhaps we are more modest and eschew such grand judgments and compare and contrast various features within these two thinkers.

Can philosophy itself mediate between the two, acting as the common ground by which philosophically relevant features can be accentuated? Confucius may not be a philosopher per se, but, knowing what philosophy is, we can select some relevant features of the *Analects*. This assumes that we know what matters or counts as philosophy. It is worth noting that in Japanese, the term for philosophy, *tetsugaku* (literally, wisdom study), is a neologism dating back to the Meiji Period and denoted a new import: Western academic philosophy. In Chinese, the term *zhexue* (哲學, from 哲, wise, and 學, study), solved the same problem as *tetsugaku* and was not coined until 1873 by Nishi Amane.[18]

What happens when we consider thinkers who take us beyond relations of coincidence and resemblance? For example, let us turn to a famous passage from the Chan classic, the *Linji Lu*, the record of the great Tang Dynasty Master Linji Yixuan (Jp. Rinzai Gigen, d. 866). A monk asks Linji about his teaching regarding the mind that remains mind (心々心), the mind that does not differ from itself from moment to moment, or in Ruth Fuller Sasaki's rendering, "where mind and Mind do not differ"[19] or in Burton Watson's rendering, "the mind that moment by moment does not differentiate."[20] Linji had presented the phrase "the mind that is always mind" as an expression of enlightened mind. Linji's answer to the puzzled monk is striking: as soon as one asks about the mind that does not differ from itself, one has already lost it. How so? In asking about the mind that does not differentiate, of course, one is differentiating it from the mind that does differentiate. A nondiffering mind is being sought in contradistinction to a differing mind. To have it in mind is already to be a differentiating mind. This separates one from one's inherent nature or Buddha nature. It drives a wedge between the Buddha mind and its expressions.

In this particular discourse, Linji proposes several striking and even shocking counter proposals. I cite here a small sample:

1. All dharmas, that is, all beings, do not have their own being. They are "without self-nature" (RL, 221). They are free from what Nāgārjuna had called the error of *svabhāva*, that is, a being being itself by having itself, by being identical to itself, by being a self-same entity. All dharmas are rather "just empty names, and these names are also empty" (RL, 221). The monk takes

these names, even the name of the mind that never differs from itself as a mind, as real. "This is a great error" (ZT, 47).
2. If you seek the Buddha, you will come into the grip of the Buddha-Māra (RL, 223), that is, the demon that tried to tempt the Buddha away from himself. The more one tries to become the Buddha, the more one falls into the trap of the Buddha devil.
3. The "true Buddha has no figure, true Dharma has no form" (RL, 228). The Buddha has no image, and the Dharma corresponds to no form or εἶδος and admits of no predicates.
4. Hence "on meeting a Buddha slay the Buddha, on meeting a patriarch slay the patriarch, on meeting an *arhat* slay the *arhat*, on meeting your parents slay your parents" (RL, 236).
5. Grasp and use what is going on right now, but never name it—this is called the "mysterious principle" (RL, 244) or "dark meaning" (ZT, 55).
6. To be clear, there is no such thing as the Dharma, yet beyond and in all names, it is decisive.

To what would we compare the Dharma when the Dharma is itself by never being itself? The Dharma takes Mañjuśrī's sword right to the heart of identities.

There is nothing obvious about the Dharma, but it as simple as learning to wash the dishes. In order for thinking to engage a text like the *Linji Lu*, it cannot assume the metaphysics that undergird comparison. Linji gives us a new way to appreciate Gilles Deleuze's critique of comparison:

> On precisely these branches, difference is crucified. They form a quadripartite fetters under which only that which is identical, similar, analogous or opposed can be considered different: *difference becomes an object of representation always in relation to a conceived identity, a judged analogy, an imagined opposition* or *a perceived similitude*. Under these four coincident figures, difference acquires a sufficient reason in the form of a *principium comparationis*. For this reason, the world of representation is characterized by its inability to conceive of difference in itself; and by the same token, its inability to conceive of repetition for itself, since the latter is grasped only by means of recognition, distribution, reproduction and resemblance in so far as these alienate the prefix RE in simple generalities of representation.[21]

Linji cuts through the assumptions of representation as such. This is nothing less than to return to the problem of philosophy itself. Nothing is so precious as philosophy, but if you see philosophy on the road, slay it.

Philosophy after comparative philosophy *ruminates* on philosophy itself. As we see in the first chapter and in many of the subsequent chapters, this book's turn to rumination is not a simple turn to thinking deeply about something or turning something over in one's mind. Nor is it the rumination of which contemporary psychology speaks, namely, an excessive worrying and anxiety that derives from obsessing on the causes of one's troubles rather than their overcoming. In its etymological sense, rumination names the overcoming that this account denies. Rumination derives from the Latin *ruminationem*, "chewing the cud," and describes the digestive process of well over a hundred ruminants, including camels, buffalo, giraffes, sheep, alpacas, antelope, impalas, and, best known, domestic cattle. After a ruminant ingests food, it travels into the first two parts of a four-part stomach, the rumen and the reticulum, where it clumps together into balls (or *boli*), which are better known as cud. The cud moves back into the mouth where it is chewed and broken down. After this second chewing, it can then make its way into the omasum and then the main stomach (the abomasum). If a ruminant cannot ruminate, if it cannot chew the cud, it cannot digest the cud. Without rumination, what provides nutrition remains poisonous. As we shall see in chapter 1 and again in chapter 5, Nietzsche thought that rumination was critical to philosophical activity. If one cannot chew the cud of the tradition and the cud of contemporary philosophical activity, it makes us sick.

This book seeks to avoid philosophical dyspepsia. In seeking *philosophy after comparative philosophy*, it ruminates on the encounter between activities that we recognize as philosophical and those that defy our powers of philosophical recognition. *After* in the second sense requires an ongoing rumination. What follows are philosophical ruminations that complicate and transgress the discipline's traditional borders, hoping to illuminate an experience of thinking in the way that lightning illuminates the night sky.

Notes

1. Friedrich Nietzsche, *Kritische Studienausgabe*, ed. Giorgio Colli and Mazzino Montinari (Munich: Deutscher Taschenbuch and Walter de Gruyter, 1980), vol. 6, 185. Henceforth KSA, followed by volume number and then the page number.

2. Rather than referring to Buddhism—a European term and a strange one at that, given that generally in these traditions there are no isms and hence no Buddhists—I will speak of Buddha Dharma.

3. Except where custom prevails otherwise, I adhere to the East Asian custom of listing the family name first.

4. From Nishida's *From the Actor to the Seer* (1927), quoted in Abe Masao, "Introduction" to Nishida Kitarō, *An Inquiry into the Good* (1911), trans. Abe Masao and Christopher Ives (New Haven, CT: Yale University Press, 1990), x. Henceforth IG.

5. Note that, except where otherwise noted, I use the pinyin transliterations. I also use the following abbreviations to indicate the source language for technical terms and proper names: Jp. for Japanese and Skt. for Sanskrit.

6. "Trust in Mind," trans. Stanley Lombardo, *Zen Sourcebook: Traditional Documents from China, Korea, and Japan*, ed. Stephen Addiss, with Stanley Lombardo and Judith Roitman (Indianapolis, IN: Hackett, 2008), 15.

7. Except where otherwise noted, I have generally relied on the two-volume edition of the *Shōbōgenzō* edited by Kazuaki Tanahashi. *Treasury of the True Dharma Eye* (Boston: Shambhala, 2010). Henceforth S.

8. Quoted in Heinrich Dumoulin, *Zen Buddhism: A History*, Vol. 1: *India and China*, trans. James W. Heisig and Paul Knitter (New York: Macmillan, 1988), 9.

9. Takashi James Kodera, *Dōgen's Formative Years in China: An Historical Study and Annotated Translation of the 'Hōkyō-ki'* (Boulder, CO: Prajñā, 1980), 118.

10. Steven Heine, *Zen Skin, Zen Marrow: Will the Real Zen Buddhism Please Stand Up?* (Oxford: Oxford University Press, 2008). Henceforth ZSZM.

11. Hakamaya Noriaki, "Thoughts on the Ideological Background of Social Discrimination," trans. Jamie Hubbard, *Pruning the Bodhi Tree: The Storm over Critical Buddhism*, ed. Jamie Hubbard and Paul L. Swanson (Honolulu: University Press of Hawai'i, 1997), 344.

12. Manu Bazzano, *Buddha Is Dead: Nietzsche and the Dawn of European Zen* (Brighton, UK: Sussex Academic, 2014), 6. There is much to admire in this spirited, lucid, and paradoxically topical yet untimely text.

13. John W. Schroeder, *Skillful Means: The Heart of Buddhist Compassion* (Honolulu: University Press of Hawai'i, 2001), 3.

14. Gilles Deleuze and Félix Guattari, *What Is Philosophy?*, trans. Hugh Tomlinson and Graham Burchell (New York: Columbia University Press, 1994), 218. Henceforth WP.

15. See Steven Burik's fine study, *The End of Comparative Philosophy and the Task of Comparative Thinking: Heidegger, Derrida, and Daoism* (Albany: State University of New York Press, 2009).

16. "When you practice under a tree or in an open field, there is no toilet, so cleanse yourself with some dirt and water from a nearby river or valley brook. You may not find ash, so use two rows of seven pellets of dirt.... Also set up a stone for rubbing [for washing hands]. Then defecate, and afterward use a piece of wood or paper. When you are done, go to the water and cleanse yourself" (S, 51).

17. "Washing the face is not merely removing filth; it is the life vein of buddha ancestors" (S, 61).

18. Lin Ma and Jaap van Brakel, *Fundamentals of Comparative and Intercultural Philosophy* (Albany: State University of New York Press, 2016), 16. "It is not necessary that X and Y share the same notion of philosophy or *zhexue*. Substantial criteria for what philosophy is need not be presupposed" (20).

19. *The Record of Linji*, trans. Ruth Fuller Sasaki, ed. Thomas Yūhō Kirchner (Honolulu: University Press of Hawai'i, 2009), 221. Henceforth RL.

20. *The Zen Teachings of Master Lin-Chi*, trans. Burton Watson (New York: Columbia University Press, 1999), 47. Henceforth ZT.

21. Gilles Deleuze, *Difference and Repetition*, trans. Paul Patton (New York: Columbia University Press, 1994), 138. Henceforth DR.

NIETZSCHE AND OTHER BUDDHAS

1

THINKING ABOUT NIETZSCHE AND ZEN

> No, this bad taste, this will to truth, to truth "at any price," this juvenile madness of being in love with the truth—is spoiled for us: we are too experienced, too serious, too jocular, too burned, too deep for it. . . . We no longer believe in the truth that remains truth when one removes its veil; we have lived too much to believe this. It is for us today an issue of decorum that we do not want to see everything naked.
>
> —Friedrich Nietzsche, *The Gay Science* (KSA 3, 352)

In *The Gay Science*, Nietzsche reflects on the gravity by which we calculate and determine what we consider to be true. "The Seriousness of the truth! How many different things human beings understand by this word! . . . And is not everything that we take *seriously* our traitor? It indicates where we give things weight and where things possess no weight for us" (KSA 3, 446).[1] Given Nietzsche's refusal to take even himself and his work seriously, that is, as something that thinking represents to itself as correct—the motto of the 1887 edition of this text vows to "laugh at every master who does not first laugh at himself" (KSA 3, 343)—what would it mean to bring Nietzsche's thinking into relationship with the classical East Asian Zen tradition?

Of course, there is little agreement as to what we might even mean by the Zen tradition. Who gets to speak for this vast and varied assemblage of practices, schools, and texts? Moreover, just as it is rather foolhardy to make Nietzsche the spokesperson of the Western philosophical tradition—for decades it was a heavy lift to make the case that he even counted as a philosopher—what sense would it make to propose one or two spokespersons for all of Zen or even to imagine that "all of Zen" is a coherent thought? Does it make any more sense to compare a single thinker, an iconoclastic one at that, with an alleged "school" of whatever Zen supposedly is? I will content myself with a small number of distinctive figures in the Chinese and Zen reception of the multifarious Mahāyāna lineage. I will do my best to avoid making claims on behalf of all of Zen. Remembering Huineng's celebrated words that "originally there is not one thing" (Zen's *mu-ichi-motsu*, 無一物, originally not one),[2] it would be peculiar to construe Zen itself as committed to the logically unitary, which would include its own supposedly selfsame identity.

Plenty of books have been written on the relationship between Nietzsche and Buddha Dharma as if comparison were an issue of weighing what one term of the comparison is, weighing the second term of the comparison, and then bringing them together in a third act of weighing and measuring (the *tertium comparationis*).[3] Nietzsche laughs at himself while Zen claims ceaselessly that there are no freestanding entities, that language lacks the power to represent (the Dharma is always indiscernible), and that all beings have their being only in dynamic interaction with other beings (*pratītyasamutpāda*). Buddha Dharma generally holds that there are no isms—there is not even a Buddhism! How then do Nietzsche and Zen appear in relationship to each other, that is, when posed within the problem of the relationship between language and truth?

We could ask our question as Heidegger famously did: Who is Nietzsche's Zarathustra?

It took time to disambiguate Nietzsche from his misappropriation by the National Socialists. Steven Aschheim recounts the Nazi argument that held that the posthumous existence of Nietzsche came to clarity only with the advent of the Nazi horizon of intelligibility: "If Nietzsche had enunciated Nazi ideas, he himself had become comprehensible only because of a particular unfolding of historical events and the creation of a new social reality." Indeed, as an "authorized spokesman [Heinrich Härtle in *Nietzsche und der Nationalsozialismus*]" put it: "Only a conscious National Socialist can fully comprehend Nietzsche."[4] Slowly but surely, a very different Nietzsche has begun to appear, and some of us eventually wondered whether Nietzsche's Zarathustra might offer some illuminating resonances with Zen. As we shall see, Zen itself has not always been free from militaristic misappropriation, and that the disambiguation process remains ongoing. Moreover, this is not to say that Nietzsche himself had studied Zen—he had never heard of Zen, although he did generally disparage what he knew about Buddha Dharma. Nor is it simply to align "ironic affinities" between the two traditions in order to celebrate a hidden cache of unexpected coincidences. When we thought we had apples and oranges and it turns out that we have nothing but apples, this does not ipso facto command apples to our attention or esteem.

We could rephrase our question anew, with both of its folds:

Who is Zarathustra such that he would care if he were a Zen master?
What kind of Zen master would care if she or he were Zarathustra?

Following the exhaustive and quite profound investigation by Bret W. Davis, "Zen after Zarathustra,"[5] we learn that we cannot approach this question except by way of the problem of the will to power: "My contention, in short, is that ultimately the *Auseinandersetzung* comes down to the question of the will, that is to say, to a confrontation between Nietzsche's radical affirmation and Buddhism's radical negation of the will" (ZZ, 90). Does the will to power, even Nietzsche's alleged experiments with twisting free from it, stand up to the will-annihilating, ego-dissipating sword of the Zen *daishi* or Great Death?

So we must go right into the heart of the will to power to see if there was a direct hit (strong coincidence) or near miss (Nietzsche moved in this direction but fell short). The guide on this treacherous path, besides Davis himself, and with greater acuity than Heidegger, is Nishitani Keiji (1900–1990).

Although Nishitani rightly detects a significant convergence between Zen and Nietzsche, there is no direct hit, chiefly for two reasons:

1. Despite its radicality and its sensitivity to the problem of nihilism, the self-overcoming of nihilism within nihilism, despite its strenuous exertion to avoid metaphysics, ends up with the centrality of the will to power (everything is "the will to power—and nothing besides") and as such, the will to power, unable to twist free of its own attachment to its own activity, remains *ontic*. It is, as Nishitani argues in *Religion and Nothingness*, "something conceived in the third person as an 'it,' it has yet to shed the character of 'being something' that is, of being a *Seiendes*" (ZZ, 104). The will to power is a new beginning, *something* to strive for, *something* to affirm in one's being. The "standpoint of the will" is not capable of *muga* (無我), of *anātman*, of being a selfless self (ZZ, 105). If the will to power is something, a being, that is, if it cannot shed its ontic dimension, then it falls prey to the kinds of things that we associate with *something* like the will: "We remain bound to a determination of a drive, a lust for power" (ZZ, 105).
2. Not only is the will to power ontic, and therefore implicitly metaphysical, the kind of something that it is presents the other chief difficulty. The very

notion of the will cannot be separated from *the somebody* who has *this something*. The "standpoint of the will" assumes some form of self-centeredness, "be that of an individual or a collective egoism" (ZZ, 105). Nishitani's *kū no ba*, his "field of *śūnyatā* (or emptiness)," emerges from the ashes of the ego (from the ashes of one who would have any kind of will whatsoever). Indeed, Davis follows up on this claim, locating in Nietzsche's writings a defense of a revised, postmetaphysical, postmoralistic, postnihilistic "elevated egoism" (ZZ, 118). "While for Nietzsche there is no ego as a given, there is the task of constructing an ego, or organizing the plurality of disparate impulses by submitting them to the role of a commanding will to power" (ZZ, 112).

At this point, one might simply wonder who constructs this ego? How does the will to power construct anything? Nonetheless, Davis turns to a quite uncompromising passage in *Beyond Good and Evil*: "At the risk of displeasing innocent ears I propose: egoism belongs to the nature of the noble soul—I mean that unshakeable faith that to a being such as 'we are' other beings must be subordinate by nature and have to sacrifice themselves" (ZZ, 113). On the other hand, there are many *Nachlaß* texts that insist upon the disparate plurality of the self; for example, from late 1882 through early 1883, we find notes like "The I contains a plurality of beings" just as it contains a plurality of forces, which remain invisible like electricity (KSA 10, 165). His "I" follows him like a dog to whatever heights he ascends (KSA 10, 165); and "as many spirits as there are animals in the sea find their home in the human—they struggle with another for the spirit of the 'I'" (KSA 10, 169). Graham Parkes is particularly strong on this point: "As we free ourselves from what Nietzsche calls 'the error of the I,' we come to recognize 'the affinities and antagonisms among things, multiplicities therefore and their laws.' This corresponds perfectly to the idea of 'no-self' (*anātman*), which is central to Buddhism and, on the basis of a radically relational ontology, applies equally to the I and to things."[6]

Nishitani and Davis's emphasis is also not without its force. Nietzsche, after all, favors figures of creation, cultivation, and affirmation, and the will to power and *amor fati* sound much more active than nirvana and the uprooting and cleansing of the three poisons.[7] The will to power, especially the way that Nishitani and Heidegger, each in his own way, centralizes it and weighs it against other movements in Nietzsche's texts, does not seem prima facie compatible with Nishitani's *kū no ba*, and, stacked against any discourse on egoism, the Great Death looks like a sword that cuts more cleanly and deeply. Parkes has nonetheless strongly objected to Davis's emphasis on the *egoism* of the will to power, and their subsequent mutual and respectful exchange, to my mind, captures most of the issues on both sides of Nietzsche's thinking on this problem and should be consulted by those wishing to sort through this issue's many ambiguities.[8]

I appreciate the force of both readings and note in agreement that neither Davis nor Parkes presents the conflicting strands as an "either/or" but rather as a "both/and." This study does not try to resolve these issues one way or another nor is it convinced that there can be a definitive final word on the issue. I settle rather for engaging a problem that gains new vigor when pursued in and between some aspects of the Japanese Zen tradition and Nietzsche's inadvertent contribution to new ways of thinking in a contemporary Zen idiom. The letter of Nietzsche likely illuminates some aspects of Zen practice in powerful and surprising ways. Certainly the spirit of Nietzsche does. This book emphasizes this opening.

If one does raise the question of some of the more aggressive and self-asserting language that sometimes surrounds the will to power, one must also in all fairness concede that Japanese Zen has not always been free of worrisome and dominating elements: one need only think of the close link between samurai culture and Zen or the dismaying complicity of some Zen monasteries with the Japanese military state during the War of the Pacific. And these anecdotes suggest that Zen is something rare even with "Buddha Dharma." The history of the latter is rife with power struggles and factionalism: the struggle between the Northern and the Southern schools, the greedy and violent monks who legendarily pursued Huineng, the violence that Dōgen encountered in Kyoto, the diminishment of some contemporary Japanese Zen temples to the crass commerce of funerary Zen,[9] or the simple fact that Zen practice is hard and that a lifetime of zazen or sitting meditation may for some simply have meant that one spent one's life sitting around.

The problem at hand is not so much a question of correctness as *it is a question of emphasis*, which in turn has everything to do with the problem of the horizon within which these figures are read together. As Dōgen demonstrates in the fascicle from the *Shōbōgenzō* called *Ikka Myōju* (*One Bright Pearl*, 1238),[10] the eponymous expression, all the universe is one bright pearl, does not *mean* anything. It is not a discursively warranted claim about the nature of things. It does not provide a philosophical account of being. It was an expression not in the sense of a proposition or a premise, for the latter, while making a claim about the Dharma, does not ipso facto *express* the Dharma. Dōgen eschewed propositional discourse about the Dharma and warned his monks to be wary of the "briars and brambles of word-attachment" (HDS, 2) and not to "get caught up in skillfully turned words and phrases" (HDS, 17) and not be "enmeshed in the traps and snares of words and letters" (HDS, 18). Dharma transmission is not accomplished through the exchange of information about the Dharma. However, "*One bright pearl* is able to express reality without naming it," and the later phrase, *to express reality without naming it*, is Waddell and Abe's admirable and creative effort to handle the elusive and critical term *dōtoku*, to speak Dao, giving its fathomless silence voice. If we merely mimic what a Zen teaching says without speaking from the standpoint of Dao, we delude ourselves.

In the *Vimalakīrti Sūtra* (*Vimalakīrti Nirdeśa Sūtra*), for instance, we learn that wisdom is the mother and *upāya* is the father. *Upāya*, skillful means, is the capacity to communicate wisdom in accordance with the idiom and mindset of one's interlocutors. It is the capacity to translate the Great Mother of wisdom; and wisdom, without *upāya*, is mere bondage. Detached from language it cannot say itself. The word for wisdom, *prajñā*, in the Mahāyāna tradition contrasts pointedly with knowledge, *jñāna*. It is not a body of knowledge of any kind, nor is it communicable through discursivity. The prefix *pra* indicates anteriority, that which precedes *jñāna*. In Greek one would say *pro-gnōsis* (γνῶσις), but with the strong caveat that prognosis is typically the art of predicting the future, of speaking for the future, rather than allowing the future to unfold itself on its own terms. (If one can speak for the future, then the future is already present and therefore not the future.) One might say that *prajñā* is at the ground of all that might be knowable, but in itself it is unknowable. *Upāya* translates *prajñā* into the word that can express what cannot say itself. The Buddha called this word, the word that skillfully carries the great sea of *prajñā* within it, the lion's roar, the word beyond all humanity that brings us the into the now and here of concrete friendship with the unfolding of the interdependent co-origination and interrelationality of nature.

So the question becomes, *Is there a manner in which we can read Nietzsche's language as expressive?* As such, is this a question not of twisting free from Nietzsche's alleged elevated egoism (à la Heidegger) but of twisting more deeply within it? Is the way beyond the will to power the way already waiting for one when one more deeply enters into it? In the fires of the will to power, fires that Nietzsche knew were waiting to disintegrate his thinking, will there ever be a real centering or will the elevated egoism of the noble be just another way of thinking the being singular plural, the singularity of Dharma experience, an experience expressed in the uniqueness of each Zen personality? The Saṅgha as partaking, sharing, the singularity that expresses one's true face before one was born?

In a sense, this would allow us to deemphasize any link between the will to power and the ego and move closer to Deleuze's reading of Nietzsche[11] when he claims that Nietzsche's thinking is an answer to the question, what is justice? "Nietzsche can say without exaggeration that the whole of his work is an effort to understand this properly" (NP, 18). There have been two mistaken but consequential failures to grapple with the problem of justice, both of which are variations on the need to vindicate or redeem life in the face of its seeming injustice. Life presents itself as intrinsically wrong, as if it were "something unjust which ought to be justified" (NP, 18). The first strategy, which Deleuze associates with Anaximander, the inadvertent forerunner to Schopenhauer, blames the gods (or the will to life) for giving us such a bad deal, such a rotten run of luck. "They see existence as criminal and blameworthy but not yet as something faulty and responsible" (NP, 20). The second strategy, the great historically dominant interpretation of Christianity, shifts the blame from the gods or the will to life and other forms of fatalism ("it's the gods' fault") to the *culpability of the earth and its human inhabitants* and their bad consciences (it is the earth's fault as well as my fault). Life is guilty; it is lacking something that it should have had because there is something intrinsically wrong with us. Both variations—*ressentiment* (there is something wrong with the way of things and life itself is responsible for not being otherwise) and the bad conscience (it is my fault that I am not otherwise than what I am)—derive from the value judgment that all becoming is somehow fundamentally unjust.

Nietzsche's justice, which he and Deleuze associate with Heraclitus, finds life neither tragically blameworthy nor theologically unjust and at fault: "Irresponsibility—Nietzsche's most noble and beautiful secret" (NP, 21). There is no need for theodicy, no call for Ivan Karamazov's infinite task of cataloguing the cruelty to which the evil ones subject the innocent. "Not a theodicy but a cosmodicy, not a sum of injustices to be expiated but justice as the law of this world; not hubris but play, innocence" (NP, 25).

One of the famous mudras or hand gestures that one can find in sculptures and paintings of the Buddha is the *bhūmisparśa mudrā*, or earth touching and witnessing gesture. In this pose, the Buddha's left hand is extended across his lap with his palm facing upward (as if to indicate that the Buddha had just been meditating) while his right hand drops over his right knee (as if he had just moved it from the meditation position), palms inward, the tips of his fingers touching the earth. In the generations after the death of the historical Śākyamuni Buddha, myths and artful teaching devices (*upāya* or skillful means) continued to accrete. In late works like the apocryphal "autobiography" of the Buddha, the *Lalitavistara Sūtra*, the demon Māra, seeking to cast doubt in the Buddha's mind, challenges him to prove that he had awoken. The Buddha responded not by evoking the heavens or transmitting some esoteric teaching or divine revelation. The Buddha responded to the obstructionist Māra (perhaps a personification of his own anxieties) by touching the earth and calling it to bear witness to the end of his somnambulance. The earth—in itself not a thing, but as such the grounding causes and conditions of things—is supremely innocent. It is suchness or *tathātā* or *dharmatā* (Jp. *shinnyo*). The way of things in the turning of the Dharma wheel is not faulty or lacking. The detachment that enables love and community with the great earth is the overcoming of the illusion of the ego that understands itself to be separate and wholly distinct from the earth, what Dōgen called *shinjin datsuraku*, the (simultaneous) casting off and falling away of body and mind.

Is there anything like the dynamic of *shinjin datsuraku* in the will to power and the eternal return of the same? I note here briefly three sample passages in Nietzsche that push against the elevated self-centeredness of the ego.

1. In *Beyond Good and Evil*, Nietzsche turns to Spinoza, who, as we know from his letters, had caught Nietzsche off guard, and Nietzsche, surprised as he was that he liked Spinoza so much, called him his "great predecessor." Spinoza, like Zarathustra, turned back to the earth, to nature. While Nietzsche, whose Zarathustra taught us "to remain true to the earth" (KSA 4, 15), applauded this movement in Spinoza, he called Spinoza's turn to the *conatus*, the will that would preserve itself, his "great contradiction" (KSA 5, 27). You have either the earth or the subject that endeavors to remain itself. Nietzsche, like Dōgen, loved mountain wandering, and one might dare here suggest, following Gary Snyder, that their writing, like their lives, was a practice of the wild. (The wild is, in fact, Snyder's own *upāya* for Dharma.)[12]
2. As we discuss in some length in chapter 5, Nietzsche regarded his earlier ignorance of matters physiological ruinous. Explaining in *Ecce Homo* (1888) why he is so clever, he confessed that his "ignorance *in physiologicus*—the accursed 'idealism'—is the real calamitous fate in my life, the superfluity and stupidity within it." He considered this ignorance to be the cause of the deviations from the "task of my life, for example, that I was a philologist—why

not at least a doctor or something else eye opening?" (KSA 6, 283). It is all just words, and the word "medicine" heals no one, or as Dōgen counseled, the painting of the rice cake is not nutritious. The Buddha himself considered his teachings not as metaphysical or ethical doctrines but as expedients, as various medicines for what is ailing one. The Buddha was the Medicine King.[13]

3. At the end of the preface to the *Genealogy*, Nietzsche lamented that he had no readers—a strange challenge, because if one accepted this challenge, it meant that one had presumably "read" it. Yet Nietzsche charged that contemporary culture lacks the necessary ingredient for *reading*: rumination, *Wiederkäuen*, to chew again. As we saw in the introduction, rumination is not simply the act of pondering something deeply. It is rather to process and digest what one reads. As the German makes even clearer than the Latinate "rumination," this is a bovine (and other ruminants) analogy. The book that one reads is the grass that the ruminant first ingests. But if the ruminant does not transform the grass into cud and chew it again, the grass will sicken and eventually kill it. Prior to rumination, grass is poison. Simply to consume it is to make oneself sick or even to destroy oneself. Rumination unleashes the nourishment latent in the poison of grass just as reading unleashes a great unsayable health within the Nietzschean word. What does it mean to *read*, to chew again, to chew transformatively, the *word* of the will to power?

It might mean that we take up again Gilles Deleuze's insistence that, in the end, Nietzsche's strange turn to egoism had nothing to do with the centering or framing of an ego-self. "When Nietzsche practices egoism it is always in an aggressive or polemical way, against the virtues, against the virtue of disinterestedness. But in fact, egoism is a bad interpretation of will, just as atomism is a bad interpretation of force. In order for there to be egoism it is necessary for there to be an *ego*" (NP, 7). Deleuze reminds us that while Nietzsche speaks of egoism (he cites the passage in the third of Zarathustra called "On the Three Evils"),[14] there is no originary ego, no abiding atomistic self (what Dōgen emphatically dismisses as the Senika heresy).[15] "The origin is the difference in the origin, difference in the origin is *hierarchy*, that is to say, the relation of a dominant to a dominated force, of an obeyed to an obeying will" (NP, 8). As we shall see in chapter 2, the will to power is a response to Schopenhauer's failed Buddhism, and the nihilistic decadence of the ego's will to nihilism is a response to the crushing weight of the egoism of the will to life. Deleuze argues that this is the crux of Nietzsche's critique of Schopenhauer's unitary or homogeneous conception of the will, despite its fourfold specifications. There is nothing in particular in the depths of the will to power. As Deleuze frames the problem:

And Nietzsche's break with Schopenhauer rests on one precise point; it is a matter of knowing whether the will is unitary or multiple. Everything else flows from this. Indeed, if Schopenhauer is led to deny the will it is primarily because he believes in the unity of willing. Because the will, according to Schopenhauer, is essentially unitary, the executioner comes to understand that he is one with his own victim. The consciousness of the identity of the will in all of its manifestations leads the will to deny itself, to suppress itself in pity, morality and asceticism. Nietzsche discovers what seems to him the authentically Schopenhauerian mystification; when we posit the unity, the identity, of the will we must necessarily repudiate the will itself. (NP, 7)

Might one also suggest that Zen practice ruminates the ego and unleashes the Dharmic life within, but the Dharma word, left to its own devices, as a theoretical or metaphysical word, is far from the Great Mother of wisdom? (Vimalakīrti says that *upāya* without *prajñā* is bondage.) Is not the will to power too a word, poisonous grass if you will, that hides its opposite: the great health of the turn not to any possible self, but to the great sea, the earth to whom we have been unfaithful? One bright pearl, a single finger, Huang-po slapping Linji upside the head, having some tea, the will to power—are these words not bondage without deep rumination?

To end with the question with which I began, who is Nietzsche's Zarathustra?

He is not simply the eponymous figure in *Also Sprach Zarathustra*. He contains multitudes. In a way he "is" Vimalakīrti, the layman bodhisattva whose outward manifestation inverted the uniform of the official Buddhist. Buddhists are monks, they leave home, they renounce the trappings of the conventional world; Vimalakīrti was no monk, did not leave his home, was not penurious, and expounded without expounding the Dharma everywhere, including houses of gambling and ill repute. This is to say that the problem of Nietzsche the Buddhist has nothing to do with wearing the external uniform of the Buddhist. In a sense, at least from some practice of the Zen perspective, there is no such thing as a Buddhist because there are no isms of any kind.

And who is Vimalakīrti? Why Huineng, of course, southern barbarian, illiterate, dirt poor, speaking poor Chinese, knowing little of the Mahāyāna canon except for a brief excerpt that he heard from the *Diamond Sūtra* while selling firewood. The legendary Huineng, the Sixth Patriarch, defied many of the external prerequisites of the Way, and in his practice figuratively killed the Buddha when he encountered him on the road. Some scholars now contend that the stories around Huineng are largely apocryphal and that Huineng's hagiography is mainly the result of propaganda and

Buddhist politics.[16] That may well be. Most of the "history" of Zen is more narrative than record, but the gap between the historical Huineng and the embellished Huineng opens up the force of Huineng's story and teaching as *upāya*. Like Vimalakīrti, Huineng does not match the requirements of the official account of a "Buddhist."

And who was Huineng? Why Zarathustra, of course, who valued a dying horse more than his own collapsing cerebration, as if he were the famous snowflake in the eighth ox herding picture:

> Thoughts cannot penetrate the vast blue sky,
> Snowflakes cannot survive a red-hot stove.
> Arriving here, meet the ancient teachers.[17]

Was not the Nietzsche that day in Turin the will to power as that melting snowflake? Much like the "historical" record of Huineng, the story of Nietzsche's embrace of the dying horse is probably not correct,[18] but this does not mean that it is not, at least in terms of *upāya*, somehow "true." It is also not *correct* that Nietzsche is a Buddhist, although it still may be "true."

This is an audacious suggestion, the defense of which comprises chapters 2 and 3.

Notes

1. "Ernst um die Wahrheit! Wie Verschiedenes verstehen die Menschen bei diesen Worten! . . . Und ist nicht Alles, was wir *wichtig* nehmen, unser Verräther? Es zeigt, wo unsere Gewichte liegen and wofür wir keine Gewichte besitzen."

2. According to legend, Huineng (638–713) was the sixth and final Ancestor or Patriarch.

3. See, for example, Freny Mistry, *Nietzsche and Buddhism* (Berlin: Walter de Gruyter, 1981) and Robert G. Morrison, *Nietzsche and Buddhism: A Study in Nihilism and Ironic Affinities* (Oxford: Oxford University Press, 1997). Far subtler and more precious is the work of thinkers like Bret Davis, Brian Schroeder, Nishitani Keiji, Tanabe Hajime, Graham Parkes, Manu Bazzano, and André van der Braak.

4. Steven E. Aschheim, *The Nietzsche Legacy in Germany: 1890–1990* (Berkeley: University of California Press, 1992), 237.

5. Bret W. Davis, "Zen After Zarathustra: The Problem of the Will in the Confrontation Between Nietzsche and Buddhism," *Journal of Nietzsche Studies* 28 (2004), 89–138. Henceforth ZZ.

6. Graham Parkes, "Nietzsche, Panpsychism and Pure Experience: An East-Asian Contemplative Perspective," in *Nietzsche and Phenomenology*, ed. Andrea Rehberg (Newcastle upon Tyne: Cambridge Scholars, 2011), 96.

7. After downplaying the importance of Nietzsche's misreading of Buddhism and arguing for the proximity of Nietzsche and Buddhist practice, Freny Mistry distinguishes them precisely on this issue: "The difference between Nietzsche's art of perfection and

the Buddhist nirvana . . . is this: Nietzsche talks of 'forming' and 'creating'; the Buddha of 'cleansing' and 'uprooting.'" Freny Mistry, *Nietzsche and Buddhism: Prolegomenon to a Comparative Study* (Berlin: Walter de Gruyter, 1981), 196. Many strains of Mahāyāna deemphasize the centrality of nirvana, insisting rather on an utterly consummate awakening (*anuttarā-samyak-saṃbodhi*).

8. See Graham Parkes's "Open Letter to Bret Davis: Letter on Egoism: Will to Power as Interpretation," *Journal of Nietzsche Studies* 46.1 (Spring 2015), 42–61 as well as his follow up to Davis, "Reply to Bret Davis: Zarathustra and Asian Thought: A Few Final Words," *Journal of Nietzsche Studies* 46.1 (Spring 2015), 82–88. Davis's rejoinder, "zebra stripes" and all, is "Reply to Graham Parkes: Nietzsche as Zebra: With Both Egoistic Antibuddha and Nonegoistic Bodhisattva Stripes," *Journal of Nietzsche Studies* 46.1 (Spring 2015), 62–81. Sarah Flavel also joins the debate, tending to side with Parkes (see "Nishitani's Nietzsche: Will to Power and the Moment," *Journal of Nietzsche Studies* 46.1 [Spring 2015], 12–24).

9. In contemporary Japan, Zen is chiefly associated with the funeral business (the Sōtōshū reports that 80 percent of laypeople visit Sōtō temples only for matters related to the funeral ceremony while less than 20 percent do so for reasons related to practice). See William M. Bodiford, "Zen in the Art of Funerals: Ritual Salvation in Japanese Buddhism," *History of Religions* 32. 2 (1992), 150.

10. *The Heart of Dōgen's Shōbōgenzō*, trans. Norman Waddell and Abe Masao (Albany: State University of New York Press, 2002). Henceforth HDS.

11. Gilles Deleuze, *Nietzsche and Philosophy* (1962), trans. Hugh Tomlinson (New York: Columbia University Press, 1983). Henceforth NP.

12. For more on this, see my *Mountains, Rivers, and the Great Earth: Reading Gary Snyder and Dōgen in an Age of Ecological Crisis* (Albany: State University of New York Press, 2017).

13. See the *The King of Medicine Master and Lapis Lazuli Light Sūtra* [*Haiṣajya-guru-vaiḍūrya-prabhā-rāja Sūtra*].

14. Here Nietzsche gives some of his most shocking formulations. The "lust to rule" is the "cruel torture that reserves itself for the very cruelest" and a "terrible teacher of the great despising." In the face of it, "the human being crawls and cowers and slaves away and becomes lower than snake and swine." Indeed, there is "nothing sick in such longing and condescension." Zarathustra declares selfishness "hallowed" and "wholesome" and "healthy" (Z, trans. Parkes, 164).

15. Dōgen in answer ten in "Bendōwa" formulates the Senika heresy: "There is in the body a spiritual intelligence . . . but when the body perishes, this spiritual intelligence separates from the body and is reborn in another place" (HDS, 21). There is nothing unitary like a soul at the seat of the self, nor does it make any sense to speak of our minds as in fundamental sense a unitary thing, permanent or otherwise.

16. See John Jorgensen, *Inventing Hui-neng, the Sixth Patriarch: Hagiography and Biography in Early Ch'an* (Leiden: Brill, 2005).

17. K'uo-an Shih-yuan, "The Ox-Herding Poems," *Zen Sourcebook*, ed. Stephen Addiss with Stanley Lombardo and Judith Roitman (Indianapolis: Hackett, 2008), 88.

18. See Anacleto Verrecchia, *La catastrofe di Nietzsche a Torino* (Turin, Italy: G. Einaudi, 1978). My thanks to Graham Parkes for this citation.

2

STRANGE SAINTS

Schopenhauer, Nietzsche, Hakuin

> Verily, the earth shall still become a place of healing.
> —Friedrich Nietzsche, "Of the Gift Giving Virtue,"
> *Thus Spoke Zarathustra* (KSA 4, 101)

WHAT IS COMPARATIVE PHILOSOPHY? DOES IT JUST BRING voices and texts from all over the world and set them next to each other and then get out a checklist and inventory the similarities and differences? Other than a fetish for lists, what is the *value* of such an endeavor? Moreover, when bringing figures like Dōgen or Hakuin into this exercise in inventory, one quickly realizes that despite being profound and difficult to understand, Dōgen or Hakuin are not doing exactly the sorts of things that we recognize as belonging to the enterprise of philosophy. Where is their epistemology or ethics? Most pressingly, where are the arguments?

This quandary, however, assumes that we have settled or even can settle what philosophy is, that its activities are self-evident and obvious, that philosophy does not require that we continue to be radically philosophical about philosophy itself. Even when philosophy itself is assumed to be the fixed term that governs what we compare, strange things can happen when the terms of the putative comparison challenge the fixed position of philosophy. Such oddities increase if one turns to someone like Nietzsche, who, we should remember, before the explosion of endless philosophical studies about him, was often not considered wrong or even insane, but also was not thought at all properly philosophical. Walter Kaufmann attempted to demonstrate that Nietzsche was not actually unhinged or a proto-Nazi but really a forerunner of Kaufmann himself. Most tellingly, at the onset of his career, Arthur Danto felt the need to help out the hapless Nietzsche and show him how to be a philosopher: "However, because we know a good deal more philosophy today, I believe it is exceedingly useful to see his analyses in terms of logical features which he was unable to make explicit, but toward which he was unmistakably groping. His language would have been less colorful had he known what he was trying to say."[1] Alas, poor Nietzsche the philosophical amateur! He "never had the discipline to write for a true public" (NAP, 200)! Had he only really understood how to philosophize, he could have more directly delivered himself over to the herd that he sought to contest.

This reluctance to even admit Nietzsche into the philosophical gates was not restricted to the West. Despite the influence he would eventually have on the Kyoto School philosopher Nishitani Keiji, Japan, taking its early philosophical cues largely from Germany, was also slow to open these gates. Graham Parkes tells us that when the great Watsuji Tetsurō, for example, wrote a dissertation on Nietzsche for the philosophy department at Tokyo Imperial University, it was rejected on the grounds that it did not count as a properly philosophical topic and he was consequently required to write on Schopenhauer.[2]

But what if we took seriously Nietzsche's contention that there is something decadent and exhausted, something that at best prefers sleep over thinking and living—"I like the poor in spirit, they help me sleep" says the chaired professor to Zarathustra (KSA 4, 33)—and at worst dramatizes a deep, pathological, reactive, *ressentiment*-driven, and ultimately nihilistic sickness operating at the provenance of the full range of what has mattered as properly philosophical?

Nietzsche had dedicated his philosophical life to making house calls on the terminal illness of the Western condition, which at its surface had many commitments, spiritual and intellectual attachments and values, but which at its heart, when honesty made its rare appearance, was virulently nihilistic. What if one brings him into dialogue with the great Tokugawa-era Rinzai reformer Hakuin? This was a Zen Master who deeply struggled with what he variously called *Zen-byō*, Zen sickness, and *kūbyō*, the disease of an attachment to emptiness (*śūnyatā*) and nothingness, in a word, the full throttle inflammation of nihilism in Zen practice.

What then is philosophy?

Our pursuit of this question first takes us through what Nietzsche considered the consummate and fully clarified expression of this malady, namely, the philosophical project of Schopenhauer, the so-called Buddha of Frankfurt. On the surface he was the *least Western of philosophers* as he attempted to extricate himself from the debilitating pain that was the veil of Māyā of human life. More deeply, he was *the most Western of philosophers*, the philosopher whose extraordinary honesty inadvertently allowed the nascently operating nihilism of Western thought to surface.

I. The Buddha of Frankfurt

Was Schopenhauer a Buddha and, as such, a saint?

Evidently he thought so.

In a handwritten note from Schopenhauer's *Nachlaß*, dated 1858, two years before he died, Schopenhauer wrote that "my teachings and those of the Buddha and the medieval Christian mystic Eckhart are virtually the same. However, while Eckhart is constrained by his Christian mythology, the same ideas are more openly propounded in Buddhism, with simplicity and clarity, as far as any religion is able to arrive at clear concepts at all."[3] Schopenhauer had to wait until he died to earn the designation the "Buddha of Frankfurt," although in his last years he actively professed himself to be a Buddhist.[4] He told his disciple Frauenstädt in an 1856 letter that he was now in possession of a foot-tall, allegedly Tibetan, bronze statue of the Buddha, which had been covered in lacquer, but which he had gilded. He placed it prominently in his apartment so that "visitors, who usually enter with considerable fright and some flap, will now understand immediately where they are: in a holy place."[5] Indeed, the following month he told Carl Grimm that it was "for domestic worship" (CN, 94) and shortly thereafter told Frauenstädt that he addressed it "Om, Mani, Padme, Hum" (CN, 94). The latter (*oṃ maṇi padme hūṃ*) is a six-syllable Sanskrit mantra popular especially among Tibetans to evoke the lotus-holding Avalokiteśvara (Tibetan: *Chenrézik*), the bodhisattva of compassion. As Schopenhauer continued to revise his collected works, he started inserting many positive references to Buddha Dharma.[6]

Although Schopenhauer had not yet discovered Buddhism when he initially wrote the first volume of his *Die Welt als Wille und Vorstellung* [*The World as Will and Representation*], he later turned to it with enthusiasm, and in the second volume he claimed that if he were to take his philosophy "as the measure of truth, I should have to concede to Buddhism pre-eminence over the others"; he was happy to see the "great confluence" between his own thinking and what he took to be the largest religion in the world (WWV II, 186; WWR II, 169). Nonetheless, Schopenhauer thought that Buddhism was the best that the genre of religion could do, given that religious language wrapped its account in the philosophically inferior garb of myth: "Never has a myth been, and never will one be, more closely associated with the philosophical truth accessible to so few" (WWV I, 421; WWR I, 356). Indeed, Schopenhauer came to understand himself as demythologizing the central Buddhist aspiration by reformulating it as the *"denial of the will-to-live"* (WWV I, 453; WWR I, 383). Schopenhauer cajoled us to "banish the dark impression of that nothingness, which as the final goal lies behind all virtue and holiness, and which we fear as children fear darkness. We must not even evade it, as the Indians do, by myths and meaningless words," which include nirvana (WWV I, 487; WWR I, 411). If one can annihilate the will, then one annihilates the "deep and painful *Sehnsucht.*" Quite simply, "No will: no representation, no world" (WWV I, 486; WWR I, 411). Wolfgang Schirmacher, president of the International Schopenhauer Association, goes so far as to conclude that "behind the mask of a pessimist Schopenhauer was a Zen master and arguably the greatest mystic of the nineteenth century."[7]

This gave rise to a sense of Buddha Dharma as nihilism in several senses: the absence of a beneficent and involved god, the vanity of all earthly things and strivings, and the evacuation of all positive values. Everything, as Nietzsche will later warn, is all in vain—*das Umsonst*! When Paul Challemel-Lacour visited Schopenhauer during the penultimate year of his life, he was treated to the Buddha of Frankfurt's familiar misanthropic vituperations, with only a few sprinkles of compassion tossed in to assuage the pain. "We are here in full Buddhism," he concluded. "These ideas are an emanation of the desperate doctrines that have been flourishing in India since the dawn of time" (CN, 101). One need only think of the last scene of Conrad's *Heart of Darkness* to appreciate the character of Frankfurt Buddhism. Marlow, having recounted that he could not tell Kurtz's widow his dying words ("The horror! The horror!"), instead mendaciously reporting that her name was his final utterance, concluded that it would "have been too dark—too dark altogether." The narrator then tells us that "Marlow ceased, and sat apart, indistinct and silent, in the pose of a meditating Buddha," and the narrator remarks that the "tranquil waterway . . . seemed to lead into the heart of an immense darkness."[8] Underneath the seeming tranquility of our interpreted world lurks the immense darkness and nothingness that does not protest either Kurtz's unhinged murderous ways or the normalized violence of the Belgian colonies in the Congo, but which also gives rise to Marlow's self-extinction and his consequent noncompliance with the horror that he witnessed.[9]

Schopenhauer may have struggled to live up to his own aspirations. Unlike the Buddha, he really craved an audience and found his solitude painfully lonely. Safranski tells us that "he did not acquire the tranquility of silence and laughter. He did not become the Buddha of Frankfurt. He found it hard to bear the silence around him. He wanted an answer, he listened for the tapping signals. When these began to swell into a roar, he was ready to die."[10] He died as the one who would be the Buddha of Frankfurt.

The Buddha of Frankfurt's thinking could be read as a kind of philosophical clarification and metaphysical justification of the Four Noble Truths, which, Magee claims, "apply, *mutatis mutandis*, to Schopenhauer's work" (PS, 342). Schopenhauer discusses them explicitly in the second volume of *Die Welt als Wille und Vorstellung*, calling them the *"vier Grundwahrheiten* [four fundamental truths]," citing them in Latin and claiming that all "improvement, conversion, and aspirational redemption from this world of suffering, this *saṃsāra*, stems from their knowledge" (WWV II, 716; WWR II, 623). The original noble truths themselves can be read as a kind of exercise in Āyurvedic medicine, as they first diagnose the disease (*duḥkha* and its etiology, the delusional craving and insatiable thirst of *tṛṣṇā*) and then prognosticate that there is a way beyond this (*nirodha*), and that the cure is the Noble Eightfold Path.

The first truth, the noble truth of *duḥkha*, what Schopenhauer cites as *"dolor"* (WWV II, 716; WWR II, 623), is the diagnosis of human living as out of whack, unbalanced, dis-eased, in turmoil, and hurting as if it were a broken wheel that can no longer progress. The theme of suffering is obviously not unfamiliar to Schopenhauer. Even in his relatively late 1851 essay "Nachträge zur Lehre vom Leiden der Welt" (from *Parerga und Paralipomena*),[11] we are told that pain belongs to the very fabric of appearance: "I know of no greater absurdity than that of most metaphysical systems which declare evil to be something negative; whereas it is precisely that which is positive and makes itself felt. On the other hand, that which is good, in other words, all happiness and satisfaction, is negative, that is, the mere elimination of a desire and the ending of a pain" (VLW, 312–313; ES, 2).

Here we are presented with "the conviction that the world, and therefore also humans, are something, that really should not have been" (VLW, 325; ES, 14); we are but a "needlessly disturbing episode in the blessed [*selig*] stillness of the nothing" and life "as a whole" is, and here Schopenhauer uses English, a "disappointment, nay a cheat," or, "to speak German," it is *eine Prellerei*, a swindle or fraud. All in all, there is "utter disappointment with all of life" (VLW, 321; ES, 10). The positivity of pain of which happiness is just a temporary alleviation is also dramatically articulated in the *Von der Nichtigkeit und dem Leiden des Lebens* discourse (chapter 46) of the second volume of *Die Welt als Wille und Vorstellung*. Suffering testifies to the vanity, inanity, and nullity—all senses of *Nichtigkeit*—of life.

Schopenhauer opposed Leibniz's cheery theodicy and countered that this is "the worst of all possible worlds" (WWV II, 669; WWR II, 583). Why? Schopenhauer's account of the "blind will to life" offers a deflationary account of time, space, and causality as the sufficient condition of being. It explains why there is something rather than nothing. However, this explanation renders any teleological, purpose-driven account absurd. There is only the blind, purposeless flow of becoming. Rather than cheerfully considering the flow of becoming as a "gift," Schopenhauer turned this upside down and declared it a "debt" (WWV II, 665–666; WWR II, 580). Indeed, time condemns all human desire to swing from boredom and ennui (too much time) to anguish need, want, craving, and *Sehnsucht* (too little time), for death and destruction, the way of all things, is nature's final appraisal of all things, revealing life to be "an enterprise that does not cover the costs" (WWV II, 658; WWR II, 574).[12] Human life, indeed, being as such, has no positive value, its nullity and worthlessness being an affront to human striving and ambition. This is the vale of tears, hell itself, where we are both victim and executioner; it is the agony of the veil of Māyā, the worthlessness of the life of *saṃsāra*.

The second truth is the noble truth of the origin, which lies in an insatiable thirst (Skt. *tṛṣṇā*) and which can be more broadly understood as the three poisons (Skt. *triviṣa*) or unhealthy roots or bewildering affects (Skt. *kleśas*). Driving the other *kleśas* is the unhealthy and toxic root of ignorance and delusion (Skt: *avidyā* or *moha*) in which I am confused about the nature of things. This in turns drives desire to the twin faces of craving: attachment (Skt. *rāga*), that is, my demand that the pleasing aspects of my life abide, that life accord with my preferences and needs, and aversion or hatred (Skt. *dveṣa*), that is, my rueful refusal of and vengeance against all of the aspects of my life that contest my attachments. Yet, as Dōgen famously remarks in the *Genjō Kōan*, in attachment the flowers still fall and in aversion the weeds still grow.

Schopenhauer reengineers this "myth" into the insatiability and *Sehnsucht* of the will to life as it blindly individuates the becoming of the spacetime realm of appearance. Pain is the inhibition, impediment, and frustration of the will (VLW, 319; ES, 8). We never get what we want, or if we do, we want more, and if we don't, we rail against life, all the time being hapless pawns in the absurd and directionless play of *Vorstellung*, the will to life: the painful and frustrating (never enough except when there is too much) nightmare that is the veil of Māyā.

The third truth is the noble truth of cessation or extinction (*nirodha*). There is a way out of the symptom of *duḥkha* and its root cause, an egress that is sometimes associated with *nirvāṇa*. For Schopenhauer, one "willingly sacrifices the existence that we know and, in its lieu, becomes what to our eyes seems like *nothing* because our existence with reference to this person is *nothing*. The Buddhist faith dubs this nirvana, that is, *Erloschen*," extinguished, gone out, as in a fire (WWV II, 583; WWR II 508, 560).

Schopenhauer's *nirodha* is to annihilate the will to life and thereby our involvement in the pseudo-reality of the universe: "To those in whom the will has turned and denied itself, this so very real world of ours with all of its suns and milky ways is—nothing" (WWV I, 487; WWR I, 412). To this Schopenhauer appended a note: "This is also precisely the *Prajna-Paramita* of the Buddhists, the 'beyond all knowledge,' that is, the point where subject and object are no more" (WWV I, 487; WWR I, 412). Schopenhauer cited Isaac Jacob Schmidt (1779–1847) and his 1836 book on the *Prajñāpāramitā*,[13] whose translation he had made from Mongolian sources (CN, 55) and which he had published less than a decade after he had translated the Bible into Mongolian. In this respect, the supreme accomplishment of the philosophical life for Schopenhauer becomes *gate gate pāragate pārasaṃgate*—gone, gone, gone beyond, utterly gone beyond as the *Heart Sūtra* has it, albeit understood from the perspective of Schopenhauer's annihilation of the will to live and thereby the annihilation of the world, whose very positivity is rife with pain.

The fourth noble truth is the truth of the path leading to *nirodha*, namely, the Noble Eightfold Path, which Schopenhauer abbreviates as the diversions of aesthetic engagement and, most critically, ethics.[14] In the latter, all actions are motivated and it is in the quality of the motivation that its moral worth can be appraised. Schopenhauer took even his beloved Kant to task for arguing that ethics is fundamentally about imperatives, that is, the task of discerning what we *should* do or *ought* to do. It is to Kant's credit that he dismissed εὐδαιμονία—clearly for Schopenhauer the optimism that we can discern the positive excellences by which we would flourish just sets us up for further pain and disappointment. However, Kant's categorical imperative begs the question,[15] confusing the principle (what it should explain, i.e., what the principle actually is) with its ground (what explains or justifies the principle)—its principle is its own ground (it justifies itself by being itself), commanding itself into existence much as Baron von Münchhausen pulled himself up by his own bootstraps. As he sneaks this little principle quietly in through the back door, it is then able raise all kinds of ruckus, allowing Kant to resurrect a theological ethics (the Mosaic voice of God pronouncing its stern "thou shalts") after the deicide that his own critical philosophy had wrought.

Schopenhauer judges an action by its motivation—what kind of character plays itself out in this action?—and here we can already detect a powerful aspect of Schopenhauer's influence on Nietzsche. When the latter uses his hammer and tuning fork to evaluate the reigning virtues of contemporary life, he genealogically detects something not to be esteemed playing itself out in them. That being said, Nietzsche will be critical of what motivates Schopenhauer's own analysis of ethical motivation.

The ethically worthy motive extirpates the misery of egoism by extending *die Menschenliebe*, the virtue of loving kindness, to one's fellow suffers, *compagnon de misères* or *Leidensgefährte*, which includes, in a rare and impassioned defense, animals, whose well-being has generally received short shrift from the Peoples of the Book. Schopenhauer associates *Menschenliebe* with the buried root of Christianity, *agapē* and *caritas* (GM, 226; BM, 228) and also links it both to the Vedas and to the Buddha, presumably alluding to *karuṇā*, compassion, critical to the bodhisattva ideal in Mahāyāna. It is also part of what Theravada extols as one of the four *brahmavihāras* or "abodes of Brahma," the four immeasurable and sublime attitudes or affective dispositions, the others being *mettā*, usually translated as "loving kindness," and an active involvement in the betterment of the lives of others; *muditā*, the opposite of *ressentiment* being the capacity to share in the joy of others; and finally, *upekkhā*, the underlying equanimity and peacefulness that facilitates such generosity. For Schopenhauer, *Menschenliebe* takes one beyond justice, which is founded on doing less or no harm to others, to *Mitleid*, compassion, "by means of which another's suffering in itself and as such immediately becomes my motive" (GM, 227; BM, 229).

One's motive, "the endpoint of all morality," is the principle, which, "like everything beautiful best distinguishes itself in the nude," can be variously formulated as "harm no one; rather, help everyone as much as you can [*neminem laede, imo omnes, quantum potes, juva*]" (GM, 162; BM, 173), or Schopenhauer's variation of a *mettā* meditation, "May all living beings remain free of pain" (GM, 236; BM, 237).

The principle is itself quite paradoxical. I am not driven to love by love itself, for that would be love as an object of the will to life, which in turn would make love just another occasion for agony. In a sense, ethics helps one more or less reengineer oneself: pain drives me to ethics, but ethics drives me away from myself, away from the misery of the blind *principium individuationis*. Selfless acts invert the movement of the will to life and its drive to involvement with this worthless and excruciating world, returning it away from the world that should never have been to the peaceful stillness of the lost unity of the pure plenum: "If multiplicity and discreteness just belong to appearance, and if it is one and the same being that presents itself in all that lives, then the view in which the distinction between I and non-I is sublated [*aufgehoben*] is not erroneous." This world is just the veil of Māyā, "that is, deceptive appearance [*Schein*], delusion [*Täuschung*], trick image [*Gaukelbild*]" (GM, 270; BM 267), seemingly like the famous final chapter of the *Diamond Sūtra* when it counsels:

> As a lamp, a cataract, a star in space
> an illusion, a dewdrop, a bubble
> a dream, a cloud, a flash of lightning
> view all created things like this.[16]

This paradoxical overcoming of all interest in pain alleviating selflessness, the realization that all individuation is just an appearance caused by the blind willing of space and time, gives rise to the great pronouncement of the principle in the *Chāndogyo Upaniṣad*: "*tat tvam asi*," "you are that" (GM, 271; BM, 268), that is, the individuated self (*ātman*) is originally the unindividuated *Brahman*. The scandal of appearance, where individuated beings struggle and compete with each other, yields to peaceful nonstriving of *neti neti*, not this, not this, and compassion emerges from and returns to this originary unity. It is a "mysterious action, a practical mysticism" (GM, 273; BM, 270), and, as such, of a piece with all mysticism east and west, including the kernel of wisdom hidden in the otherwise wretched hagiographies of the later. In such a mystical interruption of the painful grip of the world, each person, each fellow sufferer, is my emptied self as all others.

II. Nietzsche and the Inflammation of European Buddhism

In 1865, after his unhappy year as a student at Bonn, Nietzsche left the Rhineland to study in Leipzig and took a room above Herr Rohn's *Antiquariat*.

Shortly thereafter he discovered a copy of Schopenhauer's *Die Welt als Wille und Vorstellung* in his landlord's shop,[17] and the book ripped the young Nietzsche out of the measure of his time. In his *Schopenhauer als Erzieher* [*Schopenhauer as Educator*] (1874), written less than a decade later, Nietzsche tells us that Schopenhauer was a great educator because he could shatter the hold of an age's sense of itself, leaving one out of the measure of the age [*unzeitgemäß*]; he could elevate one above insufficient learning "in as much as it lay in the age and again teach one to be *simple* and *honest* in thinking and living" (KSA 1, 346). Like Diogenes, Schopenhauer distressed and saddened his audience (KSA 1, 426). Yet despite Schopenhauer's unrelenting pessimism and misanthropy, his subversive and impious sense of humor was also not lost on Nietzsche, who contended that he, like Montaigne, had a "cheerfulness that actually cheers" (KSA 1, 348).

Schopenhauer strategically remained aloof from "state and society" and avoided the "scholarly castes" (KSA 1, 351) and all other such types who could easily be bought out—it was a "great favor" that he had to work early in his life because "a scholar can never become a philosopher" (KSA 1, 409). The age that Schopenhauer rejected, however, returned the favor. He became "an utter recluse" (KSA 1, 353), retreating to the solitude that philosophy furnishes as the "asylum" of an "inward cave" (KSA 1, 354). Indeed, this was in a sense the great pain that befalls such "uncustomary humans": utter isolation and forlornness, to "drive them so deep into themselves that their reemergence each time becomes a volcanic eruption" (KSA 1, 355) like the forlorn Kleist's double suicide or the loneliness of Beethoven's music.

Nietzsche already rejected the universal pretensions of Schopenhauer's ontology—why there is something rather than nothing and why we are consequently so screwed and justly miserable—but he admired the relentless honesty with which he understood the pain of his own life and the extent to which he sought in it an antidote in justice and compassion and, as such, the "hieroglyphs of universal life" (KSA 1, 357). Nietzsche learned from Schopenhauer, Bazzano tells us, "the imperative of rigorously studying the self . . . not out of solipsism but firm in the knowledge that such investigation would be valuable to all" (BD, 17). This is also a good Buddhist teaching.

This was at the heart of Nietzsche's early analysis of Schopenhauer's Buddhism: Schopenhauer's "peculiar and supremely dangerous duality" (KSA 1, 358), namely, his peaceful and self-assured confidence in the value and power of his philosophical work and his longing or *Sehnsucht* "to be *reborn* as a saint and as a genius" (KSA 1, 358). He was pleased with his capacities even as they exacerbated his immense discontent with himself and the great earth; "in the other half lived a turbulent longing" (KSA 1, 358) that drove him to seek through ethical self-cultivation what he imagined to be the "other shore" of Buddhist awakening. "For the genius longs more profoundly for saintliness because from his lookout he has seen farther and more clearly than other humans: he has seen down into the reconciliation of knowing and being, within that the realm of peace and the denial of the will, and beyond all of that toward the 'other shore' of which the Indian [Buddhists] speak" (KSA 1, 358).

Until the last year of his writerly life, Nietzsche still considered Schopenhauer worthy of our attention—he was the last German thinker who could be considered "a European event" (KSA 6, 125). Nonetheless, abandoning God and the existence of otherworldly comforts, he refashioned the transcendent dimension of Christian redemption into the peace of the will to life's self-decimation, making him in Nietzsche's eyes a "strange saint" (KSA 6, 125)! Schopenhauer enacts a great inversion, taking the "great self-affirmation of the 'will to life,' life's form of exuberance"—here Nietzsche speaks of this as if it were the will to power itself—and subjects it to the "maleficently genial attempt" to transform it into its "counter instance," a "nihilistic total devaluation of life" (KSA 6, 125). Schopenhauer's ethics are the consummation of our war against the earth: it "is the *décadence*-instinct itself that makes an imperative out of itself, saying, 'Perish!'—as such, it is the judgment of the condemned." (KSA 6, 86). Indeed, morality "prepares poison for life and calumniates it" by showing us, Schopenhauer tells us, that with every great pain, we get what we have coming (KSA 6, 94). This is the exhaustion of *décadence*, "the will to power going down" (KSA 6, 183)—it is all just too much! The earth is consequently evacuated of all value: "Nothing is worth anything,—life is worth nothing." As religion, this is Christianity, and as philosophy, this is *Schopenhauerei* (KSA 6, 134).

For Nietzsche, Buddhism, much like Schopenhauer, is decadent, an effort to alleviate the pain. Like Christianity, it is a religion of *décadence*, but with some advantages, including the fact that it is more realistic and positivistic as well as that it goes beyond the bifurcation of the earth into good and evil (its acceptable aspects and its detestable ones). Nonetheless, as an expression of *décadence*, it suffers from "an outsized irritability of the sensibility" and hence, in the Buddhist "struggle against suffering" (and not sin), Buddhists seek, as did Schopenhauer in his own way, to mitigate the pain.

Given that the "over-spiritualization" of Indian culture—or perhaps Asian culture more broadly—tends toward the "preference for the impersonal" rather than the "person instinct" (KSA 6, 186), Buddhists, responding to the "depression" of hypersensitivity and impersonality, cultivate a "spiritual diet" to alleviate suffering (KSA 6, 187). It is not the way of beliefs but rather of "hygiene," including a hygienic response to *ressentiment*, which, in the Abrahamic West, drove the priests to process the humiliation they felt at the greatness of the earth by minimizing the power of the earth to something less threatening and challenging. Rather than build oneself a good pair of shoes, as the Buddhists do, the priests attempted to cover the earth with leather (and, since Nietzsche's time, with concrete).

Nietzsche's Buddha combated life fatigue and the deflation and depression of egoless impersonality by bringing everything back to the "person" (KSA 6, 187). Like Schopenhauer, espying the "other shore" from the watchtower of his genius, "Buddhism is a religion for the conclusion and the fatigue of civilization" (KSA 6, 189). Unlike Christianity, which is based on fantastical promises of a miraculous deliverance from the unbearable suffering of the earth to the positivity of a domain of endless and pain-free happiness, the modesty, realism, and mild-mannered positivism (no gods, no morals, no extreme asceticism, no compulsion) of Buddhism allows it to alleviate in the here and now the pain for which we are too sensitive; "Buddhism does not promise but rather delivers while Christianity promises everything, but delivers *nothing*" (KSA 6, 215).

In *The Gay Science*, Nietzsche surveyed Schopenhauer's "mystical embarrassments and subterfuges," which included his "unprovable doctrine of a *single will*"—in direct contrast to the multiplicity of the will to power—and his "denial of individuals" (all individuals are but instantiations of a single Platonic ideal), which is another diminishment and devaluation of the multiplicity of becoming. Schopenhauer's reliance on the *principium individuationis* enables not only his "nonsense" about compassion but also Schopenhauer's canard that "death is actually the purpose of existence" (KSA 3, 454). In *Götzen-Dämmerung* [*Twilight of the Idols*], Nietzsche defends a natural death, which has nothing to do with the hoax of natural law in which we are not allowed to choose our deaths—we die only when nature decides that we should, no matter how thoroughly vegetal we have become. To insist on dying with dignity is regarded as an unnatural death, suicide, and Nietzsche concludes that Christianity should never be forgiven for having abused the "weakness of the dying." To insist on the manner and time of one's own death could not be more natural because it emerges out "of a love of *living*." Schopenhauer's ethics, however, are most honestly *self-negation*, and the immense ruse of his ethics is nothing less than a lack of clarity about the suicidal implications of his thinking. Schopenhauer's suicide would "liberate life from an *objection*" (KSA 6, 135).

In the same way that Heidegger demoted poor Schelling and Nietzsche to the consummation of the Western metaphysics in subjectivity—a strange claim for two thinkers who fought the ruse of subjectivity so strenuously—Schopenhauer's Buddhism, including his renovation of the Christian saints and mystics into post-theistic Buddhists, reveals the core of European nihilism: its utter exhaustion and hostility to life. "Who has grounds to lie their way out of actuality?" Christianity did this with imaginary causes and extravagantly fantastical promises while European Buddhism embraces a slow and surgical autoextinction. These are the ones who *"suffer* from it. But to suffer from actuality means to be an actuality that has *met with misfortune*" (KSA 6, 182).

European Buddhism is the autoannihilation of the *décadence* of Christian Europe, unable to affirm the great earth now that God no longer promises an escape route and now that we have surrendered any sense of the earth's value to the conniving priests who are the cure to the sickness they promulgate. European Buddhism reveals that God was the "deification of nothingness" (KSA 6, 185). All that remains is to dull the pain of sickness, old age, and death. Hence, in the *Genealogy*, Nietzsche reflects on the misfortune of his "great teacher Schopenhauer," whose turn to an ethics of compassion and egolessness and "self-sacrifice" became the "ground of saying no to life as well as to himself." This was not an individual misfortune but rather the karmic tentacles of a Christianity that enervates everything from our grammar to our philosophical imagination:

> I saw precisely here the *great* danger to humanity, its most sublime allure and seduction—yet where to? to the nothing?—I saw precisely here the beginning of the end, stoppage, the backwards-looking fatigue, the will turning itself *against* life, the final sickness looming tenderly and with melancholy; I understood the morality of compassion, proliferating more and more and having gripped philosophers and made them sick, as the most uncanny symptom of our now uncanny European culture, as its detour to a new Buddhism? to a European Buddhism? to—nihilism? (KSA 5, 252)

In this extraordinary passage, *Schopenhauerei* is the indicator species of an ecology in runaway, the first symptom of an underlying sickness that is beginning to spread over Abrahamic Europe, a nihilistic plague in which the will to life has become so sick that it no longer expresses the power of life but rather inverts itself into the will to death. "Compassion persuades one to *the nothing*! ... [O]ne does not say, 'the nothing': one says in its place 'the beyond,' or 'God,' or 'the *true* life,' or nirvana, salvation, blessedness" (KSA 6 173). This is what Hakuin from a Zen perspective diagnosed as Zen sickness (*kūbyō*), a fixation with and attachment to *śūnyatā* or emptiness.

It is critical to note that Nietzsche is not counseling that we all become cruel or that we cease to care for each other. Nietzsche belongs to an ancient and noble lineage of thinking that extols the nonasphyxiating power of friendship with each other, with nonhuman animals (his eagles, snakes, bears, and lions), and with the earth itself. This is not the call for a moral holiday in which everyone can be mean. Like Schopenhauer, he wants to find a way to assess the value of actions without resorting to the infantilizing (theological) commands of oughts and shoulds. Schopenhauer's call to compassion (*Mitleid*), however, annihilates the self and the earth, deracinating one from the earth altogether. "It acts as a depressant" (KSA 6, 172).

The question is therefore not what we should do, but rather what is being expressed, what is playing itself out, in Schopenhauer's call to compassion? Under such compassion lurks a motivating hatred of the earth, a hatred of the self, an exhaustion with living, and an unfortunate life that seeks to assuage its pain by seducing people to annihilate their own bitterness by annihilating the earth. Pain has carried the day and its compassionate smile hides its taste for blood. Schopenhauer was what Zarathustra called a "preacher of death," and, as such, a decadent European Buddha: "They encounter a sick person or an old person or a corpse and immediately say, 'Life is refuted'" (KSA 4, 55)! This is a clear reference to the received account of the Buddha's own life, which Nietzsche knew from his study of the Indologist Hermann Oldenberg's (1854–1920) 1881 work, *Buddha: Sein Leben, seine Lehre, seine Gemeinde,* which was translated a year later into English as *Buddha: His Life, His Doctrine, His Order* (1882),[18] and which has remained in print ever since. The young prince discovers the realities of sickness, old age, and death and is "directed to that path which leads away beyond the power of all suffering" (BHL, 103). For Oldenberg, the Buddha was a "pessimist" not because he thought that this world was an illusion, a mere veneer over nothingness, but rather because life "consists of suffering and nothing but suffering" (BHL, 212). Every being is like a flame and suffering ends when the flame is extinguished (*nirvāṇa*) and all clinging to this painful world is eliminated (BHL, 234). Oldenberg, too, discovered his own exhausted culture in ancient India. To this, Zarathustra counsels, "They really prefer to be dead and so we should respect what they want" (KSA 4, 55). If "life is only suffering," then "take care that *you* stop! Take care that your life stops the life that is only suffering" (KSA 4, 56). If your eye offends you pluck it out, and if that eye is your life, just cut to the chase and end it!

The genealogy of the compassion that preaches death is sickness and exhaustion, not the value of the earth and life. "It was suffering and incapacity," Zarathustra tells us, "that created every *Hinterwelt*," every world that we believe exists as a reality beneath the painful appearance of this one, and attainment of this underlying reality, even if it is only the stillness of nothingness itself, creates "that short mad happiness that only those who supremely suffer experience." Compassion is an example of the narcotic need among those, overwhelmed by their suffering, who long for that self-annihilating mad happiness. Nietzsche evaluated the value of compassion and the value of morality more generally (Abrahamic European moral values and their consummation in European Buddhist values): "*The value of these values is put to the question for the first time*" (KSA 5, 253). Nietzsche's demotion of Buddhism to *décadence* is therefore inseparable from his struggle with the prophetic force of Schopenhauer's *décadence*.[19]

All that remains at the death knell of God is for us to die to ourselves and become nothing because the ideal or supposedly real or true world is at least not this world. This is the last gasp of the thing in itself, now emptied of the promise of the divine redemption of our pain, the "grey morning" of an "unattained and *unknown*" true world, which is "consequently also not comforting, redemptive, deontological" (KSA 6, 80). Our otherworldly aspirations, our impatience for the true world, are now a death wish, the yearning to have the awful samsaric burden of the veil of Māyā lifted.

The incipient nihilism exposed by a terminally ill Christianity and the inflamed nihilism of Schopenhauer's compassion speak to perhaps the greatest of the great occidental (Abrahamic-Buddhist European) errors: the *post hoc ergo propter hoc* fallacy (the confusion of cause and effect, mistaking a correlation for an explanation, e.g., after this, therefore explained by this) of morality itself: if you are moral, you will be happy. If you are moral, you will go to heaven or, as a last gasp, if you are moral, you will annihilate the positive pain of the will to life. If we are not moral, so the argument goes, all hell will break loose and, unrestrained by moral commands, we will do whatever we want. "I name this the great original sin of reason, the immortal unreason." It is not virtue that makes us happy but rather happiness that makes us virtuous. "The first example of my transvaluation of values" (Nietzsche setting right side up what has been set upside down) is that "a well behaved human, a 'fortunate one [ein Glücklicher],' must perform certain actions and instinctively shies away from others. . . . In a formula: his virtue is the result of his happiness [Glück]" (KSA 6, 89).

Indeed, the problem with religion is not that it is religion but rather that it is religion insofar as it dramatizes and plays out the otherworldly (or underworldly) nihilism of *décadence*. Religion is something else entirely when it dramatizes the vitality of the happy. It is no longer the desperate recourse to an imaginary cause to make the discomfort of the unknown go away. Since we are only motivated by the desire to alleviate pain, we are not choosy: "The first representation that explains the unknown as the known does just fine" (KSA 6, 93). For the fortunate ones, pain is not an automatic objection. Such a religion would be a "form of gratitude. One is thankful for oneself, and for that one needs a god," although such a god would be both "friend and enemy" (KSA 6, 182).

Dionysian religion is not a religion that worships Dionysus—it does not worship anyone or anything. It is religiosity that dramatizes a sense of plentitude and vitality. Writing against Darwin and his view of nature as a struggle over limited resources—a hungry earth grounded in lack—Nietzsche argued that while such moments speak to the part, they do not speak to the whole: "Such things happen, but they are the exception; the whole aspect of life is not the condition of distress and the condition of hunger, but rather wealth, luxuriance, even absurd prodigality. . . . One should not confuse Malthus with nature" (KSA 6, 120). The narrow ecology of human needs and enterprises cannot in itself allow the general economy of nature's wealth, the will to power itself, to manifest. As Bataille was later to warn: "Woe to those who, to the very end, insist on regulating the movement that exceeds them with the narrow mind of a mechanic who changes a tire."[20]

III. Hakuin's Great Self

Nietzsche provides an illuminating point of disclosure to begin to think of the limits and pitfalls of reducing Zen practice and its motivating force to *Schopenhauerei*. Freny Mistry argued almost four decades ago that we are unwise to put too much importance on Nietzsche's reduction of the whole Buddhist tradition to *Schopenhauerei*. "Nietzsche to be sure opposes his view of art and power to Buddhist nirvana; his perspective, however, strikes us as an approximation of the Buddhist ideal." If Nietzsche is right and Buddhist practice, including Zen, is an early Indian form of proto-*Schopenhauerei*, it is hard to defend and it merely exacerbates the crisis of the Death of God. If what Mistry sees, as well as many others, including Brian Schroeder, Bret Davis, Graham Parkes, André van der Braak, Manu Bazzano, and others, is defensible, then it opens a critical space in which Zen addresses the spiritual crises of the West.

Graham Parkes tells us that despite the many pitfalls of the early Japanese Nietzsche reception, Anesaki Masaharu (1873–1949), who went by the nom de plume Chōfū, was able to see that the selfless self of the *Übermench*, including presumably Nietzsche's strange "egoism" (an ego without an underlying self, egoism as a selfless self) could also be grasped from the Zen perspective as the nonduality of no self (*muga*, 無我, Skt. *anātman*) and the great self (*daiga*, 大我) (ERN, 181–182). Schopenhauer had only made it as far as the *muga-jakumetsu*, the "blissful dissolution" of the "I," but had not yet found his way, as Nietzsche in some way did, to the *daiga-kyūjū*, the endurance of the great self (ERN, 188).

One of the clearest—and, in an appealing way, somewhat Nietzschean—critiques of the enervating nihilism of *kūbyō*, the sickness of an attachment to the hypostatization of emptiness, is found in Hakuin. One often hears that the Rinzai School emphasizes kōan practice in order to attain awakening (*satori*), while the Sōtō School, holding that we are already awake, emphasizes what Dōgen called *shushō-ittō*, the oneness of practice and realization. There is no realization to attain at the end of some arduous process. In the end, however, such characterizations are facile, at least when weighed against their greatest teachers (Hakuin and Dōgen).

Hakuin insisted that *kenshō*, the awakening to one's original face, is just the beginning, a necessary but not sufficient condition for practice. Along with his disciples, including Tōrei, he taught *kōjō* (Chinese: *hsiangshang*) or going beyond, "never resting on an awareness," Michel Mohr tells us, "even if one is left breathless by its contents."[21] Tōrei claimed that *kenshō*, while necessary for Zen practice—you cannot go beyond if there is nothing to go beyond—is not unique to Zen but can be found in Shinto, Confucian, and Daoist practice. Zen, at least as understood by Hakuin's reformation of it, according to Tōrei, distinguishes itself "by deepening all aspects of Buddhist Dharma" (EN, 264). Hakuin and his Dharma heirs called this *gogo no shugyō* (悟後の修行), postsatori training or postrealization practice.

The Tale of How I Spurred Myself on in My Childhood[22] and *Wild Ivy* are Hakuin's two autobiographical accounts. In the first, he offers the follies of his early life of practice to spur on lay practitioners who, after having earned their dragon staff certificates from Hakuin verifying their *kenshō*, were resting on their laurels; they were pleased merely to have seen (*ken*) their own nature (*shō*) and assumed that they had achieved the endpoint of Zen. Their iron resolve to and unyielding faith in practice had gathered into the great ball of doubt, burst into the great death, and then they were done.

Hakuin recounts his own furious pursuit of *kenshō* in which he continuously "sat in zazen like a dead man." And then it happened:

> I reached the end of reason, reached the limit of words, reached the end of all human skill or ability. Ordinary mental processes, consciousness, and emotions all ceased to function. It was as though I was encased in a sheet of ice ten thousand feet thick or sitting inside a bottle of pure crystal. My breath itself seemed to hang suspended. Then, in the middle of the night, a wonderful thing happened. As the sound of a distant bell reached my ears, I suddenly broke through into great enlightenment. It was mind and body falling away; fallen away mind and body. . . . The great earth completely and utterly vanished. Not a particle remained. (HP, 25–26)

Hakuin's awakening experience alludes to Dōgen's own experience of awakening, but with a critical difference. Dōgen's *shinjin datsuraku*, the falling and casting away of body and mind, was an awakening to the great earth, the emergence of the great earth "without a particle of soil left out." Hakuin was absorbed into emptiness and "the great earth completely and utterly vanished. Not a particle remained." Emptiness usurped the earth. "From that time on, everyone I saw appeared to exist within a field of gossamer that shimmered and danced in the summer air," an awakening that ironically made him feel really good about himself and his "arrogance raced forth like an onrushing tide" (HP, 26).

This turned out to be an enervating attainment. As he later entered into kōan training with Shōju Rōjin, his pride was crushed and his aspiration for awakening and striving was reawakened. He came to see that the "silent illumination" fantasy of Zen practice, "which consists in merely achieving a state of non-seeking or non-attachment, no-thought, or no-mind," portends "the demise of the Buddha's Dharma, and [is] the fundamental reason the true traditions of Zen are dying out" (HP, 33). This is "false do-nothing" Zen, free from genuine exertion and striving, abiding in a quietistic detachment from the earth. Emptiness, Nāgārjuna taught, is, after all, empty of emptiness. It is not something to attain or a place to go.

Hakuin's *Yasenkanna* [*Idle Talk on a Night Boat*], which has remained in print since his lifetime, speaks of his suffering from Zen sickness. Hakuin realized that if he did not master Naikan meditation, meditation dedicated to balancing the "ocean of *ki*" with the earth—breathing through his feet—he would be "no better than one of those disembodied, corpse-guarding spirits that cling mulishly to emptiness" (HP, 93). The *shushiki* or "corpse guarding spirit" is a spirit detached from one's own body, disallowing emptiness to energize it, keeping it a corpse, a dead relationship to emptiness. Hakuin was suffering from a superabundance of yin (the elements of emptiness had lost their relationship to the yang elements of the earth and its myriad forms), and his body and mind were listless. As his Zen body rooted itself back into the emptiness of the earth (and not emptiness as such, emptiness without the earth), his awakening deepened. Awakening to the earth is "to churn the great sea into the finest butter, to transform the great earth into the purest gold" (HP, 104).

When *Māra* tormented the Buddha with doubts, the Buddha refuted him by touching the earth. Is this not to learn to breathe through the feet? "The Buddha himself taught that we should 'cure all kinds of illness by putting the heart down to the arches of the feet'" (HPC, 106). Is this not to remain truthful to the meaning of the earth?

Here Hakuin resonates with one of the most delicate but critical insights of Mahāyāna Buddha Dharma, one that its traditions often fail to appreciate. Emptiness is itself an expedient or purgative or physic, that is, part of the Buddha's medicine chest—he is the medicine king after all. If emptiness becomes an end in itself, if it becomes the view that we now associate with nihilism, then the cure gives rise to an even greater sickness. Nāgārjuna is perhaps the greatest and most radical of all Buddhist philosophers; he claimed in his masterpiece, the *Mūlamadhyamakakārikā*,[23] that the view, *prapañca* (hypostatization or reification), of emptiness turns that which is designed to rid one of all *prapañca* into the worst *prapañca* of all: "those for whom emptiness is a *prapañca* have been called incurable" (N, 145). His great successor, Chandrakīrti, quotes the Buddha's dialogue with Kāśyapa on this point. If the psychic or purgative to cure a disease is not itself expelled, is the person cured? Kāśyapa responded that the "illness of the person would be more intense" (quoted in N, 145). Those who hypostasize the Buddha, Nāgārjuna later argues, are "deceived" and "fail to see the Tathāgata" (N, 250). There is no one self-standing thing that either the Buddha or beings of this world are, especially not the thing called nothing. "Emptiness misunderstood destroys the slow-witted, like a serpent wrongly held or a spell wrongly executed" (N, 274).

Schopenhauer grabbed the serpent of emptiness by the head and received a mighty dose of its venom. Zarathustra bit its head off and that made all the difference. Schopenhauer could not chew the cud of nothingness, and it gave him philosophically lethal indigestion. In the impending dyspepsia of the collapse of traditional values and the virulence of nihilism, Nietzsche regarded rumination as the preeminent contemporary task. This is the advent of the Great Health to which we now turn.

Notes

1. Arthur C. Danto, *Nietzsche as Philosopher* (New York: Macmillan, 1965), 13. Henceforth NAP.

2. Graham Parkes, "The Early Reception of Nietzsche's Philosophy in Japan," in *Nietzsche and Asian Thought*, ed. Graham Parkes (Chicago: University of Chicago Press, 1991), 192. Henceforth ERN.

3. Quoted in Thomas Regehly, "Schopenhauer, Buddha and Kamadamana: The Problem of Suffering and Redemption in Thomas Mann's Novel 'The Transposed Heads,'" in *Schopenhauer and Indian Philosophy: A Dialogue between India and Germany*, ed. Arati Barua (New Delhi, India: Northern Book Centre, 2008), 190. Schopenhauer argued for the similarity of the Buddha and Meister Eckhart toward the end of the second volume of *Die Welt als Wille und Vorstellung*. While the Buddha "dared to express his ideas plainly and positively," Eckhart was "obliged to clothe them in the garment of Christian myth." *The World as Will and Representation*, 2 vols., trans. E. F. J. Payne (Indian Hills, CO: Falcon's Wing, 1958), 614. Henceforth WWR, followed by volume number and page citation and preceded by the German original, which in this case is Julius Frauenstädt's *Arthur Schopenhauers Sämmtliche Werke*, 2nd ed. (Leipzig: Brockhaus, 1891). Henceforth WWV for *Die Welt als Wille und Vorstellung*. Meister Eckhart's writings did not become widely available until Franz Pfeiffer published his edition of them in 1857 (see WWV I, 450; WWR I, 381). I have altered many of the translations in light of the German original.

4. David E. Cartwright, *Schopenhauer: A Biography* (Cambridge: Cambridge University Press, 2010), 273–274.

5. Quoted in Roger-Pol Droit, *The Cult of Nothingness: The Philosophers and the Buddha*, trans. David Streight and Pamela Vohnson (Chapel Hill: University of North Carolina Press, 2003), 93. Henceforth CN.

6. Schopenhauer was a voracious reader of research on nineteenth-century Hindu and especially Buddhist thought. Moira Nichols, who argues that Schopenhauer could not extricate himself from "substance ontology" (194) as the Buddhists do, reports that he had between thirty-eight and forty-four Buddhist titles, depending on whose accounting one accepts (204). She also provides an authoritative list of all of Schopenhauer's textual

allusions to Buddhist texts (200–203). Moira Nichols, "The Influences of Eastern Thought on Schopenhauer's Doctrine of the Thing-in-Itself," *Cambridge Companion to Schopenhauer*, ed. Christopher Janaway, 171–212 (Cambridge: Cambridge University Press, 1999).

7. Wolfgang Schirmacher, "Living Disaster: Schopenhauer for the Twenty-first Century," in *The Essential Schopenhauer*, ed. Wolfgang Schirmacher (New York: Harper, 2010), vii. Henceforth ES.

8. Joseph Conrad, *Heart of Darkness and Two Other Stories* (London: Folio, 1997), 158.

9. The influence of Schopenhauer is well known and has been well documented since his contemporary John Galsworthy first remarked on it. See Bryan Magee, *The Philosophy of Schopenhauer*, rev. ed. (Clarendon: Oxford University Press, 1998), 409. Henceforth PS. See also Nic Panagopoulos, *The Fiction of Joseph Conrad: The Influence of Schopenhauer and Nietzsche* (Frankfurt am Main: Peter Lang, 1998).

10. Rüdiger Safranski, *Schopenhauer and the Wild Years of Philosophy*, trans. Ewald Osers (Cambridge, MA: Harvard University Press, 1989), 346.

11. "Nachträge zur Lehre vom Leiden der Welt" is the twelfth chapter of the second volume of *Parerga und Paralipomena*. It can be found in Frauenstädt's *Arthur Schopenhauers Sämmtliche Werke*, 2nd ed. (Leipzig: Brockhaus, 1891), vol. 6, 312–327. Henceforth VLW, followed by the English translation found in ES.

12. The German reads: *Ein Geschäft, das nicht die Kosten deckt.*

13. Isaac Jacob Schmidt, *Über das Mahājāna und Pradschnā-Pāramita der Bauddhen* (Saint Petersburg: Mémoires de l'Académie impériale des sciences de St. Pétersbourg, 1836), vol. 4.

14. Schopenhauer, *Grundlage der Moral*, in Frauenstädt, vol. 4. Henceforth GM, followed by the English citation, "On the Basis of Morals," in *The Two Fundamental Problems of Ethics*, trans. David E. Cartwright and Edward E. Erdmann (Oxford: Oxford University Press, 2010). Henceforth BM.

15. *Petitio principii* (assuming the premise) is assuming what you have to prove such that the premise is also the conclusion.

16. *The Diamond Sūtra*, trans. Red Pine (Washington, DC: Counterpoint, 2001), 27 (chap. 32).

17. Julian Young, *Friedrich Nietzsche: A Philosophical Biography* (Cambridge: Cambridge University Press, 2010), 63–64.

18. Hermann Oldenberg, *Buddha: His Life, His Doctrine, His Order*, trans. William Hoey (London: Williams and Norgate, 1882). Henceforth BHL. Mistry lists the Buddhist and Hindu texts found in Nietzsche's library. Freny Mistry, *Nietzsche and Buddhism* (Berlin: Walter de Gruyter, 1981), 17–18.

19. Benjamin A. Elman argued that "because Schopenhauer was the vehicle by which Nietzsche came to view Buddhism, we find that many of his misconceptions concerning Buddhism resulted from Schopenhauer's influence. In most cases where we find Nietzsche discussing Buddhism, we invariably find a reference to Schopenhauer as well." Benjamin A. Elman, "Nietzsche and Buddhism," *Journal of the History of Ideas* 44.4 (October–December 1983), 684. Antoine Panaïoti argues that Nietzsche was wary that Schopenhauer would do to Europe what the Buddha had done to India and so he opposes both as variations of the same sickness. "Nietzsche turns the tables on Schopenhauer. If Schopenhauer showered merit on himself for seeing eye to eye with the Buddha when it comes to the denial of the will, Nietzsche accuses Schopenhauer of remaining caught in moralistic, life negating thinking even after he has seen through so many of Christianity's fictions." Antoine Panaïoti, *Nietzsche and Buddhist Philosophy* (Cambridge: Cambridge University Press, 2013), 76. Johann Figl also

argues that Nietzsche failed to see his proximity to the Buddha Dharma because he had allied the tradition with Schopenhauer. Johann Figl, *Nietzsche und die Religionen: Transkulturelle Perspektiven seines Bildungs- und Denkweges* (Berlin: Walter de Gruyter, 2007), 72–80. Michael Allen Gillespie refers to Schopenhauer's embrace of Buddhism as part of his "demonodicy": "Schopenhauer thus ends with the exaltation of what Nietzsche was later to call nihilistic or Buddhistic negation. Schopenhauer, however, calls it liberation." Michael Allen Gillespie, *Nihilism before Nietzsche* (Chicago: University of Chicago Press, 1995), 192.

20. Georges Bataille, *The Accursed Share*, trans. Robert Hurley (New York: Zone Books, 1991), 26.

21. Michel Mohr, "Emerging from Nonduality: Kōan Practice in the Rinzai Tradition since Hakuin," in *The Kōan: Texts and Contexts in Zen Buddhism*, ed. Steven Heine and Dale S. Wright (Oxford: Oxford University Press, 2000), 262. Henceforth EN.

22. *Hakuin's Precious Mirror Cave: A Zen Miscellany*, ed. and trans. Norman Waddell (Berkeley: Counterpoint, 2009). Henceforth HP.

23. *Nāgārjuna's Middle Way* (*Mūlamadhyamakakārikā*), trans. and ed. Mark Siderits and Shōryū Katsura (Boston: Wisdom Publications, 2013). Henceforth N.

3

CONVALESCENCE
Nietzsche, James, Hakuin

> One comes back out of such abysses, such severe lingering illnesses, as well as from the lingering illness of a severe doubt, *newborn*, having molted, and being more ticklish, mischievous, with a finer taste for joy, with a more tender tongue for all good things, with more jocular senses, with a second, more dangerous innocence in joy, simultaneously more childlike and a hundred times more refined than one ever was before.
> —Friedrich Nietzsche, *The Gay Science* (KSA 3, 351)

THIS CHAPTER CONTINUES OUR MEDITATION ON THE PROBLEM of health and convalescence by bringing Nietzsche into dialogue with an unlikely interlocutor, William James. As we did in chapter 2, we then bring our analysis of the problem into the arena of Master Hakuin's style of Zen.

For James, convalescence is fundamentally a religious experience, the "conversion" of the "sick soul." For Nietzsche, on the other hand, if one wants fresh air, one best stay out of a church! The great sickness of modernity is a symptom of the inability to affirm the death of God, nay, to bury God and dance on His grave. It is, at first glance, folly to reconcile religious rebirth with the convalescence that led Nietzsche to the "Great Health." To try to see beyond this folly, we consider carefully the site in which health emerges for these thinkers and in their practices.

I. Sick of It All

In his famous Gifford lectures on religion, *The Varieties of Religious Experience* (1902), William James distinguishes two antinomian types of human experience: healthy-mindedness and the sick soul. The former demanded a habitual and disciplined denial of evil, abjection, and horror in favor of a uniformly positive disposition toward life. One becomes "feelingless to evil" and in "these states, the ordinary contrast of good and ill seems to be swallowed up in a higher denomination, an omnipotent excitement which engulfs the evil, and which the human being welcomes as the crowning experience of his life."[1] The enthusiastic disposition that feels that everything is good, that, in a sense, there is only good, has been the ambition of much of the American talking cure, therapeutic optimism, positive thinking, and even indicated a fundamental mood of attunement in Walt Whitman's poetic exuberance. Depression, sadness, self-destructive rages, gnawing nihilism, and wilting despairs are signs of a bad attitude and an impoverished perspective. The healthy minded person contends that as soon as one thinks more positively about the world, the world soon appears likewise. (I fear that a variation of this atavistic American optimism was in part behind the magic thinking that drove many Americans to vote for a billionaire who, in an awesome non sequitur, would suddenly embrace the plight of the little person.) Perhaps for the most accomplished practitioners of this overflowing positivity, the world is revealed to have been all along without evil and ugliness. "Clear and sweet is my soul and clear and sweet is all that is not my soul," sings Whitman in "Song of Myself" (section 3).

Walt Whitman's majestic affirmation is, however, the exception that reminds us of the rule: that most all positive thinkers, like most all people, eventually hit a wall, namely, an experience of the abject that shatters the prophylactic of their healthy mindedness. An insuperable gap appears between what they believe is good and what they experience as anything but. "But it breaks down impotently as soon as melancholy comes; and even though one be quite free from melancholy one's self, there is no doubt that healthy-mindedness is inadequate as a philosophical doctrine, because the evil facts which it refuses positively to account for are a genuine portion of reality" (VR, 182).

In a sense, from a more contemporary perspective, one can discern that the movement that begin with American popular culture's incessant autosuggestion that everything is great, that positive thinking makes one more powerful by rendering illusory human life's unappetizing aspects, will culminate in a culture whose leader flaunts his "optimism" as if it were a sufficient condition to change the world and whose population trends toward self-medication as a condition for life. Megalomaniacal optimism and the Prozac nation share the same root: the conflation of health with the inflation of idealism. By the latter I mean that the problem of health is understood to be in some fundamental sense an outgrowth, a symptom, of the quality of one's subjectivity. If the subject succeeds in believing her or his own dramatic declaration of optimism and by means of a willful fallacy of collection decides that the good parts of life speak to and for the whole of life, then the evaluative mode ceases to distinguish anything. One becomes insensate to sickness and evil, which evaporate into the bright day where everything is blindingly good.

But "living simply in the light of the good is splendid as long as it will work" (VR, 182). Should the blinding light fail to protect one from the experiences that rebel against the mood of omnibenevolence, then one must render the subject even more insensate. When autocratically dictated good moods and beliefs are not enough, when the mind cure no longer repels the barbarian forces of sickness, and optimism "breaks down impotently as soon as melancholy comes" (VR, 182), one must further blunt one's sensitivity, becoming "happier and healthier," with pain medication, nonprescribed narcotics, or massive, almost sublime, levels of denial. (That the United States is suffering from a widespread opioid epidemic and that it elected Trump cannot be fully disambiguated.) One medicates the pain that dis-eases the failing optimist, allowing life once again to appear palatable and "healthy." Mother's little helper succors mother's erupting despair. Former US president George W. Bush, who presided over two failed wars and an almost fatal economic collapse, was particularly fond of the sunny yellow rug in front of his desk that his wife Laura designed. "I told Laura one thing," Bush explained in 2006; "I said, 'Look, I can't pick the colors and all that. But make it say 'optimistic person.'"[2]

The implication is clear: what James calls the "once-born," that is, those who can affirm the whole of life naturally, are either exceedingly rare, natural-born sages who humble us with their equanimity, or, as is usually the case, hucksters, the desperate, citizens of the New Age, and other dreamers, all of whom are likely headed for a rude awakening. Optimism is in this respect nascent sickness, waiting for the clarity of the dark night to flush it out.

The "twice-born," on the other hand, emerge from the dark depths of life with an increased capacity to affirm the whole of experience. Religious experience increases one's capacity for life, but it does not do so through therapeutically playing the bait and switch of either medical idealism (the decision to see life as what it is not) or medical materialism (just medicate the brain into pleasure states). Or to put it more succinctly, religious experience, as opposed to the institutional forms of religion, is not something that *I experience*. It is not an object in a subject's field of experience. It is rather an experience that alters one's very sense of self, that suggests that the search for health in the narcissistic field of egoism is itself a symptom of the most pernicious and delusional kind of sickness, a symptom that drives one to "cures" that appear as such because of the nature of the sickness. The fetish for quick and easy miracle cures as well as narcissistic self-obsession are symptoms of the original sickness. This sickness drives one to "cures" that exacerbate the root cause or in the best-case scenario merely distract one from any clarity regarding the nature of one's sickness.

In a matter that would have made Nietzsche wince, James defined religion as the "feelings, acts, and experiences of individual men in their solitude, so far as they apprehend themselves to stand in relation to whatever they may consider the divine" (VR, 36). The religion being analyzed is the *experience* of religion and not therefore the collective behavior of shared rituals, common dogmas, and mass movements. Nor is religion a merely personal matter, as if the subject were merely and perhaps mysteriously following individual preferences and more generally confusing their fancies with an experience of supreme value. Religion is first and foremost experienced in *solitude* and in some way is even the experience of solitude itself. The latter should not be confused with a state of abandoned individualism. The individual, when abandoned by others or isolated by a repressive government, knows loneliness.

Hannah Arendt distinguished loneliness, the bane of the compression of space in totalitarian states, from solitude: in the latter, "I am 'by myself,' together with myself, and therefore two-in-one, whereas in loneliness I am actually one, deserted by all others."[3] When I am starving and ask for food, it is as if I am speaking an extinct language that no one else understands any longer. This is an example of the immense loneliness of contemporary global culture. Solitude, on the other hand, is always plural ("being singular plural" as Jean-Luc Nancy felicitously articulates it). I am not one, even to myself. There is singularity or there is individualism, but one cannot be a singular individual. Singularity is paradoxically always shared.[4] This is not to say that every time I walk down a country path contemplating my past mistakes I am necessarily having an experience of religious solitude. The latter is a deepening and radicalizing of solitude. Individualism, on the other hand, is the permanent risk of loneliness, or perhaps one might even infer that the loneliness and the quiet sadness of self-interested individuals who come together with others simply because they share something of interest are symptoms of the sick souls who find themselves fundamentally forsaken.

Perhaps in solitude one still knows something of the sadness of things, but in loneliness, in being forsaken and abandoned to individuality, optimism merely postpones melancholy. As Tolstoy lamented, "Why should I live? Why should I do anything? Is there in life any purpose which the inevitable death which awaits me does not undo and destroy" (VR, 173)? Tolstoy's depression already articulated nihilistic despair, the sense that one has been forsaken by life. Tolstoy's lament about the "meaningless absurdity of life" (VR, 174) resonates with Nietzsche's diagnosis of modernity's sickness: the reactive nihilism of *das Umsonst!*—of the sense that human striving is an exercise in futility and that everything is in vain. What was the Death of God for Nietzsche if not the disclosure of the heretofore suppressed loneliness of modernity? Was not Schopenhauer, as we saw in chapter 2, the boldest and most unflinching affirmation of the loneliness of a meaningless world? For Tolstoy, "it was like a feeling of dread that made me seem like an orphan and isolated in the midst of all these things that were so foreign" (VR, 174). This for James indicated "the core of the religious problem: Help! help!" (VR, 181). We have been forsaken.

Intervening in the soul's sickness unto death (as Kierkegaard characterized despair), solitude speaks to "a second birth, a deeper kind of conscious being" than one "could enjoy before" (VR, 175). For in this experience of solitude I am not only related to others, perhaps even to all beings, but more fundamentally, I find myself standing in relation to the divine, to a two-in-one that takes me beyond myself. In the second birth, the "regenerative change" (VR, 560) of the sick soul, the forsaken ones are taken beyond themselves, drawn to a non sequitur that attenuates their affliction. "So long as the egoistic worry of the sick soul guards the door, the expansive confidence of the soul of faith gains no presence. But let the former faint away, even for a moment, and the latter can profit by the opportunity, and, having once acquired possession, may retain it" (VR, 235).

It is as if the sick soul experienced Arjuna's melancholic delirium in the *Bhagavad Gītā*, a text already known in the West by this time. At the narrative's outset, Arjuna is paralyzed on the battlefield, unable to blow the conch shell that would commence fighting. If he goes into battle, he must kill old friends and teachers. If he does not act, he betrays his own side and does not redress grave injustices. No matter what he does, the outcome is overwhelmingly bleak. His behavior cannot be motivated by the hope of a positive outcome because no matter what he does, there is none, and so he experiences the kind of despair that Hamlet personified. Krishna breaks through, drawing Arjuna away from himself, back to the life that he had long ago lost when he imagined that he was in charge of his life, standing in front of it, posed before it. The *Gītā* calls this mistaken assumption *ahaṃkāra*, the illusion that "I act." Subject to this illusion, one becomes attached to external objects (the preferences on behalf of which one is selectively motivated to act). In James's account of the second birth, or in the *Gītā*'s account of Arjuna's reclamation of his Dharma, religion, to be related to that which is otherwise than oneself, is the experience of solitude, of a conversion to the non sequitur of what is wholly otherwise.

Nonetheless, James's circumscription does not eschew all talk of individuality.[5] Individuals stand in relation to "whatever they may consider the divine," a notion that risks sounding like the claim that religion originates in the sphere of subjectivity. Indeed, James later confesses that to some extent religion is "essentially private and individualistic; it always exceeds our powers of formulation" (VR, 469). This is *not* to say, however, that in the end James collapses back into the lonely egoism of personal religious preferences. Here the language of individualism speaks to the depth of experience itself. It is not that the religious object is determined to have originated within the sphere of subjectivity; rather, it takes the subjects beyond themselves in such a way that they can no longer speak precisely and universally to the nature of the experience that shattered the frame of consciousness that characterized the sick soul. "Feeling is private and dumb, and unable to give an account of itself" (VR, 471). Individual religious experience is not the experience of a particular object that is discursively communicable but rather closer to Kierkegaard's knight of faith and the teleological suspension of the universality that comprises the ethical. Religious experience effects a crisis of communication.

And hence for James, mystical experience, of interest to those who are already so inclined, has no power to demand assent outside of the solitude in which it was born, for "mystics have no right to claim that we ought to accept the deliverance of their peculiar experiences, if we are ourselves outsiders and feel no private call thereto" (VR, 462). There is no unanimity in the description of mystical experience, nor is there any way in which to evaluate good ecstatic experiences from diabolical ones. Finally, such experiences do not readily yield the privacy of their solitude to the public life of reason and philosophical accounting. In this sense, the experience of religious solitude, to anticipate our discussion of Nietzsche, is for everyone and no one.

Yet this is in a sense a way of understanding the challenge that always confronts philosophy, namely, to "redeem religion from unwholesome privacy" (VR, 471) and find the language to communicate this solitude, without collapsing in "an absolutely worthless invention of the scholarly mind" (VR, 487) like the excesses of scholasticism. This may finally be an "absolutely hopeless" (VR, 496) task, for, quite simply, "there is always a *plus*, a *thisness*, which feeling alone can answer for" (VR, 495). This surplus haecceity that disrupts the sick soul, this electric shock of the singular plus that draws one back to a life that enchants us from its abeyance, is the return, the rebirth or recovery, of *health*. Convalescence, however, is not anchored in the alleged security of universals and other false, albeit institutionally, enshrined, gods. What is it to us that the sick soul is well again? It is the gift of solitude, and therefore the gift of health, sundered from the medical gaze and its bag of "healthy" functions and indicators. In this sense, health is an art, not a medical science—an art born of the *experience* of solitude. James and Nietzsche are insuperably separated by a difference in temperament and sensibility but are nonetheless co-illuminating in the emphasis on the *experience* of an awakening to health, the experience of twice-born convalescence.[6]

In this sense, as scandalous as it may first sound, there is a touch of Georges Bataille's radical religiosity in James, for the former claimed that religion was erotic and "eroticism is silence . . . it is solitude. But not to the people whose very presence in the world is a pure negation of silence, idle chatter, a forgetfulness of the possibility of solitude."[7]

And in writing about Nietzsche's tonic of solitude, Bataille once asked, "Is there a silence more stifling, more sound-proof, further beneath the earth?"[8]

II. Dangerously Healthy

Perhaps a hasty reading of Nietzsche would locate him among the mysteriously healthy minded, those so naturally beyond good and evil that they are beyond evaluation as such. Nietzsche would simply be that aberrant product of a nature that readily and enthusiastically celebrates life in toto, and we would enviously stand on the sidelines, resentfully wishing for such a miracle in our own lives. I think that this would not only be a misguided reading, but it would be a symptom of the sickness that Nietzsche diagnosed.

In the second aphorism of the second (1887) edition of *Die fröhliche Wissenschaft* (*The Gay Science*), Nietzsche asks emphatically, "What is it to us that Herr Nietzsche has again become healthy" (KSA 3, 347)? Herr Nietzsche has convalesced, and this is of vital importance for us all. But what was this sickness and what is this health, and how does it speak to *us*, perhaps to those who first know themselves as *us* in terms of some collective individuality? And, as we have seen, this sickness extends to the collapsing illusions of European culture and our inability to affirm the earth.

In a letter to his mother, Nietzsche, with his failing digestive system, chronic headaches and nausea, increasing blindness, and impending madness, claimed that he was the only healthy person in Europe. Indeed, the first aphorism of *The Gay Science* announces an effusive gratitude for an unexpected convalescence and indeed speaks of the *Trunkenheit der Genesung*, the drunkenness of convalescence (KSA 3, 345). How are we to understand a drunken recovery that has nothing in common with the desperate drinking that comprises our quotidian benders and that characterizes the opioid dependencies of optimism's flight from reality? Toward the end of *The Gay Science*, Nietzsche speaks of this rebirth as the Great Health.[9] It was the symptom of "the new ones, the nameless ones": "And now, after we have long been on our way in this manner, we Argonauts of the ideal, with more daring perhaps than is prudent, and have suffered shipwreck and damage often enough, but we are healthier than one likes to permit us, dangerously healthy, ever again healthy" (KSA 3, 636).

Before his convalescence, Nietzsche had long been sick, at least since contracting dysentery and diphtheria during his stint as a medical orderly in the Franco-Prussian War, which exacerbated the vision problems and headaches he had suffered since childhood. Given that these symptoms had not disappeared at the time he wrote these words, convalescence and becoming "dangerously healthy, ever again healthy" did not mean that he had returned to an allegedly *normal* state of health. Nietzsche and his pain-ridden body and looming insanity, would never have been deemed healthy by the medical gaze, but from another perspective he was healthy even in his medically diagnosed sickness. His health was not the absence of sickness but rather a health beyond the duality of health and sickness, a Great Health, a kind of *Übergesundheit*, a trans-healthiness that governs the manner in which one is sick and healthy. Such a health is not found. It is not the result of jogging and tofu. It is unleashed. "This art of transfiguration *is* precisely philosophy" (KSA 3, 349).

Thinking itself has been reborn and dares to affirm, after many centuries of sickness, a Great Health. This health has nothing to do with arriving at some culminating end state of being; health is not the fulfillment of a latent teleology. One is always ever again healthy, on the way to the overflow of life that is the eternal return of the Great Health. In this sense, the Great Health is also an increase—even a maximization—of the capacity for life. It is not the lonely and futile will to life but the unleashing of the will to power.

III. Philosophy as Medicine

One might nonetheless protest that bringing Nietzsche into dialogue with James seems inessential, perhaps eccentric. Certainly, Nietzsche was no friend of religion, famously arguing, "From the beginning there is something *unhealthy* in such priestly aristocracies and in the habits ruling there . . . [h]abits that have as a consequence the intestinal disease and neurasthenia that almost unavoidably clings to the priests of all ages; but what they themselves invented as a medicine against this sickness of theirs—must we not say that in the end that it has proved itself a hundred times more dangerous in its aftereffects than the disease from which it was to redeem them?" (KSA 5, 265/G, 15).[10]

The practice of religion involves running to a medicine—the promise of religious salvation—that in its appearance as a medicine indicates (a) just how sick one really must have been for such a thing ever to have appeared as either holy or healing;[11] and (b) that the disease will further rage, albeit invisibly, as one runs toward sickness as if it were health. The more one tries to cure oneself, the sicker one becomes. Finally, disdaining all healthy air as if it bore pestilence, the sick soul gets right with God, and becomes virtuous: "the diseased softening and moralization by virtue of which the creature 'human' finally learns to be ashamed of all of his instincts. Along the way to 'angel.' . . . [T]he human has bred for themselves that upset stomach and coated tongue through which not only have the joy and the innocence of the animal become repulsive but life itself has become unsavory" (KSA 5, 302–303/G, 43).

James for his part refers to Nietzsche's critique of the saintly as "sickly enough" (VR, 407), but asking great thinkers to understand each other in order to remain great thinkers is a symptom of the sick soul. For both, the Great Health of solitude involves the radical conversion to the plus that turns one away from oneself and toward the healing holiness of life, a turning that Nietzsche himself called *das heilige Jasagen*, the *holy [and healing] affirmation*.

Furthermore, both thinkers share lineages that intersected with each other in surprising and remarkable ways. James was, for example, directly in the lineage of thought that included his Harvard predecessor Ralph Waldo Emerson (1803–1882), a thinker whom Nietzsche greatly admired. Furthermore, religious experience for James methodologically suspends any consideration of doctrinal or institutional commitments (always good sources for pestilence) and argues for a sense of religion with which we still have not fully come to terms. Religious experience is first and foremost *experience*, not ritual, doctrines, theology, institutions, or a philosophy. Like Zen, one has to stand on one's own two feet. One cannot outsource religious experience or hide behind the decision to assent to certain institutionally sanctioned beliefs. Experience, feeling, sensation are all issues with which we are still grappling philosophically, precisely because they bring philosophy beyond its penchant for demonstrations and unambiguous formulations. (The Buddha did not consider his teachings to be positions or metaphysical accounts but rather medicine. As we saw in the first chapter, he was the Bhaiṣajyaguru, the Medicine Teacher.)

Religious experience does not, for example, unambiguously name a particular experience but a "variety" of experiences, rendering "religion" itself a "collective name" (VR, 31). James carefully attempts not to lose this *complexus* of experiences in a hasty and false universal. Yet James, a good doctor and pragmatist, favors healthy experiences that are reborn from melancholy, a deep sickness in which life no longer draws us out of ourselves and which therefore "constitutes an essential moment in every complete religious evolution" (VR, 28). What is it to us that the sick soul is healthy again?

Another figure, enjoying a small contemporary renaissance in some philosophical circles, also participates in these intersecting lineages, namely, F. W. J. Schelling. Although a thorough treatment of this kinship is best a topic for a different book,[12] I here touch upon a couple of resonant moments.

Karl Löwith was among the first to insist upon this kinship. "The utter lack of madness leads not to reason but to imbecility. The fundamental stuff of all of life and existence is, according to Schelling as well as Nietzsche, the awful [*das Schreckliche*]: a blind power and force, a barbaric principle, that can be overcome but never eliminated and which is 'the foundation of all greatness and beauty.'"[13] James's close friend and colleague, Charles Sanders Peirce, informed him in a letter that his own philosophy had been most deeply influenced by Schelling. "If you were to call my own philosophy Schellingianism transformed in the light of modern physics, I should not take it hard."[14]

It was in this sense that Schelling maintained that there is no health or sickness per se (as if these were discrete entities) any more than there is good or evil per se. Health becomes thinkable as what has been lost in sickness, the lost origin concealed within the ataxia of forces that is sickness. "Therefore each being can only become revealed in its opposite, love only in hate, unity only in strife" (I/7, 373).[15] In this sense, sickness would be the inversion of health within health itself. It is not a moving away from health, but rather an ataxia within health that turns health against itself. The soul of sickness, the opposite force (the ideal and incomprehensible force) concealed within the ataxia of sickness, is health, in the same way that Schelling claimed that "the soul of all hate is love" (I/7, 401). Health is the indivisible remainder of sickness, the unthinkable soul within sickness, just as love is topsy-turvy hate and hate is perverse love.

Evil, the moral equivalent of sickness, inverts the relationship between ground and existence and declares itself not an existent among the vast realm of evolving existents but rather the ground of existence. It pulls itself out of the center and languishes on the periphery, acting as if it were its own center. (The current ecological crisis in which humans assume that they are the ground of all things rather than interdependent existents with and among all other existents bears Schelling out.) "What causes illness other than a churlishness towards development, other than the individual strength not wanting to continue with the whole, not wanting to die away with the whole, but obstinately wanting to be for itself?"[16] Sickness, and in the ethical domain, evil, is the symptom reminiscent of *ahaṃkāra*: transposing the ground of one's existence with existence itself such that I become the center and hence the periphery becomes the ground of existence. Sickness does not name an independently existing thing. It names a relation among things, in this case, a relation that inverts ground and existence.

The sense of sickness that operates in Schelling's philosophy has some mutually illuminating features in common with Georges Canguilhem's

The Normal and the Pathological (1943).[17] Sickness has traditionally been construed in one of two ways. Either one first has health and endeavors to defend it against the barbarism of illness—"Disease enters and leaves man as through a door" (TNAP, 39)—or, as did the Greeks, one assumes that pathology indicates that the body is out of balance and must be returned to its equilibrium (TNAP, 40). Both approaches assume that the pathological opposes the normal just as sickness opposes health. Both accounts presuppose that we know what it *means* to be healthy, that there is some idea that adequately circumscribes the body's flourishing. For Canguilhem one does not begin knowing what it *means* to be healthy and hence assume that healing is the war against the looming threat of sickness. One does not first *have* health. Health is not a discernible set of functions. A healthy person is not someone who meets the formal criteria for being in good working order. We are first fallen from health, always thinking it in arrears, and hence pathology is not antilife, but rather *"another way of life"* (TNAP, 89).

For Schelling, I discover the good only in relationship to my experience of sickness and evil. For Canguilhem, "disease reveals normal functions to us at the precise moment when it deprives us of their exercise" (TNAP, 101). Nietzsche himself in a *Nachlaß* fragment claimed that "health and sickness are not essentially different things, like the old doctors and a few practitioners still believe today."[18]

Hans-Georg Gadamer, who mounted toward the end of his astoundingly long life one of the great defenses of the art of healing, similarly wrote of the revelatory movement of sickness. Health continually announces itself by what it is not and therefore as something always still to come, as a site of futurity and natality. He called this *die Verborgenheit der Gesundheit*, the mysterious *hiddenness of health*.

> Without doubt it is part of our nature as living beings that our conscious self-awareness remains largely in the background so that our enjoyment of good health is constantly concealed from us. Yet despite its hidden character health nonetheless manifests itself in a general feeling of well-being. It shows itself above all where such a feeling of well-being means that we are open to new things, ready to embark on new enterprises and, forgetful of ourselves, scarcely notice the demands and strains which are put on us. This is what health is. It does not consist in an increasing concern for every fluctuation in one's general physical condition or the eager consumption of prophylactic medicines.[19]

William James had also anticipated the mysterious hiddenness of the Great Health and its transformative emergence: "It may come gradually, or it may occur abruptly; it may come through altered feelings, or through altered powers of action; or it may come through new intellectual insights, or through [mystical] experiences.... However it comes, it brings a characteristic sort of relief;... it often transforms the most intolerable misery into the profoundest and most enduring happiness" (VR, 195).

In a letter to his mother (dated July 9, 1881), Nietzsche explained that he was refusing to honor modern medicine uncritically and that he was not going to heed his mother's demand that he seek "new treatments." He had become "his own doctor" and one day "humans will say of me that I was a good doctor—and not just for myself."[20] As Nietzsche experimented upon his sickness, he concluded that it was not just a sickness but also the emergence of a new form of life. In an 1885 *Nachlaß* fragment, Nietzsche observed that "every absolution comes suddenly, like a seismic shock: the young soul must see what comes to pass with it. This first eruption of force and the will to self-determination is at the same time a sickness that can destroy the person" (KSA 11, 665).

Health is double-sided: sickness can also be a sign of forthcoming forms of health. Health is futural and revelatory, not an attainment. One is always ever again healthy, and philosophy also belongs to the self-displacing life of this health. One could say that the Great Health divides sentient beings into an immanent typology of the fundamentally healthy and the fundamentally sick. As we have seen, in the Great Health one is sick in a healthy way and one is healthy in a healthy way. Even death itself—or perhaps more frighteningly, madness—belongs to what is joyfully affirmed in the Great Health. The sickly types, however, are both sick in a sick way and healthy in a sick way. Their alleged health, the things that they celebrate when they celebrate health, is yet another symptom of their sickness. To speak to this type of the Great Health can make them sicker. Nietzsche's poison, his medicinal shipwrecks, can be lethal to the sick who, as we have seen in the first chapter, have not learned the art of rumination. For those lacking the health of this art, sickness has a revelatory indication: sickness is the inability to hear anything healthy about the Great Health.

Philosophy is like sickness. It can be a symptom of decline and enervation, or it can harbor new openings and new adventures in thinking and living. Nihilism can be either active or passive. There are many true philosophies that, while perfectly correct, are sickly. As such, they are stupidly true. As Deleuze made this point on behalf of Nietzsche in *Nietzsche and*

Philosophy, "Stupidity is not error or a tissue of errors. There are imbecile thoughts, imbecile discourses, that are made up entirely of truths; but these truths are base, they are those of a base, heavy and laden soul.... In truth, as in error, stupid thought only discovers the most base—base errors and base truths that translate the triumph of the slave, the reign of petty values or the power of an established order" (NP, 105). It is not enough that philosophy aspire merely to be true; it must also take the measure of its own health.

IV. Poison and the Great Health

To speak of poison in relation to the Great Health invites paradox. Does not the conventional wisdom counsel that if you want health you should avoid poison? Since the Great Health is not something to be identified in advance—it is always thought in arrears and discovered anew—how can we speak of its critical relationship to poison? Some ancient and contemporary adepts of mind-expanding medicines like psilocybin mushrooms, DMT, and peyote speak glowingly of the "poison path,"[21] but how can poison ever be healthy? On this issue, Nietzsche and Hakuin again have something to say to each other.

Commenting on the last line of the *Heart Sūtra*—"Therefore, I preach the *prajñāpāramitā* [Perfection of Wisdom] mantra"—Hakuin scoffed, "Well, what have you been doing up till now?"[22] The faint of heart might find this impious, even heretical. Hakuin is not excoriating a corrupt priest or a lazy do-nothing monk. He is admonishing the *Heart Sūtra*, the "heart piece" or *shingyō* of the *prajñāpāramitā sūtra*, which is chanted on a daily basis by most Zen practitioners. What motivates him to disrespect what is celebrated as the most concise and direct formulation of *śūnyatā*, or emptiness, namely, "form is emptiness and emptiness is form"? Earlier in this discourse Hakuin had assailed this celebrated expression of *śūnyatā* by exclaiming, "*Phuh!* What could a little pipsqueak of an Arhat with his measly fruits possibly have to offer? Around here, even Buddhas and Patriarchs beg for their lives" (HC, 29). Pipsqueak of an Arhat? Buddhas begging for their lives? The *Heart Sūtra* as a slothful teaching?

After upbraiding the *Heart Sūtra* for the torpor of its teaching, Hakuin continued, "It's like having a teetotaler forcing wine down your throat. You don't get the real taste of the drink swilling cup after cup" (HC, 83). Teaching the *Heart Sūtra*—habitually and dutifully announcing that this is a good teaching and a true and wise doctrine—is like swilling wine. It is not rooted in a deep, intimate, compassionate experience of *śūnyatā*. It is just routine Zen. Or Brain Zen, that is, a merely intellectual account of Zen as if understanding the theory of Zen was the same as practicing and cultivating it. Or academic Zen, full of critical acumen but of necessity always at a distance from the experience of Zen. It is drunk but without tasting and enjoying the wine. A connoisseur of wine, a master of enological wisdom, is first and foremost a *lover* of wine and it is the love of wine that first gives contour to the demands and skills and practices of knowing that enable the pleasure of drinking wine.

Moreover, Hakuin's poison, the sowing of the Great Doubt and the emptying out of intellectual attachments, is a fine wine, but it is not something that one attains. Ingesting poison *takes away*, unblocking the impediments to what Linji dubbed "the true person of no rank." To borrow a felicitous analogy from Søren Kierkegaard, it is as if we were starving because our mouths are so full of food that we cannot not close them. The last thing that we need is more food. Rather we need to lose something, to shed our gluttony. We need a medicinal poison to take away an unhealthy poison. Kierkegaard was toxically direct about this in a footnote in the *Concluding Unscientific Postscript to* Philosophical Fragments (1846):

> When a man has filled his mouth so full of food that for this reason he cannot eat and it must end with his dying of hunger, does giving food to him consist in stuffing his mouth even more or, instead, in taking a little away so that he can eat? Similarly, when a man is very knowledgeable but his knowledge is meaningless or virtually meaningless to him, does sensible communication consist in giving him more to know, even if he loudly proclaims that this is what he needs, or does it consist, instead, in taking something away from him?[23]

In a similar sense, one can think of Hakuin's words as a kind of beneficent poison or healthy venom. Hakuin called his commentary the *Dokugo shingyō*, the *Poison Words for the Heartpiece* (or *Heart Sūtra*). It preys upon safely intellectual interpretations and those who hide behind them. It is easy for the ego to stand at a safe, merely intellectual, distance from *śūnyatā*. As we saw at the end of chapter 2, when Hakuin attacked *śūnyatā* sickness, he was wary of those who become attached to emptiness and impermanence (what we may also at this point call *Schopenhauer's sickness*, or *Schopenhauerei*). Hakuin upbraids the *Heart Sūtra*—or at least those who hide behind it—for being so preoccupied with impermanence. When Avalokiteśvara tells Śāriputra that all forms are empty, this is not nihilism and an evacuation of the earth. "If all things don't exist to begin with, what do we want with 'empty appearances'? He is defecating and spraying pee all over a clean yard!" (HC, 37).

Hakuin had not always known such salubrious toxicity. When he was young, his mother took him to a Nichiren temple in Hara, where he learned of the impending horrors of hell. The priest spoke vividly of the Eight Scorching Hells and "he had every knee in the audience quaking, every liver in the house frozen stiff with fear. As little as I was, I was certainly no exception. My whole body shook in mortal terror."[24] Hakuin was initially attracted to the Buddha Way because he wanted to avoid the Eight Scorching Hells. As poor a motivation as this was, it had a silver lining because it exposed him to something whose real value he would not appreciate until much later. We can see this in a late work of his calligraphy that reads "Homage to Hell, the Great Bodhisattva."[25] On the one hand, it was the idea of Hell that first drove Hakuin to practice zazen, although this motivation was itself born of the ego. Even though it was the ego that drove Hakuin to seek *satori*, it was a use of the ego in which the ego is eventually used against itself. The celebrated Mādhyamika philosopher Śāntideva taught that one has to use the *kleśas* or defiled emotions against themselves. One has to be impatient in one's desire to cultivate patience. One has to be angry at anger and learn to hate hate. In so doing, one inaugurates a movement that overcomes its origin. Hakuin's ego drove him to Zen, but zazen overcame the ego of the one who had originally sought the Pure Land. *Poison* poisons "poison" and health breaks through the forces that block it.

Hakuin later laughed in appreciation when his disciple Tōrei told him that his motivation for practicing Zen was "to work for the salvation of my fellow beings." Hakuin admitted that this was "a much better reason than mine" (WI, xxii). Nonetheless, in his old age, Hakuin became a tireless teacher, working "to devote my energy to liberating the countless suffering beings of the world by imparting the great gift of the Dharma; to assemble a few select monks capable of passing through the barrier into genuine *kenshō*; to strive diligently toward creating conditions for the realization of a Buddha-land on earth and, in the process, carry into practice Bodhisattva vows" (WI, 84).

In the same egoless spirit, Hakuin concluded his commentary on the *Heart Sūtra* by clasping his hands in *Gasshō* and invoking the awakened and clear mind that expresses itself outwardly as the first Bodhisattva vow:[26] "In mind, sweep clear the demons of illusion everyone, and benefit without rest the vast suffering multitudes" (HC, 87).

The image of Nietzsche clasping his hands together and taking the Bodhisattva vows is implausible. Given the obvious dissonance between the two figures, Graham Parkes has also taken note of a serendipitous co-illumination.[27] One could first note in general that neither is after a mere conception of either poison or medicine. The word "medicine" heals no one.[28] Both are deploying the salubrious powers of the poison path.

Parkes for his part avoids the twin pitfalls of assuming that they are "saying the same thing" (NH, 131) or that they are too exotic to have anything to say to each other. Despite the "striking difference in their *modus operandi*," both "have in common . . . an appreciation of the vital power of the emotions and a refusal to let that power be lost through the reduction or extirpation of affect" (NH, 131). Although Parkes is not bringing exactly the same questions to bear on the two thinkers that I am, we both in our complimentary ways find the two thinkers addressing the problem of sickness and the Great Health. As Parkes notes: "They also have a special connection with pathology, being capable themselves of engendering illness as well as participating in its cure" (NH, 125).

For Nietzsche and Hakuin, it is a new manner of thinking that unleashes the Great Health, a manner of philosophizing born of the healthy ambiguity of poison itself. When Hakuin wrote his famous "Letter to a Sick Monk Living Far Away," he shared the counsel of his old teacher (Shōju Rōjin) with his convalescing friend, warning that "deluded minds turn slight disease into major illness" and hence in the end "they are not killed by sickness but rather are eaten up by deluded thoughts."[29] Living and dying are ultimately beyond our control, but to approach an uncertain future, practice is critical. Hence, "for effective meditation nothing is better than practice while one is ill" (ZMH, 75).

Hakuin then recounts his teacher's story of a haughty priest who was afflicted with a horrible and exceedingly painful tumor. "Feeling that my life could in no way be saved, I set about practicing true meditation. Not knowing whether the pain or the meditation would triumph, I resolved to carry my attack to the utmost limits of my capabilities" (ZMH, 77). He eventually "awakened to the true principles of the non-duality of birth and death" (ZMH, 77). When the tumor was cut away and the consequent pain raged, the priest nonetheless smiled with gratitude for the tumor, which had "been unsurpassed as a good teacher" (ZMH, 78).

Hakuin also recounts the story of a Yamabushi—one of the famous mountain ascetics who practice the austerities of *Shugendō* endeavoring, some say, to live like a bear[30]—who was suffering profoundly from typhoid. When his disciples laughed at him, remarking that he no longer sounded like a fearsome taskmaster, the priest laughed in response: "Three days ago my groans sounded as though I were suffering the torments of the Hell of Wailing. Today my groans are the mysterious sounds of the Supreme Dharma" (ZMH, 78). The Yamabushi priest's "Great Health" had nothing to do with whether or not he had typhoid any more than Nietzsche's "Great Health" had anything to do with despair over his pending physical and mental collapse. Both were able to ruminate the poison, rendering it nutritious.

The rumination of philosophy after comparative philosophy enables experiences and practices of thinking to emerge from surprising places. In chapter 4, this surprise will extend beyond Zen to the True Pure Land tradition of Buddha Dharma, a tradition that prima facie seems hopelessly remote from both Zen and Nietzsche. Tanabe's metanoetic practice of rumination proves otherwise.

Notes

1. William James, *The Varieties of Religious Experience* (New York: Modern Library, 2002), 103. Henceforth VR.

2. Peter Baker, "Bush Weaves Rug Story into Many an Occasion," *Washington Post*, March 7, 2006.

3. Hannah Arendt, *The Origins of Totalitarianism* (1951) (San Diego: Harcourt, 1994), 477.

4. Jean-Luc Nancy, *Being Singular Plural*, trans. Robert D. Richardson and Anne E. O'Byrne (Stanford, CA: Stanford University Press, 2000).

5. For a discussion of the slipperiness of the term "individual" (as well of James's language more broadly), see James O. Pawelski, *The Dynamic Individualism of William James* (Albany: State University of New York Press, 2007).

6. The importance of experience to this study is further evidenced by Nishida Kitarō's critical deployment of William James's phrase "direct experience" in his inaugural work, *An Inquiry into the Good (Zen no kenkyū)* (1911). For a rich and complex series of meditations on the legacy and prospects of this work, see *Kitarō Nishida in der Philosophie des 20. Jahrhunderts: Mit Texten Nishidas in deutscher Übersetzung*, ed. Rolf Elberfeld and Yōko Arisaka (Freiburg: Karl Alber, 2014). I return to the problem of experience in my concluding remarks.

7. Georges Bataille, *L'Erotisme* (Paris: Les Éditions de Minuit, 1957), 292. *Erotism: Death and Sensuality* (1957), trans. Mary Dalwood (San Francisco: City Lights Books, 1986), 264.

8. Georges Bataille, *Inner Experience*, trans. Leslie Anne Boldt (Albany: State University of New York Press, 1988), 156.

9. *Die große Gesundheit*

10. I have used with minor alterations the following English translation of *Zur Genealogie der Moral: On the Genealogy of Morality* (1887), trans. Maudemarie Clark and Alan J. Swensen (Indianapolis: Hackett, 1998). Henceforth G and given with the KSA citation.

11. Medicine, *Heilmittel*, is literally a means (*Mittel*) for *heilen*, which is etymologically related both to healing and the holy or hallow (*heilig*).

12. See Jason M. Wirth, *The Conspiracy of Life: Meditations on Schelling and His Time* (Albany: State University of New York Press, 2003); *Schelling's Practice of the Wild: Time, Art, Imagination* (Albany: State University of New York Press, 2015); and *The Barbarian Principle: Merleau-Ponty, Schelling, and the Question of Nature*, edited with Patrick Burke (Albany: State University of New York Press, 2013).

13. Karl Löwith, *Nietzsches Philosophie der ewigen Wiederkehr des Gleichen* (1935), 4th proofed ed. based on the corrected 3rd ed. (Hamburg: Felix Meiner, 1986), 154.

14. Quoted in R. B. Perry, *The Thought and Character of William James* (Boston: Little, Brown, 1935), II: 416. See also Bruce Matthews's introduction to his translation of Schelling's Berlin lectures, *The Grounding of Positive Philosophy* (Albany: State University of New York Press, 2007), 74–75.

15. F. W. J. Schelling, *Philosophische Untersuchungen über das Wesen der menschlichen Freiheit und die damit zusammenhängenden Gegenstände* (1809), ed. Thomas Buchheim (Hamburg: Felix Meiner, 1997). I use the standard pagination, which is embedded in the Buchheim edition as well as the translation by Jeff Love and Johannes Schmidt, *Philosophical Investigations into the Essence of Human Freedom* (1809) (Albany: State University of New York Press, 2006).

16. F. W. J. Schelling, *Clara: Or on the Relationship between Nature and the Spirit World*, trans. Fiona Steinkamp (Albany: State University of New York Press, 2002), 36.

17. Georges Canguilhem, *The Normal and the Pathological*, trans. Carolyn Fawcett and Robert Cohen (New York: Zone Books, 1989). Henceforth TNAP.

18. *Werke in drei Bänden* (the so-called *Schlechta-Ausgabe*), ed. Karl Schlechta (Munich: Hanser, 1959), vol. 3, 781.

19. Hans-Georg Gadamer, "On the Enigmatic Character of Health," in *The Enigma of Health*, trans. Jason Gaiger and Nicholas Walker, 112 (Stanford, CA: Stanford University Press: 1996).

20. Friedrich Nietzsche, *Sämtliche Briefe: Kritische Studienausgabe in 8 Bänden*, ed. Giorgio Colli and Mazzino Montinari (Munich: Deutscher Taschenbuch: 1986), vol. 6 (January 1880–December 1884), 103. Pierre Klossowski's *Nietzsche and the Vicious Circle*, trans. Daniel Smith (Chicago: University of Chicago Press, 1997) provides a remarkable philosophical account of Nietzsche's sickness. See especially chap. 2.

21. For more on the "power plants" of the "poison path," see Dale Pendell's superb trilogy of "shamanic ethnobotany": *Pharmako/Poeia: Power Plants, Poisons and Herbcraft*, updated ed. (Berkeley: North Atlantic Books, 2010), *Pharmako/Dynamis: Stimulating Plants, Potions and Herbcraft* (Berkeley: North Atlantic Books, 2009), and, most germane to this chapter, *Pharmako/Gnosis: Plant Teachers and the Poison Path* (Berkeley: North Atlantic Books, 2009). One can only wonder what remarkable thinking the poison path would have produced were it available to Nietzsche and Hakuin.

22. *Zen Words for the Heart: Hakuin's Commentary on the Heart Sūtra*, trans. Norman Waddell (Boston: Shambhala, 1996), 83. Henceforth HC.

23. Søren Kierkegaard, "A Glance at Danish Literature," *Concluding Postscript*, part 2, in *Concluding Unscientific Postscript to Philosophical Fragments*, vol. 1, 275, trans. Howard V. Hong and Edna H. Hong (Princeton, NJ: Princeton University Press, 1992).

24. *Wild Ivy: The Spiritual Autobiography of Zen Master Hakuin*, trans. Norman Waddell (Boston: Shambhala, 1999), 9. Henceforth WI.

25. See WI, 11.

26. Sentient beings are numberless. I vow to free them all.

27. Graham Parkes, "Nietzsche and Zen Master Hakuin on the Roles of Emotion and Passion," in *Nietzsche and the Gods*, ed. Weaver Santaniello, 115–134 (Albany: State University of New York Press, 2001). Henceforth NH.

28. André van der Braak: "Because the healthy do not need to flee from reality, they not only have a wider range of perspectives at their disposal, but they are also capable of certain higher experiences that decadent people are not" (52). He also provides an excellent discussion of this issue centered on the self-overcoming of salvation (*Erlösung*) and enlightenment. *Nietzsche and Zen: Self-Overcoming without a Self* (Lanham, MD: Lexington Books, 2011), chap. 8.

29. *The Zen Master Hakuin: Selected Writings*, trans. Philip B. Yampolsky (New York: Columbia University Press, 1971), 74. Henceforth ZMH.

30. For more on the Yamabushi and their relationship to bears, see my *Mountains, Rivers and the Great Earth: Reading Gary Snyder and Dōgen in an Age of Ecological Crisis* (Albany: State University of New York Press, 2017), chap. 4.

4

NIETZSCHE IN THE PURE LAND
Nietzsche, Shinran, Tanabe

> It is difficult to meet true teachers
> And difficult for them to instruct.
> It is difficult to hear the teaching well,
> And more difficult still to accept it.
>
> —Shinran, *Hymns on* The Larger Sutra

I. Locating Nihilism

In the concluding chapter of his 1949 study of Nietzsche,[1] Nishitani Keiji took stock of the historical conditions of his own analysis, focusing on the "meaning of nihilism for Japan." This might seem at first curious because the entire text is dedicated to coming to an understanding of nihilism as such. Moreover, as we saw in chapter 3, the experience of nihilism is not the experience of an object that we can analyze with scholarly detachment. Nishitani for his part argued that if one wants merely to know *about* nihilism, as if it were an objective and general philosophical problem, then the question was being asked from a standpoint in which nihilism itself had already ceased to be a question (SON, 1). Nihilism is not transmittable within the terms of the information age where it would be a theory among theories about the nature of things. Nihilism comes into question only when the singular self, beyond its codification into various strategies of knowledge production, intellectual capital, and other means of defusing an intimate and urgent question by making nihilism abstract and general, takes it up as a living and transformative question.

Nihilism becomes a question for one only when one is no longer one. It does so not when one asks *about* nihilism but only when one—resonating with Augustine and Heidegger in *Being and Time* (1927)—becomes a question to oneself.[2] Nihilism undoes the individual who would inquire about it by exposing one to one's own nothingness. "By being thrown into nihility, the self is revealed to itself. Only in such encounters does nihilism (like death) become a real question" (SON, 2). Just as death is the most general (everyone dies) but also the most singular ("no one dies my death" and "death interrupts the realm of generalities"), nihilism does not confront an individual but rather interrupts individuality with the shared but nongeneralizable singularity of *my* death. Nothingness exposes me—reveals me to be a question—not as an individual example of a more general kind, but rather as the solitude of singularity. In this way, it resonates in some ways with the exposure to despair that, as we saw in chapter 3, William James analyzed as the catalyst for becoming "twice-born."

Heidegger's influence on such analyses is easy to detect. Nishitani was a student of Nishida Kitarō (1870–1945), the inaugural thinker of what came to be called the Kyoto School, and had, at his insistence, studied with Heidegger during the first two years of Heidegger's Nietzsche lectures. Furthermore, Nishida, Nishitani, and Tanabe Hajime, along with thinkers like Abe Masao, Hisamatsu Shin'ichi, Miki Kiyoshi, and Ueda Shizuteru, comprise a tradition of thinking that retained both its distinctively Japanese "personality" and "location," yet engaged in a mode of thinking that was irreducible to either the East Asian or the European philosophical traditions. Yet in taking up the question of nihilism as such, which is to experience intimately oneself becoming a question for oneself, Nishitani also considered the specific historical collectivity of Japan. What could nihilism mean for Japan when its meaning opens up in a singular suspension of meaning itself? If nihilism interrupts the fundamental status of meaning as such, what kind of paradoxical yet distinctively Japanese historical meaning could such a question have?

Nishitani, knowing full well that professional philosophy was itself a by-product of the Meiji Restoration and therefore born of Japan's rapid Westernization, argued that Karl Löwith was on to something when he claimed that Japan had uncritically accepted a historical tradition without taking into account that this tradition was suffering a crisis regarding its own foundations. Japan had imported a dead god without importing the critical awareness of its demise. "We went through this crisis without a clear realization that it *was* a crisis; and even now the crisis is being compounded by our continuing lack of awareness of our spiritual void" (SON, 175). Not only had Japan severed its roots, producing both ultranationalism and reactionary nihilism (two sides of the same coin), but it had also inherited a location and tradition of thinking that was announcing its own decadence. These were the historical conditions that led a youthful Nishitani first to turn to Nietzsche. It was the gateway of the latter that first made it possible for Nishitani to rediscover and retrieve Japan's sedimented Zen tradition. The Mahāyāna Buddhist tradition in Japan, and elsewhere, already had an ancient—but now opaque and remote—tradition of meditation on nihilism and a series of techniques for activating nihilism, in its robust, affirmative, Nietzschean sense.[3] This is not to deny that Zen remained a prominent part of Japanese culture. Its influence is widespread. Nonetheless, what is sometimes hardest to see is what is closest to home.

If one allows this circle to continue turning back on the European and European-inspired traditions, the question becomes, How does Nietzsche, returning with the activated Mahāyāna resources that we discussed in the second chapter, reactivate his original European and European-inspired settings? After all, as Nishitani argued, Nietzsche's nihilism "was backed up by responsibility towards the ancestors to redeem what is noble in the tradition. His standpoint calls for a returning to the ancestors in order to face the future, or to put it the other way around, a prophesying toward the tradition" (SON, 177). So how does Nietzsche prophesy toward the tradition when read prophetically from another tradition, especially given that this other tradition becomes accessible in a new way under the lens of Nietzsche's creative and active nihilism? What is the Kyoto Nietzsche to us? What is it to us that Nietzsche is no longer simply a "good European" but, as we saw in the first three chapters, a good, albeit inadvertent, Zen adept? This forms the central focus of this chapter, which concerns the question of history in the plurality of its trajectories. How did Nietzsche intrude upon the historical situation of the Kyoto School and how does this intrusion, in its turn, intrude again upon our own historical situation, especially given the fact that Nietzsche, right from the beginning, was *unzeitgemäß*, an intruder into history par excellence?

I take this question up not with a further examination of Nishitani's reading of Nietzsche but by turning to another, in some ways even more remarkable, reading by Nishida's colleague and sometimes unsympathetic interlocutor, Tanabe Hajime (1885–1962). This leads us into a circle of historical complications. Nietzsche was lucid about the self-overcoming movement of the valences of thinking, including his own. "Only when there are graves are there resurrections," sings Zarathustra in his "Tomb Song" (KSA 4, 145). Zarathustra warns his would-be followers: "Go forth from me and defend yourselves against Zarathustra. And better yet: be ashamed of him! Perhaps he deceived you" (KSA 4, 101). As we have seen in the first chapter, such thinking demands the all too rare practice of "rumination." And the third chapter argues that such philosophy should be regarded as a poison path: capable of unleashing the Great Health but also a risk that the sick will just be made sicker.

In the following examination of Tanabe's reading of Nietzsche, we locate three intertwined and elliptically progressive strands. (1) The valences of Nietzsche's thinking undergo a performance of their own self-overcoming and reemerge in dialogue with the Pure Land of thinking via Tanabe's retrieval of Shinran and the True Pure Land sect (Jōdo Shinshū). Given that Jōdo Shinshū is often regarded, however erroneously, as opposed to Zen, this is yet another surprise.[4] Without collapsing the various Zen and Jōdo Shinshū traditions, we will attempt to think their relationship more nondualistically.[5] (2) In so doing, we find that Tanabe not only locates the circle of self-overcoming in Nietzsche's thought but in thinking itself, albeit with a critical awareness that this can be done only within thinking's present historical location. (3) Finally, this movement, twice thought and twice performed, reemerges a third time as we reflect on Tanabe's reflection on Nietzsche's reflection on the movement of thinking. All three circles come to tell us variously of the adventure of experience in its ceaseless, circular becomings amid its diversely determined locations.

II. The Pure Land

Unlike the antinomian personalities that comprise the Zen tradition, when one thinks of Shinran (1173–1263) and the Japanese True Pure Land School (Jōdo Shinshū), it would likely be prima facie surprising if one's thoughts turned to an antinomian figure like Nietzsche. Tanabe Hajime (1885–1962), who after Nishida is one of the most important philosophers in the first generation of the Kyoto School, experienced this surprise firsthand. It was not that Tanabe, who had cut his professional teeth on Hegel, found a new research opportunity. Although the Kyoto School tended to embrace Zen, for Tanabe it was the meeting of Shinran and continental figures like Nietzsche (and most prominently Hegel) that transformed his sense of the stakes and range of philosophy. This strange and wholly unexpected meeting among

Tanabe, Shinran, and Nietzsche offers us an opportunity to reflect on what it means to think between the continental tradition and Japan, and, moreover, what might be at stake in *philosophy after comparative philosophy*.

Tanabe's magnum opus, *Philosophy as Metanoetics* (1946),[6] acknowledges the proximity of Nietzsche to Zen (PM, 113), but it does so from a surprising cast of mind that exposes a new philosophical sensibility. This new cast of mind issues from a problem that Shinran called *honganbokori* (Jp. 本願ぼこり), presumptuously flaunting the Primal Vow (Jp. *hongan*, 本願). The latter refers to the eighteenth of the forty-eight vows that the Buddha made in the *Infinite Life Sūtra* (*Longer Sukhāvatīvyūha Sūtra*) in which his own journey to the Pure Land will be contingent upon accompanying all of those who entrust themselves to him and who say his name at least ten times. This is one of the origins of the Jōdo Shinshū practice of the *nembutsu*, that is, chanting *Namu Amida Butsu* (from the Sanskrit, *Namo Amitābhāya*), "homage to infinite light," in order to give way to the "other-power" of the Buddha, enter the Pure Land, and awaken within oneself the mindfulness of the Buddha (Skt. *Buddhānusmṛti*).

Surprisingly, this does not imply that chanting the *nembutsu* is a good thing or that it makes one a good person and, unlike zazen, it cannot even technically be considered a practice to which one can actively apply oneself. In his *Tannishō* (*A Record in Lament of Divergences*),[7] written to help emend the many misunderstandings of his teachings, Shinran instructs the reader that "the moment you entrust yourself thus to the Vow, so that the mind set upon saying the *nembutsu* arises within you, you are immediately brought to share in the benefit of being grasped by Amida, never to be abandoned" (T, 661). The *nembutsu*, however, is not sufficient to bring about Amida's grasp. That is the presumption of all *jiriki* or self-power: "Since it is not performed out of one's own designs, it is not a practice. Since it is not good done through one's own calculation, it is not a good act" (T, 665). Moreover, "no working is true working" and therefore those who know themselves to be good are also not abandoned, but they have a decided disadvantage over those who do not know themselves to be good. "Even the good person is born in the Pure Land, so without question is the person who is evil" (T, 663).

If the claim that I and my acts are good is itself already in the grip of karma and defiled by the *kleśas* (the destructive emotions and mind poisons)—"Truly, how powerful our blind passions are" (T, 666)!—it does not follow that everything is permitted and I am given free license to do whatever I please. (Both Shinran and his teacher Hōnen had been banished and the *nembutsu* had been banned after prominent followers of Hōnen had allegedly used it to justify misconduct.)[8] This is another form *honganbokori*, of arrogantly flaunting the vow, and in itself is another example of the karmic grip of the *kleśas*. "Thus, Other Power lies in entrusting ourselves wholly to the Primal Vow while leaving both good and evil to karmic recompense" (T, 672). It is presumptuous to assume that entrusting in the *nembutsu* is *my* good deed, *my* good practice, or the result of *my* good character just as it is presumptuous to conclude that since I am hopelessly defiled and subject to the vice-grip of the *kleśas*, it makes no difference what I do. Other-power, *tariki*, is beyond good and evil. Even admonishing others to avoid *honganbokori* is itself an instance of *honganbokori* and "to be possessed of blind passions and defilements" (T, 672). What actions would not in and of themselves, putatively good or evil, not presume upon the Primal Vow? If we were Buddhas, there would be need for *honganbokori*, but since we are not, we can only have a "heart that presumes upon the Primal Vow" (T, 672).

For Tanabe, writing against the background of the horror of war, this is the aporia that arises when I realize that if I seek the Pure Land, I inadvertently reinforce the very thing (namely, the ego and the sense of self-power) that the Pure Land seeks to eradicate. If I do not desire the Pure Land, if I do not presume that I can enter it, then I will not seek it. If I do seek it, I presume to know what is best to do and how best to do it. If I figure that not knowing what to do, I can do whatever I please, this is the presumptuous confusion that I am doing something besides submitting to my karma. One could also extend this to Zen practice: if I do not vow to seek *satori* or to realize my Buddha nature, then I will not show up for practice at the Zendō. Yet when I enter the Zendō, I must also heed Dōgen's admonition in the *Fukanzazengi* to have no mind on becoming a Buddha.

However, the ego that desires to acquire *satori* is the same ego that blocks access to *satori*. The good person whose goodness is the key to the entry into the Pure Land is the one whose self-satisfied goodness deviates from the Pure Land. Does not the second of the four noble truths locate the source of human turmoil and *dukkha* in the unquenchable thirst of desire (Skt. *taṇhā* or *tṛṣṇā*) as it is poisonously conditioned by delusionary attachment and aversion (*avidyā* as *rāga* and *dveṣa*)? Is not desire for the Pure Land an especially grand version of desire's impossible quest for satiation and fulfillment? Do not the ceaseless cravings of the ego demand a final transport from those sufferings and in so doing reinforce the ego that makes such demands? Is not the desire for the Pure Land paradoxically the symptom of the poisoning of desire itself? Our desire for heaven belongs to the hell of desire itself.

Hoganbokori is pride in one's trust of the Amida Buddha and is thereby the necessary but misleading hope that one can inaugurate one's own liberation (entry into the Pure Land) (PM, 12). The ineluctable aporia or antinomy of *honganbokori* derives from the desire that initiates the path to *satori*. Desire wants *satori* because it somehow wants to unify itself with the enlightened state, wanting a "unity founded on the principle of identity" (PM, 15). But "since the Buddha is the one who seeks nothing, one falls into self-contradiction if one *desires* directly to become the Buddha. But if one does not seek at all to become the Buddha, one will never be able to awaken one's Buddhahood" (PM, 8). This is the paradoxical movement of *self-overcoming* (to borrow Nietzsche's term) rather than the mistaken image of straightforward progress at the heart of the Buddha Way.

This antinomy also manifests in the desire to read well, to initiate a line of understanding between the desiring subject and the text at hand. The desire that draws the reader to the text, the desire to want to understand the text, is the same desire that obfuscates the reader's access to the text. An enlightened practice of reading in the desire to read well also requires that the desire that inaugurates the way to *satori* perish in order to liberate what it otherwise obfuscates. One dies to the text just as one dies to oneself, allowing the text to expose "oneself" to *oneself* as a question. Desire expires in order to be resurrected in a non sequitur that is otherwise than what it once was.

> To consider the Buddha as the one who seeks 'no-thing' means that Buddhahood is inaccessible to those who make it the object of their search, since their efforts drive them in exactly the opposite direction. Only those who can resign themselves to accepting the total annihilation of all objects of desire as well as all desiring subjectivity—only those whose desire is free of all desire—can face their own death with 'naturalness' and be restored to life as one who has died to the world and to self. (PM, 119–120)

In the case of the *honganbokori* of reading, the desire to comprehend the text that initiates the act of reading must die to itself in the act of reading. The reader who has come under the enlightening force of the text is not the reader who was originally capable of grasping the text. The two selves, the latter a non sequitur born out of the shell of the former, stand in discontinuous and, as we shall see, circular relationship to each other. An awakened reading is a resurrection in the sense of a radical *metanoia* (μετάνοια), an unexpected revolution of the heart.

Nowhere is this more evident than in Tanabe's metanoetic reading of Nietzsche, a thinker whose *Also Sprach Zarathustra* "had been a closed book to me. No matter how many times I tried to read it, I could not understand it. But now it has become one of my favorite books, and this is due, strangely enough, to metanoetics. In the doctrine of the superman, which at first seemed so contrary to my own way of thinking, I found proof of metanoetics and could hardly contain myself for joy" (PM, 115). Tanabe, the Hegel scholar, lover of Kierkegaard, and defender of the interconnectedness of all beings,[9] the religious thinker who unselfconsciously uses words like *metanoēsis*, resurrection, and grace, could not, prima facie, seem farther away from Nietzsche. "Not without reason, his thought had long been a locked treasure house as far as I was concerned. Now that metanoetics has given me a key, it seems worthwhile to try and open it up and have a look inside" (PM, 102).

Nietzsche would remain impenetrably obscure to "ordinary, ignorant people like me" (PM, 102) because Tanabe, turning to Shinran's radical humility, realized that no matter how much he tried, he would never be able to read Nietzsche on his own steam (*jiriki*). He required power from somewhere radically other (*tariki*), wholly otherwise than himself. The circular overcoming of *honganbokori* that occluded Nietzsche for Tanabe is the same self-overcoming that Tanabe, resurrected as the one who can read Nietzsche, finds dramatized by Nietzsche who now appears as the holy person (Ch. *shenren*, 神人), or sage (Ch. *shengren*, 聖人), or "true person" (Ch. *zhenren*, 真人) of Classical Chinese Daoism. Nietzsche, the godless, heartless, hammer-wielding, iconoclast reappears "beneath the exterior garments," as having "the heart of a sage overflowing with infinite love" (PM, 113). Nietzsche's purported egoism, at the heart of our discussion in the first chapter, "is actually nothing more than a disguise" (PM, 112).

III. This I Fully Avow

The *honganbokori* of reading requires the reciprocal play of death and resurrection. "It would not be going too far to say that the only way for old fools like me to become disciples of Nietzsche is to walk the way of metanoetics" (PM, 115). Tanabe does not adapt the self-deprecation peculiar to the True Pure Land Way as an institutional affectation. To read Nietzsche—indeed, to read or think at all—one must first die to oneself. It is this mood of death and collapse, of the shipwreck of a life built exclusively upon the delusion that one lives by one's own means, of the moon becoming visible only after the house has burnt down, that opens Tanabe's own text written in the final months of the Second World War. "In my case, *metanoēsis* was aroused because I had been driven to the limits of my philosophical position as I confronted the desperate straits into which my country had fallen" (PM, liv). Writing in a Japan on the brink of ruin brought the failure of Tanabe's own thinking into dramatic relief. What could one say? What words were adequate? In a way, Hegel was not just to die at the gates of Auschwitz but also amidst the unfathomable heat and black rain of Hiroshima and Nagasaki as well as the dark specter of Imperial Japan's quest for the domination of Asia.

Tanabe does not make this catastrophe about himself. He does not mourn his own lamentable fate, as if the erstwhile honor of philosophy were being sullied by its internecine context. Although Tanabe was not working in the war factories or championing the cause of Japanese imperialism, he proclaims first and foremost his own guilt, his own failings, and he announces with great repentance the scales that ineluctably obscured his own philosophical vision as if he were Oedipus, who, in an act of auto-enucleation, repented for an act for which he could not be reasonably held responsible. Like Oedipus, who did not denounce the gods or life itself, who prima facie seem like worthier and more reasonable culprits, Tanabe, an exhausted Kyoto professor of philosophy recovering in the mountains and retreating from the quite reasonable fear that Kyoto would be destroyed (and, as one might remember, Kyoto was one of the early candidates to be hit with the atom bomb), holds himself first and foremost responsible. Tanabe was not an architect of a New World Order. He had, as his tombstone proclaimed, searched for "truth, and it alone" (PM, vii). Yet Tanabe hastened not to disguise his own guilt—and thereby preserve his own ego—in the more deplorable actions of others.

Such *metanoia*, in its opposition to its prevailing attachments, echoes Levinas's partiality to Dostoyevsky's insistence (in the voice of Zosima and his student Alyosha Karamazov in *The Brothers Karamazov*) that "we are all responsible for everyone else—but I am more responsible than all the others." I do not hide my ego behind the failings of others. This is not to excuse the behavior of others, but it is to insist primarily upon one's own guilt. "Of course, I despise the shamelessness of the leaders primarily responsible for the defeat who are now urging the entire nation to repentance only in order to conceal their own complicity. *Metanoēsis* is not something to be urged on others before one has performed it on oneself" (PM, lx). *Metanoēsis*, the circle of repentance that leads, in the loss of the self, to conversion, to the rebirth of a new self, is the Way (道) or *Dao* of *zange*, that is, *zangedō* (懺悔道).

Metanoēsis (μετανόησις), derived from metanoia (μετάνοια), names both repentance and conversion, and Tanabe thinks both resonate in their reciprocal nonduality. I repent because I converted but I could not have converted had I not repented. Having a new cast of mind, I repent for the failings of my old cast of mind, but I could not have a new cast of mind had I not already repented my former cast of mind even though, in the original cast of mind, I do not grasp precisely what I am repenting. Only in turning toward the past in order to loosen its karmic hold can I thereby simultaneously affirm what Schelling had called *die Unvordenklichkeit* or unprethinkability of the future. Thinking of *metanoia* univocally as repentance, as it was sometimes earlier translated, lopsidedly concentrates the act upon the past (regret for what has been done, punishment or atonement for past misdeeds) and thus occludes its radical futurity.

As the Japanese Jesuit and Zen practitioner Kadowaki Kakichi argues, *metanoia*, "a change of heart," is "not just the puny act of repenting for the sins of the past: it is to turn in the direction of an entirely new reality, the 'kingdom of God,' and throw oneself into creating a new way of life."[10] Mark speaks of John the Baptist's namesake act as *metanoia* (Mark 1:4) while Matthew declares that it is the gateway to the kingdom of God, which is already at hand (Matthew 4:17). It is simultaneously a turning away from and a turning toward—a circular way of death that gives rise to new birth, which gives rise to death, which gives rise to new birth. It does not begin with death and give rise to birth any more than it begins with birth and gives rise to death. It is a circle, which has no point that one can rightly call the beginning, although, as the paradox of *honganbokori* demonstrates, one nonetheless has to enter the circle somewhere, knowing that one cannot enter at the beginning. One cannot begin at the beginning. In this respect it is worth noting that a Japanese translation for *saṃsāra*, the endless cycle life, death, and rebirth, is *shōji* (生死), "birth and death" or "life and death." Everything comes down to the great matter of life and death and how one enacts their reciprocal nonduality. This is one way of reading Nāgārjuna (in the *Mūlamadhyamakakārikā*) and Dōgen's claim (in the *Shōbōgenzō* fascicle *Shōji*) that *nirvāṇa* is not the escape from *saṃsāra* but rather that *saṃsāra* rightly grasped is *nirvāṇa*.

Tanabe repents that *his*, or any philosophy, could ever hope to have done enough, even though, as the *honganbokori* of philosophy announces itself, this failure can be born only of the necessity for philosophy to always strive to do its utmost and act as if it could finally say enough. This structure is replicated in *metanoēsis* or *zangedō*. If I succeed in repenting for the finitude that has already betrayed the Pure Land, then I affirm what restricts access to the Pure Land, namely, the ego that imagines that it could successfully repent. *Honganbokori* is the ineluctable conceit of the ego that expects to be rewarded in the Pure Land, or simply to have articulated the Good and satisfied the demand that we act always as if we could act on behalf of the Good even though we do not know what this would have looked like. One aspires to succeed while knowing that one has already failed. "I feel especially obliged to share in the corporate responsibility for irrationalities like the injustice and prejudice evident in our country. I feel responsible for all of the evils and errors committed by others, and in so doing find that the actual inability of my philosophy to cope with them compels me to a confession of despair over my philosophical incompetence" (PM, 26).

Tanabe's solution to the problem of *honganbokori* is to understand *upāya* ("skillful means") in a circular fashion. As we already saw in both the introduction and the first chapter, *upāya* is the capacity to speak within the linguistic and value world of prevailing discourses. That is to say, in speaking not in my terms, but in terms that are not my own, I attempt to say what is true in a discourse that is technically not correct. I try to tell true lies. I attempt to speak the truth in the language of the false. I do not lose the true in the false nor do I assume that the false is the true per se. This is famously exemplified with the parable of the burning house in the *Lotus Sutra*—a kind of *upāya* about *upāya*. The Buddha asks Śāriputra to imagine a wealthy man whose house has caught on fire. It would be easy for him to flee the house, but he cannot find a way to get his children to understand that they should do so as well because they are so delusionally enthralled by their playthings (attachments and addictions) that they are unable to realize the immanence and ferocity of the fire. Every time he attempts to tell them the "truth," they are "unalarmed and unafraid ... for they do not even know what a 'fire' is, or what a 'house' is, or what it means to 'lose' anything."[11] The only way to get them out of the burning house is to entice them with even more alluring playthings outside the house. Such *upāya* is not correct—the point is not to replace old and feeble obsessions with new and shiny obsessions—but it skillfully points to the *true*.

Upāya is the true *as* the false and the false *as* the true. This *as* is a critical term for the whole Kyoto School and Tanabe carefully deploys it. *As* or *qua* or *sive* translates the Sino-Japanese copula *soku* (即), which, for Tanabe names a pivot around which opposites progressively turn without a Hegelian resolution or mediation (*Aufhebung*). Discussing this term in relationship to Nishida's famous articulation of the absolutely contradictory identity of being, James Heisig explains that Nishida, in refusing "self-identity" as "A is A," was not therefore affirming the inverse, namely, "A is not A." (The denial of the principle of identity, in relying upon negation, paradoxically affirms what it seeks to deny.) Nishida and Tanabe, each in his own way, was rather saying "A *soku* not A," which is more like "A-*in*-not-A is A." What is otherwise than A within A is also A, but in a way opposite to the way that A is A.[12] As Tanabe explains, "The copulative—in—translates a Chinese character of notorious ambiguity (usually pronounced *soku* in Japanese). Its meanings include 'i.e.', 'at the same time', 'and also,' 'or', 'forthwith,' and 'as such.' The common ingredient is the connecting of two items or attributes, the second of which is attached to the first as a matter of course" (PN, 65). For Nishida and Tanabe, one could say then "that 'A transforms B and B transforms A' in virtue of 'something common to both'" (PN, 66).

Hence, the "not A" or "B" that volatizes every A is, to borrow Schelling's term, a "barbarian principle" and an "irreducible remainder" that operates more like Plato and Schelling's *mē on* (μη όν), nonbeing, which is not to be confused with *ouk on* (οὐκ όν), the outright negation of being. The *ouk* marks the dismissal of A as not being the case. The *mē on*, however, does not negate A and, in fact, Schelling endeavored to do something that for the Kyoto School goes back at least as far as Nāgārjuna, namely, to think without negation and thereby without discrete identities.[8] The *mē on* names that which opposes A within A and hence cannot in any way be assimilated by A but which nonetheless belongs to A. "A" and "not A" are more like contraries that belong to the deeper life of a unity. In the Kyoto School we find something like what William Blake (1757–1827) in *Jerusalem: The Emanation of the Giant Albion* activated in his thinking, namely, thinking without negation but rather with the progression of contraries. "Negations are not Contraries! Contraries mutually Exist: But Negations Exist Not: Exceptions & Objections & Beliefs Exist not: nor shall they ever be organized for ever & ever: If thou separate from me, thou art a Negation."[13]

Upāya in this respect is the movement of contraries by which one says the true by way of the false and simultaneously repents for having betrayed the true in the false. This is not an avoidable mistake. It is the condition for the possibility of speaking at all and hence conversion's constant circulation with repentance. In *upāya* one gains oneself by constantly dying to oneself—becoming utterly a question to oneself—in the *soku* circulation of *metanoēsis*. One sacrifices one's own power (or *jiriki*) and is resurrected as Other-power, as the gift or grace of *tariki*.[12] "It is no longer I who pursue philosophy, but rather *zange* that thinks through me" (PM, 1). But since *upāya*, the becoming the proxy of Other-power (*tariki*), is still *jiriki soku tariki*, the self is both grateful to have become the gift of *tariki*, yet repentant that every reception of the Pure Land is also its betrayal.

The way of *zange* is both repentance for the betrayal of the Pure Land and gratitude for the eternal gift of the Pure Land. This is not enacted by the actions of an agent. It is no longer I who act or read. In this sense one can appreciate why Shinran after his 1207 banishment to Echigo referred to himself as Gutoku (愚禿, the Baldheaded Fool). It is rather the enactment of the circle of *zangedō* or, to use Tanabe's adaptation of Daoist language, it is *wu wei* (無爲), the "action of non-action," or "effortless naturalness," or "action without an acting subject." From the perspective of *zangedō*, every minute enacts the circle of repentance and conversion, death and resurrection. The death in every minute is what Shinran called *ōsō*, the expulsion from oneself on the way to the Pure Land as the Great Death of absolute nothingness as one lives *sub specie mortis* (PM, 127). Resurrection is the gift of *tariki* or Other-power and hence is *gensō*, the return from the Pure Land in order to aid others and to engage the non sequitur of each new moment compassionately. *Zangedō* is the eternal revolving circle of *ōsō* and *gensō*, of departure ("going toward" the Pure Land) and return (returning to "this world" from the Pure Land) (PM, 3), of eviction and reunion, of death and rebirth. The Pure Land speaks in the *upāya* of the impure land, silence speaks in the *upāya* of language, emptiness expresses itself in the *upāya* of form, the Dao births itself as the ten thousand things, and the absolute future always ironically negates itself as the present. It "is the world of mediation through which such a reciprocal transformation enables relative beings to move toward nothingness and to return to the world to serve as a means of enlightenment and salvation for others" (PM, 22).

The self in this respect is a kind of pivot, the nonentitative and nonidentitarian *soku* around which opposing forces turn. The *soku* is the copula (e.g., A *is* not A) around which opposites circulate elliptically, much in the way that the *Zhuangzi* speaks of the Pivot of the Dao.¹⁴ "When even This and That have lost all sense of themselves, we call it the Pivot of the Dao, and when the pivot is born into the middle of the great circle, it serves without end."¹⁵ The self is a pivot of *upāya*, both the skillful means of nothingness to express itself as something and the ongoing realization that something is fundamentally an expression of nothing. For the pivot really to turn, its center really must die to itself as Hakuin's Great Doubt transforms itself as the Great Death. "No one can live a genuine life except through death. Living in death, acting as one who has died, becomes the way to true life" (PM, 163).

In a metanoetic reading, Tanabe links the circle of *zangedō* (*jiriki soku tariki* and *tariki soku jiriki*) to Nietzsche's self-turning circle of the eternal return of the same. Despite being unable to understand *Zarathustra* for years and having written him off as a fad of the Japanese youth, Tanabe returned to Nietzsche during the height of the war (when Nietzsche was, in a cruel irony, the official Nazi philosopher) and found him to be the exact opposite of Tanabe's earlier understanding. Tanabe's access to Nietzsche had turned full circle. Nietzsche's circle of absolute affirmation operates in its own way like Tanabe's circle of absolute renunciation. Even though Nietzsche, as does Zen practice as articulated in the first three chapters of this book, enters the circle from the side opposed to Tanabe (affirmation rather than renunciation), he nonetheless affirms the circle (albeit as a near "sage" who is inaccessible to "old fools" like Tanabe).¹⁶ There is after all no right place to enter a circle. One enters where one can. Both the Nietzsche/Zen and the metanoetic entry points into the circle require the perpetual overcoming of the ego that inhibits the circle's ongoing realization—*honganbokori* solved by Nietzschean self-overcoming. "In this sense the structure of *metanoēsis* is one of infinite spiral process. It is, so to speak, an 'eternal returning' (Nietzsche's *ewige Wiederkunft*) in the true sense of the term, namely a genuine 'repetition' through the power of the transcendent, and is therefore the fulfillment of the movement by eternity" (PM, 5–6).

The eternal return is not the return of any particular entity or event, but rather the eternal realization and advent of the Pure Land or the Buddha lands. In other words, what returns is not the *object* of the return, but rather the *medium* of the return, that is, what returns is the *return itself*. As

Deleuze articulated this with respect to Nietzsche, the eternal return of the same is the "principle" of "difference and its repetition," and, as such, it is "an answer to the problem of *passage*" (NP, 49). If beings are, as in Zeno's famous paradoxes, themselves *in* time, how can the same being remain itself yet move through time? If it moves through time, it cannot be the same being in time$_1$ and time$_2$; if it is itself, it is at rest as itself in each point in time and hence cannot move into the next point. X is therefore not an X in time but rather a nonentitative and discontinuous expression of time, the *upāya* of time (time *soku* being). The eternal return of *honganbokori* and its repentance and conversion are the discontinuity of passage.

If one translates the eternal return into the language of *karma*, in which the past exercises a grip on the present, relegating the present moment reactive, the gnashing teeth and *ressentiment* of the "it was," the eternal return can be heard in a new register. "According to the Buddhist notion of *karma*, which sees karmic links of the past as reaching back to an infinite past, there is no escape from *karma*: each present moment is ordained by the *karma* of the past" (PM, 111). To escape this trap, the eternal return does not ask the present moment to be otherwise than it is; it does not react against the karmic necessity of time. *Amor fati* loves the moment—each discontinuous moment—without asking that it be like the moment before. As Nietzsche expresses the affirmation of the eternal return in *Zarathustra*: "*So das ist das Leben? Wohlan! Noch einmal!*" So that is life? Well then! Once more! The affirmation of eternity in each moment is done anew in every moment. *Karma* does not have to manifest exclusively as the continuous and implacable hold of the past on the present. Affirmation *soku* renunciation, to coin a phrase, affirms yet renounces each *now* in order to remain open to all future *nows*. In slave morality, as karmic pressure "reaches its peak, the wheels of time grind to a halt and finally cease to turn. Life passes into a state of stagnation and suffocation" (PM, 111). Bad and unconsciously operating *karma* asphyxiates the self-turning wheel of the child. "But if life, faced with this outermost limit, can move beyond itself, abandon itself, and accept death, the time of the present, which has stopped, will be transfigured into the fullness of a moment possessed of the weight of infinity. Here is the manifestation of infinity transcending life and death" (PM, 111). This is not to suggest that one can escape karma but rather that one can be free for its discontinuous becoming.

The metanoetic pivot, the eternal return of the same (thought variously as either renunciation *soku* affirmation or affirmation *soku* renunciation or, to use a transfigured Nietzschean idiom, philosophizing with a hammer *soku* philosophizing with a tuning fork) is not a repetition of a self-same operation or process. This was the failure of the Hegelian dialectic, namely, that it refused to die of its own antinomies. "Hegel holds firm to the self-identity of reason . . . and clings throughout to a logic based on self-power" (PM, 55). Tanabe was much more sympathetic to Schelling whose progression of opposites does not admit of closure or final conclusions. Embracing a theme that Schelling also celebrates as paramount in the *Philosophical Investigations into the Essence of Human Freedom* (1809), only in love, that is, the abdication of the self as ground and the affirmation of the *soku*, can the *circulation without mediation* emerge. "It is therefore through the Other-power [*tariki*] of love, not through the self-power [*jiriki*] of reason, that ethics achieves fulfillment as an ethics of *gensō*. In this sense, Schelling's logic of conversion and transformation accords with . . . metanoetics, and I can agree with it completely" (PM, 139).[17]

Tanabe was, to phrase this from a different perspective, a thinker of the problem of difference. The eternal return of the metanoetic pivot is closer to Deleuze's characterization of repetition as "the dark precursor" or "the differenciator of difference,"[18] of difference repeating itself as difference, as the repetition of itself as the self-displacement of itself. This discontinuous passage of circular movements (the pivot of the *soku* of death and resurrection) does not emanate from a shared center. The pivot of the *soku* does not retain its center in time. Time is rather the resurrection of new centers out of the Great Death of former centers. There is no integral locus by which to center thinking in order to prevent it from dying (and being reborn) of its own antinomies. Thinking cannot orient itself to its own activity but rather affirms itself discontinuously as the self-displacing pivot. In such humility and generosity, the *honganbokori* at the heart of the gift of reading, Nietzsche resurrects as a (near) sage.

The Kyoto Nietzsche returns as the Zarathustra written "for everybody and for nobody." As we seek the *new* Nietzsche, the Kyoto Nietzsche teaches us that Nietzsche can only be Nietzsche in ever being Nietzsche *anew*. New places and new voices allow Nietzsche to rescue the Buddhist tradition from the narcissism of the New Age Movement (which ironically operates in perpetual flight from the *renewal* of thinking) and bring it to bear again on the generosity and creativity that is the Pure Land of the whole earth of thinking. This not only requires open-mindedness but also the selflessness of "our original face," the cultivation of what James Heisig has felicitously dubbed "a community of the disestablished."[19]

IV. Philosophy after Comparative Philosophy

Tanabe's metanoetic readings of Nietzsche in particular and philosophy more broadly—exercises in his way of rumination—provide us with two valuable lessons for *philosophy after comparative philosophy*.

First of all, the *experience* of philosophy *as* metanoetics is a foolish endeavor. This is not to say that it is not worthwhile—it is among the most precious activities of the human mind. It is to say that discursive prowess, rigor, and creativity, necessary conditions for philosophical activity, are nonetheless not sufficient. Metanoetic philosophy is the experience of fools—those wise enough to affirm with gratitude their foolishness—whose humility and generosity opens them to the unprethinkable, unexpected, and surprising non sequiturs of thinking. Despite what is generally true of the history of philosophy as we officially recognize it, the self-congratulatory posture is unbecoming for a philosopher. Compassion and service on behalf of the unheard and the unthought—Rancière's "poor"—talking truth to power and opening the horizon of thinking to include all sentient beings is more apt. Preserving philosophy's identity crisis and being more philosophical about what it means to be philosophical honor philosophy's inherent foolishness.

Correlatively and second, this is the experience of philosophy's horizons expanding to include any and all beings. The horizons increase in proportion to the diminishment of the philosopher's ego. As the Franco-Czech author said of Nietzsche in relationship to his impact on the novel, "'I think.' Nietzsche cast doubt on this assertion dictated by a grammatical convention that every verb must have a subject. Actually, said he, 'a thought comes when "it" wants to, and not when "I" want it to; so that it is falsifying the fact to say that the subject "I" is necessary to the verb "think."'"[20]

This not only radically opened the horizons of novelistic thought, but it also expanded the horizons of philosophy. Leaving each path to itself even as they meet and enhance each other, Kundera extolled Nietzsche's gift to both paths: "Nietzsche's refusal of systematic thought has another consequence: an immense *broadening of theme*: the barrier between the various philosophical disciplines, which have kept the real world from being seen in its full range, are fallen, and from then on everything human can become the object of a philosopher's thought. That too brings philosophy nearer to the novel: for the first time philosophy is pondering not epistemology, not aesthetics or ethics, the phenomenology of mind or the critique of reason, etc., but *everything human*" (TB, 175). Nothing is too great or small to be philosophical. Philosophy ponders everything and anything, anyone and everyone, and it does so with grateful foolishness and the *wu wei* and effortless naturalness of egoless humility.

This experience of philosophy also speaks to the spirit of chapter 5, where food—historically ignored as a philosophical problem—is no less (or more) important than ontology. Its philosophical activity after comparative philosophy invites Deleuze to accompany Nietzsche *after* one of Japan's most extraordinary Zen practitioners, Eihei Dōgen.

Notes

1. Nishitani Keiji, *The Self-Overcoming of Nihilism*, trans. Graham Parkes and Aihara Setsuko (Albany: State University of New York Press, 1990). Henceforth SON.

2. As Heidegger quotes Augustine in *Being and Time*: "I have become to myself a land of trouble and inordinate sweat" (§9). Martin Heidegger, *Being and Time: A Translation of* Sein und Zeit (1927), trans. Joan Stambaugh (Albany: State University of New York Press, 1996), 41.

3. From Nietzsche's *Nachlaß*:

> Nihilism. It is *ambiguous*:
> Nihilism as symptom of the enhanced power of the spirit: active nihilism.
> Nihilism as the decline and regression of the power of the spirit: passive nihilism.
> Friedrich Nietzsche, *Werke in Drei Bänden*, ed. Karl Schlechta (Munich: Carl Hanser, 1956), 557.

4. Nishida, as well as his childhood friend Daisetz Teitarō Suzuki, in the end came to embrace Shinran and the Jōdo Shinshū tradition. Nishida admitted that there "can be no religion of self-power [*jiriki*]." *Last Writings: Nothingness and the Religious Worldview* (1945), trans. David A. Dilworth (Honolulu: University Press of Hawai'i, 1987), 80. Religious repentance "must be an abandoning of the self in its existential depths—a feeling of shame concerning the very existence of the self" (77). Nishida, following the lead of Suzuki, finds this "logic" at work in the *Diamond Sutra* in the "dialectic of 'is' and 'is not' [*soku hi*]": "Because all dharmas are not all dharmas. Therefore they are called all dharmas. Because there is no Buddha, there is Buddha; because there are no sentient beings, there are sentient beings" (70). For more on this problem in the *Diamond Sutra*, see Nagatomo Shigenori's lucid exposition, "The Logic of the *Diamond Sutra*: A Is not A, Therefore A," *Asian Philosophy: An International Journal of the Philosophical Traditions of the East* 10.3 (2000), 213–244. Toward the end of his life, Nishida drew closer to Tanabe. For an account of this complicated relationship, see Nishitani Keiji, *Nishida Kitarō*, trans. Yamamoto Seisaku and James W. Heisig (Berkeley: University of California Press, 1991), esp. 161–191.

5. In a 1602 power struggle, the Hongan-ji, the Kyoto-based headquarter temple of Jōdo Shinshū, split into two opposed factions: the Nishi (or Western) Hongan-ji and the Higashi (or Eastern) Hongan-ji. There are three schools of Zen, which generally do not cooperate much with each other: Rinzaishū (the Linji lineage founded in the twelfth century by Eisai and whose most celebrated practitioner was Hakuin); Sōtōshū (associated with Dōgen and derived from the Chinese Caodong school, where Dōgen had practiced); and Ōbaku (formed in the seventeenth century and associated with Manpuku-ji outside of Kyoto in Uji). Despite their historical autonomy from and occasional antipathy for each other, it is less convincing to hold that such divisions belong ineluctably to the vision of practitioners like Shinran, Hakuin, and Dōgen.

6. Tanabe Hajime, *Philosophy as Metanoetics*, trans. Takeuchi Yoshinori, Valdo Viglielmo, and James W. Heisig (Berkeley: University of California Press, 1987). Henceforth PM.

7. Shinran, *Tannishō* (*A Record in Lament of Divergences*), *The Collected Works of Shinran*, trans. Dennis Hirota, Hisao Inagaki, Michio Tokunaga, and Ryushin Uryuzu (Kyoto: Jōdo Shinshū Hongwanji-ha, 1997), 659–682. Henceforth T.

8. See Kikumura Norihiko, *Shinran: His Life and Thought* (Los Angles: Nembutsu, 1972), 107–116.

9. This is not to suggest, however, that Nietzsche did not have his own account of interconnection. Near the conclusion of the fourth and final book, for example, Zarathustra sings in the "Somnambulist Song" that "everything is chained together, entwined, and in love" (KSA 4, 402).

10. Kadowaki Kakichi, *Zen and the Bible*, trans. Joan Rieck (Maryknoll, NY: Orbis Books, 2002), 23.

11. *Scripture of the Lotus Blossom of the Fine Dharma*, trans. Leon Hurvitz (New York: Columbia University Press, 1976), 59. Henceforth LS.

12. In his introduction to Nishitani's *Religion and Nothingness*, Jan van Bragt explains that he translated *soku* as *sive*, evoking Spinoza (e.g., *Deus sive natura*). "Put between two contradictory concepts (for instance in the formula, 'emptiness-sive-form, form-sive-emptiness'), it is meant to draw off the total reality of the two poles into itself as their constitutive and ontologically prior unity" (RN, xxx).

13. William Blake, *Jerusalem: The Emanation of the Giant Albion* (1804–1820), ed. Morton D. Paley (Princeton, NJ: Princeton University Press, 1991), 156 (plate 17).

14. Takeuchi explains that the *soku* "functions as a sort of pivot around which two terms revolve and interchange with each other as mutually defining elements in a single dynamic" (PM, 297).

15. Zhuangzi, *The Essential Chuang Tzu*, trans. Sam Hamill and J. P. Seaton (Boston: Shambhala, 1998), 11. This is from the second of the Inner Chapters.

16. Tanabe carefully qualifies his newfound esteem for the "near sage" Nietzsche: "Although fundamentally a sage, Nietzsche is not without his imperfections, a finite historical individual forever denied the fullness of his sagehood. We would do better to say that he was not an actual sage but only a potential one. The way of Zen, which seeks to awaken people to the Buddha nature latent within them, is close to the thought of Zarathustra here in its teaching of the will to power" (PM, 113). Tanabe's ultimate hesitation over Nietzsche and Zarathustra as well as his sense of Nietzsche's relevance for Zen brings us back to the debate between Parkes and Davis that we touched upon in the first chapter.

17. Tanabe was not in complete accord with Schelling because he considered Schelling's account of love in the *Freedom* essay finally to be too abstract, to have ceased with the

thought of love rather than enacting *acts* of love. "In this sense, we may say that Schelling stops at a *metaphysics* of love without arriving at a *religious witness* to love" (PM, 142). Whether Schelling's later positive philosophy addresses this limitation is the subject for another inquiry.

18. "Given two heterogeneous series, two series of differences, the precursor plays the part of the differenciator of these differences" (DR, 119). "It is the in itself of difference or the differently different—in other words, difference in the second degree, the self-different which relates different to different by itself" (DR, 119). It "perpetually displaces itself within itself and perpetually disguises itself in the series" (DR, 120).

19. James W. Heisig, *Nothingness and Desire: An East-West Philosophical Antiphony* (Honolulu: University Press of Hawai'i, 2013), 3.

20. Milan Kundera, *Testaments Betrayed: An Essay in Nine Parts*, trans. Linda Asher (New York: HarperCollins, 1995), 149. Henceforth TB.

5

PLANOMENAL NOURISHMENT

Nietzsche, Deleuze, Dōgen

> A good set of teeth and a good stomach—
> These I wish you!
> And once you first stomach my book,
> You will surely be able to stomach me!
> —Friedrich Nietzsche, "To My Reader," *The Gay Science* (KSA 3, 365)

I. Why the *Records* Were Damp

Nietzsche's short poem relies on a wordplay. If readers are able to stomach (*vertragen*) *The Gay Science*, that is, digest it rather than be sickened by it or vomit it up, then they will get along (*sich vertragen*) with its author. Turning to the issue of food and nourishment—historically not philosophically germane problems—we can anticipate that this will reveal other facets of the problem of rumination. How do both food for the body and food for thought become nourishing?

At the heart of this chapter and our investigation of this problem is the incomparable Dōgen, whose words on food, its preparation, and its relationship to the great matters of thinking and living seem more relevant than ever in this age of fast food and industrial food production. We begin by looking at a beautiful poem about Dōgen written well over a half millennium after his death:

> Now when I take the *Record* of Eihei Dōgen and examine it,
> the tone does not harmonize well with usual beliefs.
> Nobody has asked whether it is a jewel or a pebble.
> For five hundred years it's been covered with dust

just because no one has had an eye for recognizing Dharma.
For whom was all his eloquence expounded?
Longing for ancient times and grieving for the present, my heart is exhausted.

One evening sitting by the lamp my tears wouldn't stop,
And soaked into the records of the ancient Buddha Eihei.
In the morning the old man next door came to my thatched hut.
He asked me why the book was damp.
I wanted to speak but didn't as I was deeply embarrassed;
my mind deeply distressed, it was impossible to give an explanation.
I dropped my head for a while, then found some words.
"Last night's rain leaked in and drenched my bookcase."[1]

When the author, the "Great Fool" Ryōkan Taigu (1758–1831), a celebrated and marvelously eccentric Sōtō hermit monk, considered the works of his tradition's founder, Dōgen Zenji, after having been "covered with dust" for a half millennium, he soaked them with his profuse tears. On the one hand, their dusty surface suggests that they had been unduly neglected by his own tradition, which, indeed, they largely had. Dōgen is a daunting thinker; not only is he technically difficult, but his recondite reformulation of the tradition also requires diligent scholarship. More important, these texts require that readers undergo a recasting of their minds in order to encounter Dōgen "Buddha to Buddha [*yuibutsu yobutsu*]." Dōgen calls this experience *ichibutsu-nibutsu*, one Buddha and two buddhas, that is, two buddhas realizing their mutual interdependence in the great expanse of the Buddha mind. Dōgen transmits his Buddha mind to readers by awakening their own Buddha minds. It takes a Buddha to know a Buddha. One does not simply grasp the intellectual transmission of arguments and perspectives. Such communication is as difficult as it is rare.

On the other hand, this negligence was not merely the accretion of centuries of ignorance, apathy, and oblivion, as if Sōtō monks and priests had simply been indolent in their inquiries. It is not merely a personal failing but rather an earthquake in consciousness when one realizes the constrictions of one's mind. This is also the dust of the *sahā* world, the enduring world of dull, somnambulist, suffering consciousness. As we have seen in the introduction, access to Dōgen's writings requires something more than discursive athleticism and scholarly diligence: they are covered in dust "because no one has had an eye for recognizing Dharma." In addition to the *Eihei Kōroku*, to which Ryōkan alludes, Dōgen is now celebrated once again as the author of the magisterial *Shōbōgenzō*, a collection of almost a hundred fascicles that seek to scratch the dusty scales off the somnambulist eye and mind just as the Buddha did in the teaching story of his first transmission. Holding up a flower, the Buddha blinked and Mahākāśyapa smiled. The Buddha responded, "I possess the true Dharma eye, the marvelous mind of Nirvana, the true form of the formless, the subtle Dharma gate that does not rest on words or letters but is a special transmission outside of the scriptures. This I entrust to Mahākāśyapa."[2]

As we saw at the beginning of this book, the standpoint of the true Dharma eye is not in itself philosophical, but it is related to the possibility of philosophy as such. This question of philosophy's bond to its antecedent, the prephilosophical plane of nonphilosophy, demands that one philosophize about the nature of philosophy. As we saw in the introduction, Deleuze and Guattari argue in *What Is Philosophy?* that "the plane of philosophy is prephilosophical insofar as we consider it in itself independently of the concepts that come to occupy it, but nonphilosophy is found where the plane confronts chaos. *Philosophy needs a nonphilosophy that comprehends it; it needs a nonphilosopical comprehension just as art needs nonart and science needs nonscience.* They do not need the No as beginning, or as the end in which they would be called upon to disappear by being realized, but at every moment of their becoming or their development" (WP, 218).

A plane of immanence offers the possibility of moving from the nonphilosophical to the prephilosophical. The latter "does not mean something preexistent but rather something *that does not exist outside of philosophy*, although philosophy presupposes it. These are its internal conditions" and as such it "constitutes the absolute ground of philosophy, its earth" (WP, 41). The plane of immanence is a "like a section of chaos," a prephilosophical slice of the utterly nonphilosophical, and, as such, it "acts like a sieve" (WP, 42). It is like a "desert that concepts populate without dividing up" (36). Working in tandem, concepts allow the prephilosophical ground of philosophy to appear in thinking. The prephilosophical plane of philosophical concept creation is not itself a phenomenon, but a *planomenon* (WP, 35), "the horizon of events, the reservoir or reserve of purely conceptual events" (WP, 36). The planomenal negotiation of chaos is not in itself a concept but rather the possibility of coordinated concept creation. It is, rather, "the image of thought, the image thought gives itself of what it means to think, to make use of thought, to find one's bearings in thought. . . . The image of thought retains only what thought can claim by right" (WP, 37).

In this sense, perhaps one can begin thinking about Dōgen's relationship to philosophy as an attempt to express *an image of thought that allows one to think the image of thought as such*. This image is unimaginable, that is, it is not an image or a representation of something. It is rather a prephilosophical intuition as to what belongs to or counts as philosophy. Deleuze and Guattari locate a new image of thought, an image of thinking as paradoxically having no image, in the imageless-image of the vampire. "Thought is like the Vampire; it has no image, either to constitute a model of or to copy. In the smooth spaces of Zen, the arrow does not go from one point to another but it is taken up at any point, to be sent to any other point, and tends to permute with the archer and the target."[3] The Zen arrow is captured in no particular image, although it accompanies all possible images.

What do we mean in this context by "thought"? For Dōgen, like Nietzsche, in the phrase "I think," there is either "I" or "thinking." When the fixed "I" relents, "thought" emerges in the simultaneous "casting and falling away of body and mind [*shinjin datsuraku*]." Can one say that Dōgen, in opening the true Dharma eye in the casting and falling away of the body and mind, expressed definitively what Deleuze and Guattari call the plane of immanence? Such a claim is unbecoming, yet, as Deleuze and Guattari insist, "We will say that THE plane of immanence is, at the same time, that which must be thought and that which cannot be thought. It is the nonthought within thought. It is the base of all planes, immanent to every thinkable plane" (WP, 59). This is not, however, to again lament the tribulations of finitude but rather to unleash its forces. "Perhaps this is the supreme act of philosophy: not so much to think THE plane of immanence as to show that it is there, unthought in every plane" (WP, 59).

In this chapter I contend that Dōgen was adept at the supreme act of both philosophy and fundamental practice: showing that the plane of immanence is there and exposing thinking and living as expressions of it. In so doing, I call to mind Ryōkan's tears, cast not only at the opening of the true Dharma eye but also at the infinite vastness that emerges with its opening. This vastness later inspired Nishida to recall the words of the great twelfth-century poet, Saigyō Hōshi (1118–1190): "Though I know not what is enshrined, my tears flow in the face of its awesomeness" (IG, 110). Yet when confronted about his tear-drenched text, Ryōkan became a bit embarrassed and thought how to explain himself, given that "it was impossible to give an explanation." He then "found some words": "Last night's rain leaked in and drenched my bookcase." It is premature to write off these words as mere evasion, a polite lie to someone who would not understand the truth anyway. Ryōkan is *expressing* the truth: his tears are *a force of nature*, for they are in a sense Dharma rain.

In an era when we proclaim to be "after" nature, "beyond" nature, or otherwise "done" with nature, does anything remain to be said with this word? For Dōgen, who was "after" nature *avant la lettre*, it is *Sansui-kyō* (*Mountains and Waters Sūtra*), that is, "nature" as the dynamic and interdependent play of form (mountains) and emptiness (waters).[4] *Sansui-kyō* does not refer to a sūtra (*kyō*) about mountains and waters, as if the issue at stake is a treatise on nature. It is nature, that is, mountains and waters, itself as a sūtra, or, as John Daido Loori has put it: "The whole point of Zen training in a natural environment is to make us open and receptive to the insentient, to nature as the teacher." Loori called this "being born as the earth."[5] To think what Dōgen calls "the great earth" is to think form and emptiness at its most encompassing level and to do so, as we saw in earlier chapters, has its advantages. This chapter considers the "great earth" in a smaller and quieter way. Dōgen gave equal weight to the great and the small, the dramatic and the quotidian. Activities like washing one's face, cleaning one's teeth, sewing one's robes, cleaning the pots, and cooking rice are not more important and not less important than the mind's grandest gestures (the plane of immanence, the true Dharma eye, time-being, the great earth). In this spirit, we again turn to Nietzsche, this time accompanied by Deleuze and in dialogue with Dōgen about something largely ignored in both quotidian life and the canon of Western philosophy: food.

II. Nietzsche's Nutritious Food for Thought

Many philosophical considerations of Dōgen rightly concentrate on the big themes like time and being, issues whose breadth resonates well with the aspirations of much of the Western philosophical tradition. Indeed, Dōgen has much to contribute to these discussions, and fascicles like the celebrated *Uji* (*Time Being*) rightly command our attention. Such a univocal approach, however, risks assuming that if we can get the big picture straight and metaphysics in order, then everything else falls into place. It also implies that this is where we should start, that first philosophy is always what is most important. Dōgen, however, just as provocatively started with little things, things so minor that they often escape our attention and rarely command our respect.

Attentiveness to what conventional habits of seeing take for granted is also at the heart of Dōgen's *Tenzo Kyōkun* (1237), *The Instructions to the Tenzo*, which was one of the six sections of his *Eihei Shingi*, *The Record of Zen Pure Monastic Standards*, a work that articulates in minute detail the responsibilities of the various offices of Dōgen's monastery (Eihei-ji in present day Fukui prefecture). The *tenzo* is the monastery's head cook, a position many cultures considered obviously necessary but not of great importance. The *tenzo* is not a celebrity chef at a Michelin-starred restaurant. She is just a cook. She is not an important philosopher and metaphysician, or a great master dispensing earth-shaking kōans or giving powerful Dharma talks. The denigration of quotidian activities has also generally been the prejudice of European philosophical traditions where, at least until recently, food has not traditionally been an important philosophical topic. Food is primarily fuel and for some also a delectation, but it is philosophically irrelevant.

Nietzsche, like Montaigne before him, is a remarkable exception. He eventually characterized his earlier ignorance of matters physiological as ruinous. Explaining in *Ecce Homo* (1888) why he is so clever, he confessed that his "ignorance *in physiologicus*—the accursed 'idealism'—is the real calamitous fate in my life, the superfluity and stupidity within it." He considered this ignorance to be the cause of the deviations from the "task of my life, for example, that I was a philologist—why not at least a doctor or something else eye opening" (KSA 6, 283)? Thinking is about health and nutrition, just as the Buddha's teachings were medicine. Lost amid such accursed idealism, food remains necessary yet curiously inconspicuous.

Although it is conceded that one must eat in order to live and one must be alive in order to philosophize, food nonetheless cannot compete with the traditionally important issues to which one must first give one's philosophical attention. What is a carrot measured against epistemology or spinach before the majesty of metaphysics? In *The Gay Science* Nietzsche asked, "Does one know the moral effects of nourishment? Is there a philosophy of nourishment? (The noise that again and again breaks out for and against vegetarianism already proves that there is still no such philosophy!)" (KSA 3, 378). Despite his strong reservations about the embrace of vegetarianism by both his brother-in-law and Richard Wagner, Nietzsche was not antagonistically advocating the consumption of animals. Nietzsche's defense and embrace of animals, including his final (albeit likely mythic) embrace of the dying horse in Turin, demonstrate a rare sensitivity to nonhuman forms of life. (This is one of the values that he shared with Schopenhauer.) Rather, the "accursed idealism" in which one becomes convinced that some *ism* addresses the problem of nourishment indicates that one does not have a mindful, attentive, philosophical relationship to food. Food remains inaudible amidst the din of ideologies, invisible amidst the blur of the priority and preeminence of ideation.[6] What *ism* orients my thinking in general and what derivative *ism* organizes my relationship to food? The spirit abandons the body and dwells in the heavens. Wagner's empyrean puffery around vegetarianism, for example, "converted" Nietzsche to the other side (KSA 6, 281).

This abstract (idealistic) relationship to food in which theory instructs the body—played out, for example, in Wagner's bizarre and intrinsically antisemitic vegetarianism, which inspired Hitler's own vegetarianism—is an example of what Nietzsche in *Götzen-Dämmerung* considered the first of the four great errors. The *post hoc ergo propter hoc* fallacy ("after this therefore because of this"), that is, the confusion of correlation with causation or what Nietzsche calls "the error of confusing cause and consequence," is at the crux of how we generally think of diet. Nietzsche's case study is Luigi Cornaro, a Venetian noble who died in Padua in 1556 at the ripe old age of ninety-eight. As he entered middle age, he realized that his hedonistic lifestyle, replete with alimentary and sexual exuberance, was taking a great toll on his health. He soon adhered to a rigorously parsimonious lifestyle, which he discussed in his *Discorsi della vita sobria*. When he was in his eighties, he detailed his diet in *The Art of Living Long*, which was widely translated and remained in print for centuries, voraciously consumed by those who wanted to maximize their chances of becoming centenarians.

With the exception of the Bible, Nietzsche doubted whether any other book had "abbreviated" so many lives and made so many people "unhealthy." There was indeed a clear *correlation* between Cornaro's diet and longevity, but it was not because his diet caused him to have a long life. It was rather because he made the healthy decision to listen to his body (he had an exceptionally slow metabolism) that he changed his diet (KSA 6, 88–89). Many people, eager to extend their lives, followed his diet, hoping that it would cause them to live long, but they became unhealthy, sometimes fatally so. This is the same fallacy at the heart of some of our grandest values. For example, I assume that being moral (adhering to the mores of my culture, doing good and avoiding evil) will cause me to be good or that going to Mass will cause me to be religious in any defensible sense. Rather, it is an *experience* of value (transvalued value as Nietzsche would say) that gives rise to acting generously and cultivating ethical values and perhaps even "religious" practices. One does not begin with an ideology about food and expect to live long and well, yet it is telling that we generally continue to entrust the issue of diet, including the sourcing of food, to the prevailing mores of our time. Rather than cultivating our bodies to incorporate great truths, we depend on puny half-truths and base ideologies to "nourish" our bodies.

Despite medical diagnoses to the contrary, Nietzsche insisted that his maladies were gastric, not cerebral.[7] Nietzsche indeed may have suffered from irritable bowel syndrome,[8] but as we saw in the third chapter, Nietzsche's understanding of the Great Health refused the paradigm that health is the absence of disease and poison. The same holds for his understanding of nutrition and digestion. A nutritious diet is not the automatic result of ingesting what the medical industrial complex and Big Pharma prescribe as health food. Not only does diet depend on attuning to the singularities of one's own body and using a hammer against the ideology of health, but it also relies on being able to digest and process what one eats so that it transforms food into nourishment. As our bovine neighbors demonstrate, without digestive prowess, even the healthiest diet is poisonous. Those who emphasize nourishment as selecting items from a class of healthy foods commit at least two mistakes: (1) the hasty generalization that all bodies have the same capacities for nourishment, and (2) that correlatively food is intrinsically healthy or unhealthy (the post hoc fallacy that we discussed above) and not a question of a healthy digestion that can transform its dietary intake into nourishment.

Since thoughts happen in the body and not in a spiritual stratosphere, thought can also be metaphorically nutritious. Food for thought—thought that can be ruminated and digested—is critical for philosophy. Nietzsche regarded his decadent era as dyspeptic, unable to digest the death of God and its poisonous nihilism. Self-overcoming, active forgetting, and active nihilism—even rumination (as we saw in the first chapter)—can be understood as digestion metaphors, the capacity to process poison (as we saw in chapter three) into healthy modes of thinking and living. For Nietzsche, Silke-Maria Weineck argues, "No defecation, no philosophy. Those who write before they digest are worthy of only scorn."[9]

In the first of his "Why I Am so Clever" reflections, Nietzsche counsels one to get to know the "size" of one's stomach (KSA 6, 281), that is, to attune oneself to its particular capacities. Ironically, it was the absence of health and nourishment as serious philosophical issues that allowed him to digest the European Buddhism of Schopenhauer's ethics and "will to live." The horrors of Leipzig cuisine helped him get over Schopenhauer's monomaniacal illusion by undermining Nietzsche's own "will to live"! (KSA 6, 279). Nietzsche charged "the German spirit" with being "an indigestion. It is finished with nothing" (KSA 6, 280). In a difficult to translate play on words and a repurposing of Christian theology, he chastised *Sitzfleisch*, literally "sitting flesh" (as in the sedentary body), as "the actual *sin* against the Holy Spirit" (KSA 6, 281). The sin was abandoning the body. The sedentary lifestyle with its head in the clouds cannot ruminate its thoughts and digest cultural poisons, transforming them into nourishment. Hence Nietzsche urged attention to one's diet and counseled one to get off one's feet and think in the open air. "All prejudices originate in the intestines" (KSA 6, 281). Christianity is rotting in and blocking the guts of modernity. Rumination—altogether lacking in the dyspepsia of the death of God and the collapse of values—transforms thinking into nourishing thoughts. In this instance we can respect Nietzsche's considering "digestion" worthier of "veneration" than Kant's praise of the moral law within and the starry heavens above (KSA 12, 317).

His discourse on digestion is, to borrow from the Mahāyāna traditions discussed in this book, one of Nietzsche's many exercises in *upāya*, one that helps us think the will to power and affirmation less metaphysically and more experientially. It allows us to pose the question of *philosophy after comparative philosophy* in a new way: to what extent are the dominant forms and practices of philosophy dyspeptic, that is, unable to process their prior forms in order to transform them into new forms? The strangeness of this question—in a way, it hardly registers in the dominant philosophical culture as a sensible philosophical concern—cannot be separated from the neglect of food (and philosophical nourishment) as a relevant or intelligible philosophical problem. Having a healthy philosophical digestive system is not the demand that one do a particular *form* of philosophy—philosophy, like diet, is also a question of knowing the size of one's stomach (and the contours of one's philosophical temperament and capacities)—but it is an experience of philosophy becoming less ideological and more philosophical. If "all prejudices originate in the intestines," and this is surprising to us, it is in part because philosophers have a tendency to take the nature of philosophical activity for granted. In so doing, they are oblivious to the *granting* (the opening of the Dharma eye, philosophy as metanoetics, etc.) and genesis of what comes to count as philosophy.

III. The Bifold Nonappearance of Food

Our philosophical incuriosity about food and nourishment should alarm us. Contemporary industrial food production and the advertising complex that cloaks it exacerbate this incuriosity. In 1975, Peter Singer's classic *Animal Liberation* seemingly came out of nowhere to illuminate this mysteriously obscure problem. As he and Jim Mason argued three decades later, we "don't usually think of what we eat as a matter of ethics."[10] At the time they wrote their book, the food industry spent eleven billion dollars every year trying to excite our desire for specific food products, food substitutes, and pseudo-foods (WWE, 4). Desire for these food products does not include knowledge or even curiosity about where they come from and what is involved in their production. Food appears almost ex nihilo. Advertising habituates us to loyal consumption, yet the origins of beloved brands are obscured. Fast-food restaurants serve "must eat" food while spending millions on lobbying efforts to make sure that consumers will never learn its origins or ingredients.

The violence of factory farming, furthermore, is by and large purposively hidden from public scrutiny. The notorious American Legislative Exchange Council (ALEC), for example, has helped several states construct so-called ag-gag bills, including the Animal and Ecological Terrorism Act, which makes the taping or filming of the treatment of animals on a factory farm an act of terrorism and places those who do so on a terrorist registry. Efforts to promote the truthful labeling of food (including genetically modified organisms, GMOs) are fought by their powerful and highly capitalized corporate producers. We consequently see what we are meant to see: the food we should desire, most all of which appears not with a merely absent origin but with a purposively concealed one. Singer and Mason report some of the accounts of the secretive production of food: "Well, our objective is just to be quiet, to just get out of the public eye as quickly as possible" (WWE, 11) and "You're not going to see a beef-packing plant be transparent. They can't. It's so shocking to the average person" (WWE, 12).

Increasingly prolific warnings have come from works like the book and film version of *Fast Food Nation*; Robert Kenner's documentary, *Food,*

Inc. (2008); the documentary series, *Rotten* (2018); Nikolaus Geyrhalter's extraordinary, narration-free cinematic study, *Our Daily Bread* (2005); and, most germane to our present context, Doris Dörrie's inspiring exploration of Dōgen, Edward Espe Brown, and the Zen practice of the *tenzo*, *How to Cook Your Life* (2007). Despite these, the radical transformation of the food supply places us in what Michael Pollan has dubbed, following Paul Rozin, the omnivore's dilemma. We go into a supermarket and it is as if we were foraging at the dawn of humanity, having little idea what items are foods and what are indigestible poisons. Aside from the individual considerations involved in knowing the "size of one's stomach" and adjusting one's diet accordingly, one first must know how to distinguish potential food from its opposite. Before cultural repositories of food memory were formed, almost everything we encountered posed a dilemma: Should I eat this? Is this food? Is it potentially nourishing or is it deadly? One could imagine that the trial and error experimentation involved with answering such questions exacted some unfortunate costs.

It now seems that this hard-won knowledge is disappearing. Contemporary cultural repositories of traditional food knowledge (and food production) are increasingly compromised and bankrupt. The food industry provides myriad bewitching choices, most of whose blinding sparkle incites desire while simultaneously obscuring any insight into what one is consuming or where it originates. Even the explosion of health food and vitamin supplements is not exempt from this problem. At its worse, the rapid explosion of healthy alternatives risks confusing the problem of digestion with the post hoc fallacy that some foods are universally and intrinsically pure. Our efforts to awaken from this consumerist somnambulance brings to the fore what Pollan calls "an American paradox—that is, a notably unhealthy people obsessed by the idea of eating healthily."[11]

The proliferation of diets and their evanescent reigns, the inverse relation between the unprecedented wealth that circulates in late capitalist economies and the prevalence of poor discernment in food choices, and the fact that never have we eaten so much with so little idea of what we are doing indicate the dominant manner of appearance of food as somewhere between the obvious (nothing to think about) and the mysterious (what the hell is this thing on my plate?). Mindlessness rules this intersection, couriosity with bewilderment. This intersection is the bifold nonapod. It is as if the dinner table were Plato's cave, and we feasted on the shadows cast before us or, somehow making our way to the entrance of the cave, we found ourselves blinded by the solar violence of the omnivore's dilemma. Do we not need a philosophy of nourishment?

It may therefore at first appear strange in the light of this bifold nonappearance of food—itself a special case of the manifold nonappearance of "nature" that spurs the inattentiveness enabling the prevailing ecological crisis—to bring this reading of Nietzsche into dialogue with Dōgen. He was the ardent proponent of *shikantaza*, just (*shikan*) sitting, nothing but sitting. In the question and answer section of the early work *Bendōwa*, however, we find the following exchange:

> You have told us all about the sublime merits of zazen. But an ordinary person might ask you this: "There are many entrances to the Buddha Dharma. What is it that makes you advocate zazen alone?"
>
> Answer: Because it is the right entrance to the Buddha Dharma. (HDS, 14)

If one only sits, how does this confront the bifold nonappearance of food or the vast and complex ecological degeneration of the earth? When urgent action is needed, what good is just sitting about, communing with the cosmos, seemingly dropping out of the very field in which one's actions are so desperately required? Furthermore, what is the relevance of zazen to the demand that we better understand the mess we have created for ourselves? As we have already discussed, Dōgen eschews our customary reliance on the primacy of theoretical discourse. In his first work, finished on his return from China, the *Fukanzazengi* (*Universally Recommended Instructions for Zazen*), Dōgen warns against confusing zazen with getting a better conceptual grasp on things. "You should therefore cease from practice based on intellectual understanding, pursuing words and following after speech" (HDS, 3).

Although Dōgen warns us not be seduced by the "splendor of the words," he did not dismiss any of the rival Buddha Dharma teachings, including Kegon and Shingon. "You should know that in the Buddha house we do not discuss the superiority or inferiority of the teaching" (S, 9). By calling zazen the entrance, Dōgen is saying that it is the *shōmon*, literally, the front gate, the way into any possible teaching, without which the teachings would be mere word attachments. Yet how is zazen as the "front gate" not a wholesale retreat into a quietist attachment to sitting around? Dōgen was pressed on this issue: "How can you be certain that if you pass your time sitting idly in zazen, enlightenment will result?" (HDS, 14). Dōgen responds that the equation of *shikantaza* with "sitting idly" is "as profound illusion as to declare that there is no water when you are sitting in the midst of the ocean" (HDS, 14).

First of all, zazen has only the most superficial resemblance to regular sitting. The point of "just sitting" is not to remain in one's sitting posture. It is to actualize the Zen mind in all the activities of one's life. It is to live and think wakefully and mindfully. Zazen, first practiced in the sitting posture, comes to be practiced in everything that one does. The *tenzo* practices zazen by procuring and preparing food. There is even the zazen of dying (HDS, 4). Zazen is a transformative relationship to the whole, to the "ocean" (the plane of immanence). It is not that one is in the ocean but rather that the ocean circulates in and through one without one being either the source of that circulation or the point of reference for it.

This does not mean that one becomes conscious of a new, heretofore concealed, set of objects, or to a limiting point beyond which lies ineffable transcendence. Consciousness is thoroughly and yet infinitely immanent, and, as Deleuze and Guattari argued, immanence is not immanent *to* something. "Transcendence enters as soon as the movement of the infinite is stopped." At such a point, thinking degenerates into religion in the worst sense. Immanence is not a prison from which transcendence must save us (WP, 47). It is rather a transformation of the very nature of consciousness itself, from an *I experience, I think, I sit* into the general circulation of infinite immanence without the latter naming anything abstract, but rather the concreteness of each and every singular moment.

IV. The Planomenal Way of the *Tenzo*

The *Tenzo Kyōkun* is the lead essay of the *Eihei Shingi*, and rather than being a dry laundry list of regulatory details, it is something quite remarkable. Its careful protocols are practices to awaken the *tenzo*. When the late Uchiyama Kōshō (1912–1998), the former abbot of Antai-ji, reflected on his own early training in Sōtō Zen (Dōgen's lineage), he confessed that he had not taken the position of *tenzo* seriously:

> It was after the War, and we lived at a starvation level. . . . In those days, when I was assigned the duty of *tenzo*, I could sneak extra food for myself. I thought that was the only benefit of being a *tenzo*. But when I worked as *tenzo* in the kitchen with such a secretive and underhanded spirit, I discovered that there was something haphazard in my work. Not only when I was thinking about snitching a little food, but even when I was thinking about zazen and trying to clarify its meaning, I made careless mistakes in my work as *tenzo*. (NIH, 93–94)

In a sense, one could say that the young Uchiyama was not mindful of food preparation, and food was consequently not present to him. He was like the monk that Dōgen observed at Kennin-ji who had the position of *tenzo* "in name only, without him really doing it at all. He did not yet discern that this was Buddha's work. How could he possibly understand and comply with the Way?" (DPS, 45).

It was not the food that was hiding but rather Uchiyama who had not yet opened his true Dharma eye. Dōgen admonishes the *tenzo*: "When you take care of things, do not see with your common eyes, do not think with your common sentiments" (DPS, 37). This is not simply an admonishment to dehabituate one's thinking nor is it the fantasy of attaining a lofty, transcendent viewpoint. It is not to blur all things into the transcendent indistinction where "everything is one." As we have seen, Nishitani, like Hakuin before him, admonished that "the 'solid frozen all sameness of the *Tathātā* [suchness],' the 'ice of the one Dharma nature,' the 'ice covered absolute one or absolute identity,' etc. refer to those higher attachments to self and law that lie hidden at the level beyond ordinary attachments to self and law." Only when one breaks through this hidden source of narcissism, when the Great Mirror Wisdom tears one asunder, does the infinite fragrance of life emerge.[12] Mañjuśrī's sword slices through the ego's secret hiding places in the dark night of ecstatic raptures.

Hence Dōgen instructed the *tenzo* not to lose either "the eye of oneness [the true Dharma eye] or the eye that discerns differences [the capacity to be present and mindful to food and its preparation]" (DPS, 38). At the end of Dōgen's fascicle, we find the phrase, "Written in the spring of 1237 to instruct later wise people who study Dao."[13] The *tenzo* is the one who cultivates mindfulness in response to the bifold nonappearing of food. One practices to find the Dao of food preparation.[14] "If you do not have the mind of the Way, then all of this hard work is meaningless and not beneficial" (DPS, 33). The *tenzo* should strive to interrupt this nonappearing. Dōgen cites an ancient master: "When steaming rice, regard the pot as your own head; when washing rice, know that the water is your own life" (DPS, 33). The *tenzo* prepares food *nyohō*, in accordance with Dharma (DPS, 39). If one can prepare food in accordance with Dharma, from the general circulation of Dao, then one can practice "one flavor Zen," that is, Zen mind beyond the invidious and reductive falsification of Zen into schools and approaches and competing philosophies. If one falls short, then one is subject to "five-flavor Zen," to the Zen partitioned into competing approaches (DPS, 43).

The Zen practitioner, philosopher, and poet Gary Snyder has argued that we should extend this to our ecological sensibility, hoping that Dōgen's *"Instructional Text for Forest Management, Ocean and Wetland Restoration, and Third World Crisis Intervention* would be that guide for Dharma activists and administrators—the 'Tenzo-kyōkun,' 'Instructions to the Head Cook.'"[15]

Dōgen also recounted his own youthful obliviousness to food. In May 1223, when Dōgen had journeyed to China, his ship was docked at Qingyuan. There he met an old Chinese man of the Way who had practiced for forty years and who had recently been assigned the office of *tenzo*. He had come aboard to buy some shiitake mushrooms in order to make noodle soup for his monks. Dōgen invited him to stay. He figured that the *tenzo* still had a long journey back to the monastery in front of him, and certainly the *tenzo* had assistants who could assume the task of preparing the food in his absence. Nonetheless the *tenzo* adamantly insisted that he had to get back promptly to the monastery to cook. Dōgen was perplexed. It was just cooking after all. Anybody could do that. "Venerable *tenzo*, in your advanced years why do you not wholeheartedly engage the Way through zazen or penetrate the words and stories of the ancient masters, instead of troubling yourself by being *tenzo* and just working? What is that good for?" (DPS, 41).

Dōgen invited the Chinese *tenzo* to skip the seemingly unimportant task of food ("just working") and to concentrate on the more important Zen practices. What was really important in training, namely, *bendō*, that is, the rigorous wholehearted of negotiation of Dao through Zen practice, and *watō*, stories and sayings from the Zen record, a technique now most commonly associated with the Rinzai lineage and its practice of *dokusan*, or kōan training under the tutelage of a Zen master. It is not that one should not do these things, but the Chinese *tenzo* laughed heartily at Dōgen's ignorance regarding why they are important and how they should be engaged. Dōgen did not yet grasp either *bendō* or *watō*. "Just working" does not penetrate what opens up when one is *just working*. More broadly, one could say that Dōgen did not yet understand Zen practice or Zen language. Zazen is neither a task to be accomplished in pursuit of a remote goal nor a theory to be taught. Dōgen felt both shame and surprise, embarrassed and shocked by his inability to grasp what was purportedly fundamental to his whole life endeavor. He implored the *tenzo* to tell him what *bendō* and *watō* really were. The *tenzo* did not comply, and instead made the query as to the nature of *bendō* and *watō* a kind of *bendō* and *watō* for Dōgen. "If you do not stumble over this question, you are really a true person" (DPS, 42).

At a later time, Dōgen had the good fortune of seeing the Chinese *tenzo* again, but he still had not figured out what was so important about cooking, and what that had to do with Zen practice and language. The Chinese *tenzo* answered his questions regarding the nature of language and practice. What are Zen words and stories (*watō*)? "One, two, three, four, five." It is not so important what words say as what they express. If one is not careful, they become the briars and brambles of word attachment. "Today what I see of *watō*, of words and phrases, is also six, seven, eight, nine, ten" (DPS, 43). To use language mindfully does not reduce to rehearsing a language *of* mindfulness. Zazen encompasses all ways, not just special ways, all days, not just holidays. Everything is practice. "When searching for the black dragon's pearl, you will find they are numerous" (DPS, 43). There is nothing strange in the Dharma.

And what is *bendō*? "Everywhere, nothing hidden." There is no special place where practice resides, hidden from the ordinary mind. The problem was not with something hiding but with the ordinary mind not opening the true Dharma eye. As Graham Parkes observed, Dōgen realized that "the buying of mushrooms, and everything else connected with eating, is itself, like zazen, a practice that can be profoundly enlightening."[16] It is not a question of holding or promoting the superior doctrine, or of confusing *shikantaza* with sitting around. With authentic practice, humans "have flowed into the Way drawn by grasses and flowers, mountains and running water. They have received the lasting impression of the Buddha-seal by holding soil, rocks, sand, and pebbles." Everything is practice. Even a "single mote of dust suffices to turn the great Dharma wheel" (HDS, 17).

The true Dharma eye enables a vast capacity for mindfulness. In the *Tenzo Kyōkun*, Dōgen encourages the tenzo to practice mindfully as if mind itself was trivalent: *kishin* (joyful mind), *rōshin* (the nurturing mind akin to that of a parent or grandparent for a child), and *daishin* (great or magnanimous mind). In joyful mind (*kishin*) "you must reflect that if you were born in heaven you would cling to ceaseless bliss and not give rise to Way-seeking mind. This would not be conducive to practice. What's more, how could you prepare food to offer to the three jewels [Buddha, Dharma, and Sangha]?" (DPS, 47). Joy is the realization that one can *just prepare food*. The *tenzo* does not have to dream of paradise to take joy in preparing food. Even when the ingredients are meager and the prospects for satiation are dim, it is enough simply to be able to practice in the kitchen. This is the *tenzo*'s version of *amor fati* and her gratitude for things just as they are.

With *rōshin* (the nurturing mind of a selfless parent), one regards "the three treasures as a mother and father think of their only child. Even impoverished, destitute people firmly love and raise an only child" (DPS, 48). Love the rice as if everything depends on it, because it does. Do not take the practice of preparing nourishment for granted. Protect practice as if you were protecting your life—and since you are interdependent with all other beings—as if being itself were at stake.

Finally, *daishin* (great mind) is "like the great mountains or like the great ocean; it is not biased or contentious mind" (DPS, 49). Dōgen recommends that one study the character for *dai* (大), which is based on the pictograph of a person, whose arms reach out in embrace. In contrast, the character for small (小) has the arms dropped, no longer reaching beyond itself. "You should know that former great mentors all have been studying the character for great, and right now freely make the great sound, expound the great meaning, clarify the great matter, guide a great person, and fulfill this one great cause" (DPS, 49). As we saw in the second and third chapters, Nietzsche refused the small-minded nihilism of his day and with his particular version of *daishin* embraced and digested its poison.

Hence in the third fascicle of the *Eihei Shingi*, the *Fushukuhanpō*, "The Dharma for Taking Food," a meticulous set of directions for receiving and eating food, we learn that "if dharmas [phenomena] are the Dharma nature, then food is also the Dharma nature. If Dharma is suchness, food is also suchness. If the Dharma is the single mind, food is also the single mind" (DPS, 83). Food does not hide itself. Lacking the true Dharma eye, it is we who do not see food. Like the hapless followers of Luigi Cornaro, we are lost in mindless ideas about food. It is not, however, that we don't just see food, but that we don't see at all, and hence we do not even see that we do not see. If one cannot see food, one cannot see anything. If one sees at all, one sees food.

As audacious as it may sound, the awakening of the true Dharma eye resonates with what Deleuze and Guattari called a "plane of immanence," although it is approached without the seeming serenity of *shikantaza* (although zazen is not without its own bouts of anguish). "We head for the horizon, on the plane of immanence, and we return with bloodshot eyes" (WP, 41). While some might regard this resonance as too much of a stretch,

Deleuze and Guattari did not think so. We find the following footnote in their discussion of the plane of immanence: "We refer also to the Zen text of the Japanese monk Dōgen [*Shōbōgenzō*], which invokes the horizon or 'reserve' of events" (WP, 220). I unpack this allusion in the next section, but its relevance for the experience of *philosophy after comparative philosophy* is striking. It also follows other allusions to East Asian planomenal thought. In *A Thousand Plateaus*, for example, they refer to Dao as "a field of immanence in which desire lacks nothing and therefore cannot be linked to any external or transcendent criterion" (TP, 157). The true Dharma eye is planomenal, as wide as the Great Buddha Sea. Deleuze and Guattari are right to lament that "*we lack resistance to the present*" (WP, 108). In Buddha Dharma, the kitchen is as important as Hegel, the billowing grasses as vital as the ruins of Greek temples, and shit as much a vehicle of Dao as fine wine. Food—its sourcing, preparation, consumption, and digestion—is planomenal.

V. The Planomenal Dharma Eye

The discussion of the plane of immanence was not Deleuze's only allusion to Dōgen. He also turned, however briefly, to Dōgen in his analysis of Ozu Yasujirō (1903–1963), whose cinema Deleuze considered an exemplary practice of the cinematic time-image.[17] Although Ozu's cinema is not overtly concerned with food and nourishment, a brief consideration of it further clarifies Deleuze's admiration for Dōgen and indirectly elucidates the concerns of this chapter.

Deleuze argued that in Ozu's time-images, "the action image disappears in favor of the purely visual image of what a character is, and the sound image of what he says, completely banal nature and conservation constituting the essentials of the script" (C2, 13–14; C2F, 23). To elucidate Ozu's sense of the banal, we can contrast it with its cinematic deployment in Akira Kurosawa's classic *Ikiru (To Live)* (1952). Kurosawa carefully creates a situation whose exigent tensions simmer until they burst into action. (One need only think of the slow exposition in *Seven Samurai* that suddenly explodes when the samurai rescue the peasant village.) In *Ikiru*, partially inspired by Tolstoy's *The Death of Ivan Ilyich* (1886), the agonizing banality of bureaucratic life is the ground that gives rise to the central character's decisive action. The ground initially intensifies when the somnolent bureaucrat Watanabe Kanji (Shimura Takashi) is diagnosed with stomach cancer, which produces a long, brooding crisis. How will Watanabe live his final days under the shadow of his fast approaching death? The inactivity of his bureaucratic life initially yields to his flailing attempts to come to terms with his impending fate through excessive drinking and carousing. This double paralysis (the dull, purposeless life of a bureaucrat and the aporia that the proximity of death induces) is suddenly and decisively broken by Watanabe's decision to build a playground for the poor, despite the adversarial bureaucracy of his own department.[18] As Deleuze said of Kurosawa more generally: "One must tear from a situation the question which it contains, discover the givens of the secret question which alone permit a response to it and without which even the action would not be a response."[19] Watanabe acted decisively, motivated by the dawning disclosure of the question, and thereby interrupted the banality of the quotidian, which holds death itself in abeyance.

The situation is much different with Ozu, where "everything is ordinary or banal, even death and the dead who are the object of a natural forgetting" (C2, 14; C2F, 24), something "close to a kind of Zen wisdom" where "nothing is remarkable or exceptional in life" (C2, 14; C2F, 25)—"everything is ordinary and regular, everything is everyday" (C2, 15; C2F, 25).[20] There is, therefore, no "breathing space or encompasser to contain a profound question, as in Kurosawa (C2, 15; C2F, 26). As a kind of intellectual experiment, we could imagine that Ozu's signature low-camera position with its stationary shots, the famous "tatami" perspective with its immobile view from the floor, are also the point of view of a person doing zazen. In the latter, one neither moves the body nor judges with the mind. Zazen lets the constant coming and going of beings flow. In the stationary view from below as it gazes upon the noise and chaos of the quotidian, the lens presents itself as the opening of the true Dharma eye. It becomes like a mirror that in Mahāyāna famously does not discriminate in what it reflects but receives all images equally. As images are received without judgment, they are also received in the immensity of their original ambiguity.

This is not to say that Ozu publicly proclaimed himself to be a Zen filmmaker. His statements about the subject are ambiguous, although he was eventually interred on the grounds of a Zen temple (Engaku-ji) and had a one-character epigraph inscribed on his grave: nothingness (*mu*, 無). This is the great (Buddha) sea out of which one, as Ozu famously said of his own approach to films, makes the tofu again and again. The *mu* on Ozu's gravestone does not express a theory about either life or death. Even death, which people generally consider exceptionally meaningful (it is what spurs Watanabe out of his indolence and into action), here no longer has that distinction. This absurdity, however, is not the disappointing whimper of a mere lack. That nothing is special means also that everything is special, although nothing is especially special. If everything is special, then everything is worthy of cherishment—beyond high and low. As Zen Master Yunmen Wenyan (J. Ummon Bun'en, d. 949) famously counseled his monks: "Every day is a good day." Time does not parcel itself into a hierarchy of the high and the low, the good and the bad, the important and the quotidian.[21]

Deleuze articulates this by borrowing a fascinating argument from Leibniz (who had an abiding interest in China): "The world is made up of series which are composed and which converge in a very regular way, according to ordinary laws. However, the series and sequences are apparent to us only in small sections, and in disrupted or mixed-up order, so that we believe in breaks, disparities and discrepancies as in things that are out of the ordinary" (C2, 14; C2F, 24). Everything happens in its time and, as such, in its *justesse* (how it happens is how it should happen, how it is appropriate for it to happen), but since we inevitably do not see events in their *justesse*, we confuse our lives and exacerbate our pain. This is what the historical Buddha called the "second dart," namely, the supplemental mental pain that physical pain causes us. We think about our pain in the terms that it sets for us and hence think painful thoughts about our pain. While there is no cure for the first dart, that is, no cure for sickness, old age, and death, one can cultivate oneself so that attachment, aversions, and delusions that govern the second dart are pacified.[22] "This is Ozu's thinking: life is simple, and man never stops complicating it by 'disturbing still water'" (C2, 15; C2F, 25).

Deleuze explicitly connects this planomenal perspective to Dōgen. There is a small but critical typo in the English translation of *Cinema 2*. In the early discussion of Ozu's cinema as paradigmatic of the time-image, footnote 30 incorrectly cites Dōgen, while the following footnote (31) cites Antonioni, making it appear as if the latter were suddenly making Zen pronouncements. The footnotes are obviously off by one, something discernible even by considering the context of Deleuze's analysis as it appears in the English translation. The correct reference to Dōgen refers to the following, quite remarkable passage: "Time is the full, that is, the unalterable form filled by change. Time is 'the visual reserve of events in their appropriateness.'" [*Le temps, c'est le plein, c'est-à-dire la form inalterable remplie par le changement. Le temps, c'est "la réserve visuelle des événements dans leur justesse"*] (C2, 17; C2F, 28).

Deleuze is not here referring to an actual line or passage by Dōgen but rather to the 1980 French translation of the Japanese title of Dōgen's magnum opus, *Shōbōgenzō*, of which the translators, Ryōji Nakamura and René de Ceccatty,[23] made a small selection and provided philosophically expansive (albeit controversial) translation choices. Their translation of the word *Shōbōgenzō* is quite unusual and merits examination. The kanji 正 (*shō*) is typically read "right or true" but is here being read as *dans leur justesse*, that is, in a fitting matter, in their appropriateness, suitability, propriety, or aptness. Most strikingly, 法 (*bō* or *hō*), which is the kanji for Dharma, is read as *les événements*, that is, the events, happenings, or occurrences, although such language should not automatically be ceded to Heidegger's *das Ereignis*. 眼 (*gen*) is the kanji for "eye" and 蔵 (*zō*) is the kanji for "treasury" or *réserve*. Typically, one speaks of the eye as a true eye (as when it becomes a Dharma eye and when one plucks out Bodhidharma's eyeball and makes it one's own). Here, however, the translators associate the eye with the treasury itself (*la réserve visuelle*) and the true as the propriety of events, that is, things not understood as entities but rather as occurrences of Buddha nature (Jp. *busshō*, Skt. *tathāgatagarbha* and *Buddha-dhātu*), with no intrinsic natures, but in each occurrence proper and apt. The translators strictly demarcate their use of *l'événement* as a translation of *hō* (法),[24] Dharma, from any connection to Heidegger's *Ereignis* (event): "*Hō* does not concern either being or presence. ... [H]ō is a synchronic plane where events interlace, cling, and go 'on peregrination.'[25] The proper is only the 'proper of the Buddhist event.' Every rapprochement with the texts that Heidegger devoted to the event (... "the donation of the present is the proper of the event [*la donation du présent est le propre de l'événement*], *Die Gabe von Anwesen ist Eigentum des Ereignens*) is excessive" (RVE, 133).

From the standpoint of the Dharma, each event is as it should be. Contrary to the American director Paul Schrader's emphasis on a kind of Zen transcendence (beyond the realm of human affairs) in Ozu's cinema ("a hierarchy from the Other-oriented to the human-oriented"),[26] Deleuze rightly insists that there is "no need at all to call on a transcendence (C2, 17; C2F, 28).[27] Or if we insist on the language of alterity, otherness, and the transcendence of the nonhuman—for the Dharma is not found in the seeming obviousness of the quotidian world (what Mahāyāna called the dust of the *sahāloka* or *sahā* world, the world of projections, discriminations, hierarchies, etc.)—then we should take more seriously how the Japanese director Yoshida Kiju understands the problem apropos of Ozu's masterpiece, *Tōkyō Story* (1953): "However, it is noteworthy that a phrase like 'the view from the sacred other side' does not necessarily contain religious meaning. It is unclear whether Ozu-san believed in life after death. It is most convincing to think that he did not. In any case, as long as all human beings die in the end, it is simply word play to distinguish the world before and after death, calling them this side and the other side. We should only use these terms in order to enrich our ways of expression and communication. We can also talk about them more freely without any religious connotations."[28]

The other side is the perspective of absolute death on human events. In this respect, Yoshida sees the other side haunting the funeral scene toward the conclusion of *Tokyo Story* where the mother, Tomi (Higashiyama Chieko), has died after a visit with her husband to Tokyo where they experienced their children's indifference toward them: "Since Ozu-san refused to regard human deaths as sacred, this scene became unforgettable" (OA, 110). Yoshida characterizes the film as a "revelation" of "silence" that "drives" the audience "to silence" (OA, 88), a silence in which the other side is the haunting presence of the dead, "a chaotic world of human beings . . . filled with the gazes of the dead," which are the "only measures that human beings are given for the order of the world" (OA, 117). The images of our *sahā* world are brought into stark relief by the plane of immanence that is the absolute time of death, haunting everything, high and low, cherished and hated, wise and stupid. It is the time of the absolutely ordinary, vast emptiness with nothing sacred.

There is nothing ordinary, that is, nothing common or obvious, about Ozu's planomenal intuition of the ordinary. His ordinary profundity of the everyday is hard won and easily lost. From this standpoint—from the standpoint of Nishitani's *kū no ba* or "field of *śūnyatā* (or emptiness)" discussed in the first chapter—to say that food is quotidian is not to banish it to the domain of the unimportant. It is to liberate it from Nietzsche's "accursed idealism," which is philosophy's heady predilection to lose itself in the clouds. Food is no more important or no less important than death or ontology. The planomenal excludes nothing. Everything is important although nothing is especially important. Not only does this expand the horizon of philosophy indefinitely, even infinitely, it also makes possible a philosophy of nourishment and allows philosophy itself to become more nourishing. That being said, we inevitably complicate things and disturb the still water (C2, 15; C2F, 25). From this perspective, *philosophy after comparative philosophy* is not only the art of stepping back from the roiled waters of our lives and our earth but also the art of convalescence in which we find our way back, this time into the still depths of these waters.

Notes

1. "Reading the *Record of Eihei Dōgen*," trans. Taigen Daniel Leighton and Kazuaki Tanahashi, *Moon in a Dewdrop: Writings of Zen Master Dōgen*, ed. Kazuaki Tanahashi (Berkeley, CA: North Point, 1985), 224.
2. Quoted in Heinrich Dumoulin, *Zen Buddhism: A History*, vol. 1, *India and China*, trans. James W. Heisig and Paul Knitter (New York: Macmillan, 1988), 9.
3. Gilles Deleuze and Félix Guattari, *A Thousand Plateaus*, trans. Brian Masumi (Minneapolis: University of Minnesota Press, 1987), 377. Henceforth TP.
4. For more on this, see my "Dōgen and the Unknown Knowns: The Practice of the Wild after the End of Nature," *Environmental Philosophy* 10.1 (Spring 2013), 39–62; also my *Mountains, Rivers, and the Great Earth: Reading Gary Snyder and Dōgen in an Age of Ecological Crisis* (Albany: State University of New York Press, 2017), chaps. 1 and 2.
5. John Daido Loori, *Teachings of the Earth* (Boston: Shambhala, 2007), 12.
6. For several instructive approaches to some aspects of this problem, see *Nietzsche and Science*, ed. Gregory Moore and Thomas H. Brobjer (Hampshire, VT: Ashgate, 2004). For a retrieval of the philosophical question of food, see *Cooking, Eating, Thinking: Transformative Philosophies of Food*, ed. Deane W. Curtin and Lisa M. Heldke (Bloomington: Indiana University Press, 1992).
7. See Robert T. Valgenti: "Even though the famous physician Professor Oppolzer of Leipzig diagnoses his illness as cerebral and not gastric, Nietzsche commonly rejected the advice of doctors who suggested treatments that limited his intellectual activity; instead, he favored dietary remedies and treatments for his stomach." "Nietzsche and Food," *Encyclopedia of Food and Agricultural Ethics*, ed. P. B. Thompson and D. M. Kaplan (Dordrecht: Springer, 2014), 1440.
8. Valgenti, "Nietzsche and Food," 1441.
9. Silke-Maria Weineck, "Digesting the Nineteenth Century: Nietzsche and the Stomach of Modernity," *Romanticism* 12.1 (2006), 37. She corroborates her pithy claim with a passage from Nietzsche's *Menschliches, Allzumenschliches* (*Human, All Too Human*): "There are dyspeptic authors who write only when when they cannot digest something, even if it got stuck in their teeth" (37; see KSA 2, 441).
10. Peter Singer and Jim Mason, *The Way We Eat: Why Our Food Choices Matter* (Emmaus, PA: Rodale, 2006), 3. Henceforth WWE.
11. Michael Pollan, *The Omnivore's Dilemma: A Natural History of Four Meals* (New York: Penguin, 2006), 3.
12. Nishitani Keiji, "The I-Thou Relation in Zen Buddhism," trans. N. A. Waddell, *The Buddha Eye: An Anthology of the Kyoto School* (New York: Crossroad, 1982), 58.
13. *Dōgen's Pure Standards for the Zen Community: A Translation of Eihei Shingi*, trans. Taigen Daniel Leighton and Shōhaku Okumura, ed. Taigen Daniel Leighton (Albany: State

University of New York Press, 1996). Henceforth DPS. I very occasionally and ever so slightly modify this translation, not in order to correct it but to align its style with that of this essay. I also rely heavily upon *Nothing Is Hidden: Essays on Zen Master Dōgen's Instructions for the Cook*, ed. Jisho Warner, Shōhaku Okumura, John McRae, and Taigen Daniel Leighton (New York: Weatherhill, 2001). Henceforth NIH. I also greatly benefited from the translation of *Tenzo Kyōkun* therein by Griffith Foulk.

14. As Edward Brown, the celebrated *tenzo* of the San Francisco Zen Center, put it: "One shifts out of the mind-world of 'What's in it for me?' into the world of mutual interdependence and interconnectedness. And this is not simply something to talk about but something to be done" (DPS, xiv). Brown and the *Tenzo Kyōkun* are the focus of Doris Dörrie's wonderful documentary, *How to Cook Your Life* (2007).

15. "Mountains Hidden in Mountains: Dōgen-zenji and the Mind of Ecology," *Dōgen Zen and Its Relevance for Our Time*, ed. Shōhaku Okumura (San Francisco: Sōtō Zen Buddhism International Center, 2003), 165.

16. Graham Parkes, "Savoring Tastes: Appreciating Food in Japan," *New Essays in Japanese Aesthetics*, ed. A. Minh Nguyen (Lanham, MD: Lexington Books, 2018), 114.

17. For more on Ozu in this respect, see my "On Not Disturbing Still Water: Ozu Yasujirō and the Technical-Aesthetic Product," in *New Essays in Japanese Aesthetics*, ed. A. Minh Nguyen (Lanham, MD: Lexington Books, 2018), 353–365. Deleuze's analysis of Ozu's cinema appears in *Cinéma 2: L'image-temps* (Paris: Les Éditions de Minuit, 1985); *Cinema 2: The Time Image*, trans. Hugh Tomlinson and Robert Galeta (Minneapolis: University of Minnesota Press, 1989). Henceforth C2 with the French citation followed by the English citation.

18. Deleuze understood the question to be, "'What is a man who knows he is allowed only a few more months of life to do?' Everything depends on the givens" (C1, 191).

19. Gilles Deleuze, *Cinema 1: The Movement-Image*, trans. Hugh Tomlinson and Barbara Habberjam (Minneapolis: University of Minnesota Press, 1986), 189. Henceforth C1.

20. *Tout est ordinaire et régulier, Tout est quotidian!*

21. The importance of time for Dōgen (he speaks of *uji*, being time, time as being, and being as time) and for Deleuze's "time-image" should not be underestimated. The illusion of movement in cinema (still frames connected in the sensory motor apparatus as if they were continuous and therefore moving) allows movement to give us a derivative sense of time (the time it takes x to go from one point to another, the length of a scene, etc.). Ozu's cinema is an example of time itself—not sequential movement relying on our habits of perception—expressing itself in an image. Ozu enacts cinematic *uji*.

22. *Early Buddhist Discourses*, ed. and trans. John J. Holder (Indianapolis: Hackett, 2006), 91.

23. Dōgen, *Shōbōgenzō: La réserve visuelle des événements dans leur justesse*, ed. and trans. Nakamura Ryōji and René de Ceccatty (Paris: Éditions de la différence, 1980). Henceforth RVE. Translations from this text are my responsibility.

24. 法 is read *hō* when it is read on its own and not as part of the compound phrase *Shōbōgenzō* [正法眼蔵] where it is read as *bō*.

25. See, for example, Dōgen's claim in the *Sansui-kyō* that "mountains walk."

26. Paul Schrader, *Transcendental Style in Film: Ozu, Bresson, Dreyer* (New York: Da Capo, 1988), 6. "Oriental art in general and Zen in particular aspire to the Transcendent" (17). Although he admits that there is some difficulty in using a term like transcendence in a Zen context, he nonetheless speaks, following Suzuki Daisetz, of the "realm of transcendence" (18). He also says "Zen art and thought is the civilization, film is the veneer" (18). Although I remain sympathetic to Schrader's insistence on a Zen sensibility in Ozu, I do not think

that one needs to speak of it as (a) a unitary tradition; (b) having anything whatsoever to do with transcendence ("everywhere, nothing hidden" as we cited Dōgen's words of the Chinese *tenzo*); (c) a classically Zen approach (the Dharma is neither conservative and reactionary nor is it modern and trendy). It is not really Zen to be "Zen." Nonetheless, I happily grant his general observation: "Like the traditional Zen artist, Ozu directs silences and voids" (28).

27. Deleuze and Guattari will link this problem to two of the most pernicious "illusions" in philosophy, namely, those of transcendence and universality. The former, perhaps at the heart of all other philosophical illusions, has the "double aspect of making immanence immanent to something and of rediscovering a transcendence within immanence itself." The illusion of universals confuses concepts (which populate a plane) with the plane itself. It is important to note that Deleuze here associates the plane of immanence with Dōgen's *réserve visuelle des événements dans leur justesse* (WP, 49, 220).

28. Yoshida Kiju, *Ozu's Anti-Cinema*, trans. Daisuke Miyao and Kyoko Hirano (Ann Arbor: University of Michigan Press, 2003), 103. Henceforth OA.

CONCLUDING THOUGHTS

Pure Experience and Philosophy after Comparative Philosophy

In his critique of Auguste Comte's positivistic stupidity (*bêtise*), Gustave Flaubert (1821–1880) lamented that "ineptitude consists in wanting to conclude.... It is not understanding twilight, it's wanting only noon or midnight.... Yes, *bêtise* consists in wanting to conclude."[1] *Philosophy after comparative philosophy* welcomes twilight as the life vein of philosophy. This is emphatically not to confuse philosophy with sophistry—the sophist hides in and exploits the shadows and takes advantage of thinking's vulnerabilities. *Philosophy after comparative philosophy* endeavors to stand in clear relationship to twilight. There are therefore no final conclusions, no resting places, no once and for all statements. We are finally done with final proclamations, as performatively paradoxical such a proclamation may be.

Although this book argues against *philosophy after comparative philosophy*'s capacity to come to a final resting point, books thankfully come to an end, however provisional. This book ends where it began: with the problem of experience in philosophy. Given that this book does not emphasize Zen as a philosophical system but rather explores it as a widening of experience—an opening of William Blake's "doors of perception"—that amplifies our expectations of what could count as philosophy, it is critical to articulate what we mean by experience as the prephilosophical plane of any possible philosophy.

Experience is a notoriously elusive and slippery term with a fraught history in the dominant strands of European and post-European philosophy. There is no need to rehearse this history because the empiricism at hand is not derived from the main currents of these traditions. It is closer to Deleuze's empiricism, which he characterized as "a mysticism and mathematicism of concepts" (DR, 3). It is not the experience in the sense of a sensuous intuition of a particular object. It is what the early Nishida called *junsui keiken* (純粋経験), pure experience, which he also linked to Schelling's intellectual intuition: "There is no distinction between subject and object in any state of direct experience—one encounters reality face to face" (IG, 31). As such, direct experience precedes a denotative account of experience in which a subject experiences certain objects. Pure experience is an intuition that the partitioned and discrete objects of experience have been abstracted from a pure state of awareness that precedes judgments. No meaning of any kind is given in pure experience. "A truly pure experience has no meaning whatsoever; it is simply a present consciousness of facts just as they are" (IG, 4). Nishida would later distance himself from such language, claiming that it was too psychological. There are other and better ways to articulate what Nishida gestured toward throughout his philosophical endeavors. Nonetheless, he suggested the prephilosophical dimension of philosophical activity in a manner that remains valuable and instructive.

Nonetheless, the Mahāyāna recourse to pure experience has suffered severe and sometimes warranted critiques by folks like Robert Sharf as well as the Critical Buddhists. After such criticisms, how can the opening of the true Dharma eye and pure experience as a prephilosophical plane of philosophy be defended? Moreover, as this book has argued, if this defense remains an exclusively academic exercise, we risk forgoing the power of some strands of Buddhist practice: its capacity to cut through deeply seated illusions and awaken, here and now. It does not promise any private and epistemically privileged experiences or data but rather a different mindset. It is closer to Pope Francis's claim that "the ecological crisis is also a summons to profound interior conversion" and an "ecological conversion."[2]

This is the opportunity to be more philosophical about the powers and relevance of *philosophy after comparative philosophy* and to disambiguate what is skillful in the use of words like "experience" from the many ways in which such words give cover to being vague and obscure at best and reactionary and autocratic at worst.

I. Cutting through the Somnamulance of Ideology

In his famous *Prison Notebooks*, Antonio Gramsci critically analyzed the assumption that common sense naturally proceeds from the obvious and self-evident. Common sense, which he understood in a manner akin to what Noam Chomsky later memorably dubbed the manufacture of consent, secludes hegemonic interests and privatizes thinking. The privileged owners of the truth put the common sense of the masses on a need to know basis. Proudly nonelitist common sense and straight talk is consequently duped into unabashedly celebrating what "everybody knows" and "what no one can deny," forming an immense, invisibly operating consensus that operates without publicly legitimating or defending itself. Gramsci opposed the hegemonic force of "common sense" to the liberating force of "good sense." The former serves the privatized assumptions of a minority as if they were public goods. The hegemonic reign of ideology operates like Plato's cave. Grounded in the surreptitious control of the domain of sense, the cave is a great feat of misdirection: the prisoners have no critical curiosity about their shadow world or about the chains that keep them bound to it, but they always come to preordained conclusions that they continuously assume to be natural and obvious. They sense what they are made to sense.

Common sense represses or is otherwise unaware of the subjective assumptions that set the terms for thinking. Common sense is hence always about power, but as such, it renders those subject to common sense philosophically impotent. This was also at the heart of Herbert Marcuse's infamous critique of the abdication of good sense tacitly operating in the demotion of philosophy to a one-dimensional "ordinary language philosophy": "The self-styled poverty of philosophy, committed with all of its concepts to the given state of affairs, distrusts the possibilities of new experience. Subjection to the rule of facts is total—only linguistic facts, to be sure, but the society speaks in its language, and we are told to obey."[3]

Regimes of common sense and ideology also include what Charles Mills has provocatively analyzed as the Racial Contract. Metaphorically negotiated among the small group of signatories who will consequently emerge as the ones who have mattered, it packages its political act as the triumph of civilization over what now contractually appears as nature. Among the many privileges accorded the beneficiaries of the ideology of white supremacy, whether they are signatories or not, is not only a sense of cultural triumphalism, but also the luxury of not even noticing, thanks to a "certain schedule of structured blindnesses and opacities,"[4] that white supremacy is a constitutive feature of one's culture and world. This extends to philosophy, which not only ignored the virulent racism of some of its most celebrated practitioners (e.g., Hume, Kant, Hegel), but scarcely recognized race as a significant philosophical problem. This exhibits "at best a disturbing provincialism and an ahistoricity profoundly at odds with the radically foundational questioning on which philosophy prides itself and, at worst, a complicity with the terms of the Racial Contract itself."[5] These traditions not only assume that philosophy belongs to white culture but also that it does so to such an extent that other candidates for what and whom might matter philosophically do not count. The matter self-evidently appears always already the case. The Racial Contract is not the only way of narrowing what and who matters. There has long been a Gender Contract as well as a Heteronormativity Contract and a Class Contract. Late Capitalism itself is not exculpated from ideology's hostile conquest of thought and practice.

In strands of the Buddha Dharma tradition(s), ideology can be read as a contemporary variation of an ancient problem: it is as if the mirror of the mind were covered in dust. No matter what the mirror reflects, it reflects it in a dusty way. Giving the mirror brighter or better things to reflect cannot solve this problem; one must first find a way to wipe the dust off the mirror, and to do that, one must first somehow realize that the mirror of one's own mind has been dusty all along—no small feat since the mirror is too dusty to know that it is dusty. Or it is as if there is a piece of shit hanging from the tip of one's nose: no matter what one smells, one smells shit. In order to smell Zen's infinite fragrance of the universe, one has to first wake up to the fact of one's own shitty nose and find a way to wipe it clean. But how will I dream of smelling the infinite fragrance of the earth's luminosity when all that I know about my nose is that it is the vehicle through which I know the relentlessly shitty smell of my life and world? *Duḥkha*— Gautama Buddha's first noble truth of the stress of life out of whack—is experienced not as the truism that everyone and everything suffers. It is *suddenly* experienced as an *epiphany* shattering the shitty and dusty common sense of the *sahā* world. The very desire to practice—to wipe the mirror clean—is itself a great awakening, Dōgen tells us.

But how does common sense awaken to good sense? How does sense come to see that the problem was not just misinformation ("fake news") and hucksterism—although those are indeed mighty problems—but one's own mind? If good sense defies common sense, common sense, left to its own devices, could not come up with the possibility of good sense. Good sense does not belong to the mindset of common sense precisely because the logic of common sense dictates that common sense itself is good sense. The prisoner in the cave did not free herself from her chains. She did not originally even know that they were chains or that she was a prisoner or that she might want to try to liberate herself.

In strands of the Mahāyāna, especially the ones that predominated in East Asia, this problem is famously addressed as the problem of *upāya* or skillful means. As we saw in the fourth chapter, it receives one of its most forceful formulations at the beginning of the *Lotus Sutra* with the parable of the burning house. Echoing the central image of the Buddha's famous Fire Sermon, Śāriputra is asked to imagine a man of great wealth whose house has caught on fire and although he knows that he can easily escape, his children are so absorbed in their games (attachments and addictions) that they cannot experience the fire raging all around them. When the father tries to alert his children to the problem, they are "unalarmed and unafraid . . . for they do not even know what a 'fire' is, or what a 'house' is, or what it means to 'lose' anything" (LS, 59). Of course, one could lose money, fame, and power—all the most valuable and real things! How could anything else matter?

The father cannot tell his children directly what is happening any more than good sense can announce itself to common sense. The father therefore devises an expedient but technically fictional mean—a clever antidote designed to penetrate the walls of the mind's own cave. He must speak in a way that his drunken, somnolent, insane children can understand. He hence caters to the logic of their besotted desires and promises to give them whatever they want, in this case, some even more extraordinary and resplendent playthings waiting for them outside the house. The children, their hearts aflame, rush from the house.

The Buddha asks Śāriputra if the father is guilty of telling a lie, and Śāriputra already sees that the father has put his sons on the path to realization, even though they do not yet understand it. For the Buddha, this means that the teaching of the Three Vehicles was merely an expedient means "in order to entice the beings" (LS, 64), to turn them from their dull minds to a direct experience of the truth already concealed within these tacitly expressive words like a hidden jewel sewn into one's clothing. One suddenly comes to see that the Buddha was everywhere and everything, even the burning house itself. That is to say, the burning house (the first noble truth of *duḥkha*) drives us to the Buddha Dharma, but the latter comes to be seen as expressing itself as all beings, even the burning house that first appeared wholly and irreconcilably opposed to Buddha Dharma. The problem was not the burning house per se, but rather our own inability to break through the barrier of our own common sense, dusty mirror, and shitty nose. The burning house was our own ignorance (*avidyā*, literally, non-seeing).

In *suddenly* waking up to a different manner of consciousness, to the non sequitur of a heretofore-unimaginable manner of attunement, one is not waking from the somnolence of alt-facts and fake news to the sunny European Enlightenment world of objective truths. In the Great Death, heaven and earth are born anew. In the language of the *Lotus Sutra*, one has attained the Buddha's *bodhimaṇḍa* or seat of awakening—on the *bodhimaṇḍa* "he was able to achieve the Fruit" (LS, 23). In characterizing this awakening as *sudden*—what has come to be called subitism[6]—what is being stressed is not the velocity of the awakening. It is not quick rather than the snail's pace through generations of reincarnation stressed by the gradual approach. Whether the shit-covered nose smells the roses for minutes or for years, it always smells shit. The suddenness marks the non sequitur of a new manner of mind. One could even say that the gradual (you will get there one day if you keep trying) is the *upāya* in which the sudden is sewn into language like a jewel was sewn into our clothing during our drunken stupor. One day we wake up and suddenly see that the Buddha lands were always there—suddenly: everywhere, nothing hidden as the Chinese *tenzo* told a young Dōgen. The moon was not hiding, waiting one day to reveal itself. That is not why the blind person failed to see it.

The *Lotus Sutra* speaks of the teaching specific to the seat or place of this mind as "beyond reckoning and calculation" and as the *anantanirdeśa* or immeasurable doctrine (literally the infinite or boundless counsel, advice, or instruction). As such, this is the *single* (*eka*) and *great* (*mahā*) vehicle of all possible approaches to Buddha Dharma—the *Ekayāna* and Mahāyāna. This is not to say that this is the one thing or substance or doctrine that characterizes all approaches to Buddha Dharma. That is precisely what the *Ekayāna* denies. The Dharma rain falls equally on all, but each receives it in his or her own way. One vehicle, ceaseless *upāya*, but at the heart of all *upāya*, the hidden jewel sewn into the garments of all possible teachings, is the *anantanirdeśa* or immeasurable doctrine, a word that in its way ends all words.

II. Experience *After Comparative Philosophy*

This sort of thinking has come on hard times in some quarters. Bernard Faure has called it somewhat disparagingly the "rhetoric of immediacy."[7] He has gone to great lengths to disambiguate the many strands of Buddha Dharma from the Chan and Zen insistence on this moment "in order to deconstruct the tradition, that is, to reveal it in its essential multiplicity."[8]

Even the teaching of the *Ekayāna*, however, does not imply that there is one way, a single *upāya*, which addresses the needs of every kind of practitioner. The distinction, rather, is between skillful/helpful and unskillful/unhelpful, and that is in part determined by the myriad entanglements of the webs of karma, or by one's culture, by the diversity within that culture, by one's personal abilities and predilections, by historical exigencies, and so on. The Buddha's medicine bag was big and full of many different kinds of medicines for many different kinds of exigencies and needs. This is not to say that there have not been doctrinally imperious self-understandings of various schools and teachers—the dogmatism that proclaims: *our* teaching is the *one* teaching. The various legacies of the transmission of the Buddha Dharma have had more than their share of partisanship and tribal egoism. (Dōgen's infamous insistence that whoever speaks of a *Zenshū*, a school or sect of Zen, is a "devil," is largely lost on Sōtōshū.) It is simply to insist that the non sequitur of the *Ekayāna* remains the challenge to learn to embrace the multiplicity of its expressions.

Robert Sharf has levied a quite substantive and consequential critique of the reliance on the concept of experience.[9] He rightly notes that the idea itself is a newcomer, both philosophically and linguistically, and as a point of fact, this was not a way in which any of these traditions, even Chan and Zen, previously understood themselves. The term itself is borrowed from Western philosophy (RE, 274) and is admittedly imprecise; its wide array of meanings is so extensive that in the end it says little if anything. The term is "exceedingly broad, encompassing a vast array of feelings, moods, perceptions, dispositions, and states of consciousness" (RE, 268). This is all well and good and an important corrective, but what Nishida and Suzuki emphasized broadly under a rubric-like "experience" is in no way exhausted by such terms, nor is the use of such a term implying that this is somehow the best or truest way to speak of and from this practice. They are ultimately just trying to be helpful. Unlike its vague use in religious studies, Nishida and Suzuki and others nonetheless attempted to use this term in a precise fashion and not confuse it with the morass of meanings in modern European philosophy.

Did Suzuki in his "approach to Zen, with its unrelenting emphasis on an unmediated inner experience" (RE, 274), naïvely state all of this as an absolute fact, unsullied by linguistic and historical contingencies and karma? Or was this not in some sense *upāya*—an attempt to communicate at the moment in which Western values were threatening to obfuscate this sensibility? Is this not the work of a Zen teacher rather than a historian who imagines that he is merely interrogating the historical record? Was not Suzuki's gift the challenge of *upāya* not only for a new cultural context but also for academic philosophical and religious discourse? Yes, we can grant that the "very notion that one can separate an unmediated experience from a culturally determined description of that experience is philosophically suspect" (RE, 271). Indeed, this is the impossibility of thinking in pure terms, of jettisoning the linguistic karma that underlies language as *upāya*. The historical and cultural criticism (HCC) position as discussed in the introduction will always serve as a valuable and sobering corrective. The fair and penetrating charge that, as Heine tells us, Zen "apologists deliberately cloak Zen in a shield of opaqueness" in order "to avoid or to claim immunity from the careful scrutiny of historical examination" (ZSZM, 8) should be welcomed, and it has the potential to make Zen stronger, clearer, more inclusive, and more open. Many terrible things and a lot of terrible behavior have hidden in the shadows of Zen obscurantism. Practice thrives when it can be actively and rigorously self-critical, and when it vows, as did Nietzsche, to "laugh at every master who does not first laugh at himself" (KSA 3, 343).

Sharf's most salient concern, however, needs to be taken seriously. "The category experience is, in essence, a mere place-holder that entails a substantive if indeterminate terminus for the relentless deferral of meaning. And this is precisely what makes the term experience so amenable to ideological appropriation" (RE, 286). Hence, recourse to some vague and ethereal realm of experience is "often used rhetorically to thwart the authority of the 'objective' or the 'empirical,' and to valorize instead the subjective, the personal, the private" (RE, 267). This is the looming danger of the "ideological aspect of the appeal to experience—the use of the concept to legitimize vested social, institutional, and professional interests" (RE, 269). Experience exceeds philosophical and political scrutiny and hence cannot be subject to critique and need not concern itself with the travails of the mundane.

This latter point is also the most serious charge that has come from the Critical Buddhists, some of whom claim that talk of things like direct experience does not even belong to Buddha Dharma. Their strength has been the manner in which they worry that *hongaku shisō* (original enlightenment)—at least in its historical practice— is reactionary, anti-intellectual, and implicitly autocratic. From the safety of the *anantanirdeśa* or immeasurable doctrine, they are beyond critical reproach. What do critical words matter to those taking refuge in the absolute silence of the *bodhimaṇḍa*? Moreover, what does the *sahā* world with its sufferings, tribulations, and injustices matter? They will eventually reach the other shore, if not in this life, then in another. Or sentient beings cannot be freed because they are hapless victim of the *mappō*, the ten thousand year period of the Dharma's inaccessibility. The downtrodden are Buddhas in the absolute, so it does not matter that they are humiliated and oppressed in the mundane. These kinds of sentiment have been alarmingly prevalent and in need of trenchant critique. As the poet, Zen practitioner, and ecological activist Gary Snyder reflected almost fifty years ago, "The 'truth' in Buddhism and Hinduism is not dependent in any sense on Indian or Chinese culture; and ... 'India' and 'China'—as societies—are as burdensome as any others; perhaps more so. It became clear that 'Hinduism' and 'Buddhism' as social institutions had long been accomplices of the State in burdening and binding people, rather than serving to liberate them. Just like the other Great Religions."[10]

Such autocratic and exclusionary practitioners are still around, and this ideology and rhetoric remains a grave occupational hazard of Buddhist practice. Nonetheless, Critical Buddhists like Hakamaya Noriaki overdetermine their case. Hakamaya, for example, dismisses the Kyoto School and Nishitani for touting "an indigenous East Asian ethos of original enlightenment tinged with German idealism," which is just another manner of catering to the Japanese obsession with their cultural uniqueness.[11] Even more problematically, Nishitani's adaptation of Nishida's "direct experience"[12] is "totally unrelated to Buddhism" (CP, 78). Hakamaya charges Nishitani and the Kyoto School more broadly with abandoning the dirty and dusty vicissitudes of history for the safety of eternity: "But the topical philosophy that Nishitani advocates is ageless, perennial, unchanging. Just as the philosophy of Chuang-tzu [Zhuangzi] is called a "philosophy of death," so is Nishitani's. Because the topos exists primordially and is separated from time, it rejects aging and the changes of life. The goal of topical philosophy is, literally, to die and become one with the topos" (CP, 79).

This is not the *Ekayāna* and it is certainly not at all what Nishitani meant by the Great Death, which brings one into more intimate relationship with the infinite fragrance of the great earth. This characterization of pure experience resembles, as we saw in the second chapter, Schopenhauer's own serious misunderstanding of the Great Vehicle as the eclipse of the suffering will as it reaches the other shore of the pure continuum of the absolute. In Schopenhauer's account, the Buddha's third noble truth (*nirodha*), is to annihilate—to dissipate into pure nothingness—the will to life and thereby our involvement in the pseudo-reality of the universe: "To those in whom the will has turned and denied itself, this so very real world of ours with all of its suns and milky ways is—nothing" (WWV I, 412; WWR I, 487). To this Schopenhauer appended a note: "This is also precisely the *Prajna-Paramita* of the Buddhists, the 'beyond all knowledge,' that is, the point where subject and object are no more" (WWV I, 412; WWR I, 487). Nietzsche, in marked contrast, understood this as the clearest symptom of Christianity's hidden truth and the burgeoning of what he called (in critical response to Schopenhauer) "European Buddhism," that is, the advent of a virulent nihilism. To those under such a toxic spell Zarathustra counsels, "They really prefer to be dead and so we should respect what they want" (KSA 4, 55). If "life is only suffering," then "take care that *you* stop! Take care that your life stops the life that is only suffering" (KSA 4, 56). Yes, we are wise to leave the dead to the dead.

Schopenhauer's Buddhism suffers from what Hakuin called *kūbyō* or *śūnyatā*-sickness. In so doing, he echoed one of the most delicate but critical insights in all of Buddha Dharma, one that its own tradition nonetheless often fails to appreciate. If emptiness, itself an expedient or purgative or physic, that is, part of the Buddha's medicine chest, becomes an end in itself, if emptiness replaces all other views with the view of nothingness (nihilism), then the medicine backfired. The poison was not ruminated and it made the patient sicker. As we saw at the end of the second chapter, Nāgārjuna claimed that the view, *prapañca* (hypostatization or reification), of emptiness turns that which is designed to rid one of all *prapañca* into the worst *prapañca* of all: "those for whom emptiness is a *prapañca* have been called incurable" (N, 145).

Moreover, the strangest aspect of Schopenhauer's Buddhism is its conception of the role of compassion. I am not driven to love by love itself, for that would be love as an object of the will to life, which in turn would make love another occasion for agony. In a sense, ethics helps one more or less reengineer oneself: pain drives me to ethics, but ethics drives me away from myself, away from the misery of the blind *principium individuationis*. Selfless acts can intervene and invert the movement of the will to life and its drive to involvement with this worthless and excruciating world, loosening the grip of a world that should never have been and returning one to the peaceful stillness of the pure plenum. Self-hatred born of pain is the original motivation for the will-abnegating turn to the absolute compassion at the heart of *mettā*, loving-kindness, and compassion.

This is a far cry from the *Lotus Sutra*'s turn to Avalokiteśvara, who hears all the cries of the world. These cries become audible when one's own mind realizes its capaciousness to hear and carry them all, and this is the experience not of emptiness for the sake of emptiness, but of the nonseparation of all beings. *Prajñā* (wisdom not as knowing wise facts but as a wise mode of knowing) suddenly interrupts ideology's spell of presence in which we are frozen and alienated subjects knocking at a distant world of objects with our petty truths, alt-facts, or cold abstractions. Wisdom within is expressed as compassion without. "This bodhisattva-mahāsattva [Avalokiteśvara] in the midst of terror, emergency, and trouble can confer the gift of fearlessness" (LS, 315). Critical thought, try as it may, cannot all by itself confer this gift, the gift by which we in these fearful times embrace with love the world of all sentient beings and their suffering.

This is not to cloak Zen in a so-called rhetoric of immediacy that shrouds it in mystery and immunizes it from critique nor is it to muddy the waters of philosophy, condemning them to sophistry and other philosophical vices that flourish in the turbidity of obscurantism. It is rather to take seriously how deep human problems run. We are in a dusty world where contemporary politics are merely the most odious symptom of the *duḥkha* of a common sense that cannot imagine a world where all beings matter, where we are not addicted to fossil fuels, and where we could anticipate the possibility of a world beyond capitalism rather than its rapacious rage upon the earth. After the many parables in the *Lotus Sutra*, "the earth trembled and split, and from its clefts there welled up simultaneously incalculable thousands of myriads of millions of bodhisattva-mahāsattvas" (LS, 225). Every expression of the earth has always been a Buddha. They emerge when we suddenly learn to experience them. "Even a mote of dust is sufficient to turn the Dharma wheel," Dōgen tells us. We need both a *sudden earth awakening* and the good sense to think of and from it. This is, as Nietzsche's Zarathustra counseled us, to "remain true to the earth" (KSA 4, 15).

This makes all the difference in this age of ecological crisis and political and economic turmoil. It also makes all of the difference for the future of *philosophy after comparative philosophy* where what is at stake is not comparing and contrasting various philosophies but rather renewing a more philosophical commitment to exploring and unleashing the powers of philosophy.

Notes

1. Quoted in Jacques Derrida, *The Beast and the Sovereign*, vol. 1, trans. Geoffrey Bennington (Chicago: University of Chicago Press, 2009), 161.
2. Pope Francis [Jorge Mario Bergoglio], *Encyclical Letter "Laudato Si'" of the Holy Father Francis: On Care for Our Common Home* (Vatican City: Vatican Press, 2015), 158–159.
3. Herbert Marcuse, *One-Dimensional Man* (Boston: Beacon Press, 1964), 178.
4. Charles W. Mills, *The Racial Contract* (Ithaca: Cornell University Press, 1997), 19.
5. Mills, *The Racial Contract*, 31. As Eric S. Nelson argues, "The question of *who* can philosophize, and *who* counts as a philosopher, is a quintessential philosophical question." *Chinese and Buddhist Philosophy in Early Twentieth-Century German Thought* (London: Bloomsbury, 2017), 2.
6. Coined in Paul Demiéville's influential article, "The Mirror of the Mind," in *Sudden and Gradual: Approaches to Enlightenment in Chinese Thought*, ed. Peter N. Gregory (Honolulu: University Press of Hawai'i, 1987), 13–40.
7. Bernard Faure, *The Rhetoric of Immediacy: A Cultural Critique of Chan/Zen Buddhism* (Princeton, NJ: Princeton University Press, 1994).
8. Faure, *The Rhetoric of Immediacy*, 4.
9. Robert H. Sharf, "The Rhetoric of Experience and the Study of Religion," *Journal of Consciousness Studies* 7.11–12 (2000). Henceforth RE.
10. Gary Snyder, *Earth House Hold: Technical Notes and Queries to Fellow Dharma Revolutionaries* (New York: New Directions, 1969), 114.
11. Hakamaya Noriaki, "Critical Philosophy versus Topical Philosophy," in *Pruning the Buddha Tree: The Storm over Critical Buddhism*, ed. Jamie Hubbard and Paul Swanson (Honolulu: University Press of Hawai'i, 1997), 78. Henceforth CP.
12. Hakamaya quotes Nishitani in dialogue with Yagi: "When your eyes are opened the Buddha is there, sentient beings are there—everybody is there. When they are not present—well, that cannot be called direct experience" (quoted in CP, 78).

BIBLIOGRAPHY

Abe Masao. *A Study of Dōgen: His Philosophy and Religion*. Edited by Steven Heine. Albany: State University of New York Press, 1992.
_____. *Zen and Western Thought*. Edited by William R. LaFleur. Honolulu: University Press of Hawai'i, 1985.
Addiss, Stephen, with Stanley Lombardo and Judith Roitman, editors and translators. *Zen Sourcebook: Traditional Documents from China, Korea, and Japan*. Indianapolis, IN: Hackett, 2008.
Allison, David, editor. *The New Nietzsche*. Cambridge, MA: MIT Press, 1977.
_____. *Reading the New Nietzsche:* The Birth of Tragedy, The Gay Science, Thus Spoke Zarathustra, *and* On the Genealogy of Morals. New York: Rowman and Littlefield, 2001.
Arendt, Hannah. *The Origins of Totalitarianism*. San Diego: Harcourt, 1994. First published 1951.
Aschheim, Steven E. *The Nietzsche Legacy in Germany: 1890–1990*. Berkeley: University of California Press, 1992.
Azzam, Abed. *Nietzsche versus Paul*. New York: Columbia University Press, 2015.
Babich, Babette E. *Nietzsche's Philosophy of Science: Reflecting Science on the Ground of Life and Art*. Albany: State University of New York Press, 1994.
Baker, Peter. "Bush Weaves Rug Story into Many an Occasion." *Washington Post*, March 7, 2006.
Bataille, Georges. *The Accursed Share* (1949). Translated by Robert Hurley. New York: Zone, 1988.
_____. *L'Erotisme*. Paris: Les Éditions de Minuit, 1957. *Erotism: Death and Sensuality*. Translated by Mary Dalwood. San Francisco: City Lights, 1986.
_____. *Inner Experience* (1943). Translated by Leslie Anne Boldt. Albany: State University of New York Press, 1988.
Bazzano, Manu. *Buddha Is Dead: Nietzsche and the Dawn of European Zen*. Brighton, UK: Sussex Academic, 2006.
Benson, Bruce Ellis. *Pious Nietzsche: Decadence and Dionysian Faith*. Bloomington: Indiana University Press, 2008.
Bergoglio, Jorge Mario [Pope Francis]. *Encyclical Letter "Laudato Si'" of the Holy Father Francis: On Care for Our Common Home*. Vatican City: Vatican Press, 2015.
Blake, William. *Jerusalem: The Emanation of the Giant Albion* (1804–1820). Edited by Morton D. Paley. Princeton, NJ: Princeton University Press, 1991.
Bodiford, William M. *Going Forth: Visions of Buddhist Vinaya*. Honolulu: University Press of Hawai'i, 2005.
_____. "Remembering Dōgen: Eiheiji and Dōgen Hagiography." *Journal of Japanese Studies* 32.1 (2006), 1–21.
_____. *Sōtō Zen in Medieval Japan*. Honolulu: University Press of Hawai'i, 1993.
_____. "Zen in the Art of Funerals: Ritual Salvation in Japanese Buddhism." *History of Religions* 32.2 (1992), 146–164.

Bonardel, Françoise. "Giants Battle Anew: Nihilism's Self-Overcoming in Europe and Asia (Nietzsche, Heidegger, Nishitani)." In *Nietzsche and Phenomenology: Power, Life, Subjectivity*. Edited by Élodie Boublil and Christine Daigle, 80–100. Bloomington: Indiana University Press, 2013.

Burik, Steven. *The End of Comparative Philosophy and the Task of Comparative Thinking: Heidegger, Derrida, and Daoism*. Albany: State University of New York Press, 2009.

Canguilhem, Georges. *The Normal and the Pathological*. Translated by Carolyn Fawcett and Robert Cohen. New York: Zone, 1989.

Cartwright, David E. *Schopenhauer: A Biography*. Cambridge: Cambridge University Press, 2010.

Clarke, J. J. *Oriental Enlightenment: The Encounter between Asian and Western Thought*. London: Routledge, 1997.

Connolly, Tim. *Doing Philosophy Comparatively*. London: Bloomsbury, 2015.

Conrad, Joseph. *Heart of Darkness and Two Other Stories*. London: Folio, 1997.

Corriero, Emilio Carlo. *Nietzsche's Death of God and Italian Philosophy*. Translated by Vanessa Di Stefano. London: Rowman and Littlefield, 2016.

Curtin, Deane W., and Lisa M. Heldke, editors. *Cooking, Eating, Thinking: Transformative Philosophies of Food*. Bloomington: Indiana University Press, 1992.

Danto, Arthur C. *Nietzsche as Philosopher*. New York: Macmillan, 1965.

Davis, Bret W. "The Enlightening Practice of Nonthinking: Unfolding Dōgen's 'Fukanzazengi.'" In *Engaging Dōgen's Zen: The Philosophy of Practice as Awakening (Commentaries on Dōgen's "Shushōgi" and "Fukanzazengi")*. Edited by Jason M. Wirth, Brian Schroeder, and Bret Davis. Boston: Wisdom, 2016.

_____. "Forms of Emptiness in Zen." In *A Companion to Buddhist Philosophy*. Edited by Steven Emmanuel, 190–213. West Sussex, UK: Wiley-Blackwell, 2013.

_____. "Letting Go of God for Nothing: Ueda Shizuteru's Non-Mysticism and the Question of Ethics in Zen Buddhism." In *Frontiers of Japanese Philosophy 2*. Edited by Victor Sogen Hori and Melissa Anne-Marie Curley, 226–255. Nagoya: Nanzan Institute for Religion and Culture, 2008.

_____. "Naturalness in Zen and Shin Buddhism: Before and beyond Self- and Other-Power." *Contemporary Buddhism* 15.2 (July 2014), 433–447.

_____. "The Philosophy of Zen Master Dōgen: Egoless Perspectivism." In *The Oxford Handbook of World Philosophy*. Edited by Jay Garfield and William Edelglass, 348–360. New York: Oxford University Press, 2011.

_____. "Reply to Graham Parkes: Nietzsche as Zebra: With Both Egoistic Antibuddha and Nonegoistic Bodhisattva Stripes." *Journal of Nietzsche Studies* 46.1 (Spring 2015), 62–81.

_____. "The Step Back through Nihilism: The Radical Orientation of Nishitani Keiji's Philosophy of Zen." *Synthesis Philosophica* 37 (2004), 139–159.

_____. "Toward a Liberative Phenomenology of Zen." In *Yearbook for Eastern and Western Philosophy*, vol. 2. Edited by Hans Feger, Xie Dikun, and Wang Ge, 304–320. Berlin: De Gruyter, 2017.

_____. "Zen after Zarathustra: The Problem of the Will in the Confrontation between Nietzsche and Buddhism." *Journal of Nietzsche Studies* 28 (2004), 89–138.

_____. "Zen's Nonegocentric Perspectivism." In *Buddhist Philosophy: A Comparative Approach*. Edited by Steven M. Emmanuel, 123–143. West Sussex: Wiley-Blackwell, 2017.

Davis, Bret W., Brian Schroeder, and Jason M. Wirth, editors. *Japanese and Continental Philosophy: Conversations with the Kyoto School*. Bloomington: Indiana University Press, 2011.

Deleuze, Gilles. *Cinema 1: The Movement-Image*. Translated by Hugh Tomlinson and Barbara Habberjam. Minneapolis: University of Minnesota Press, 1986.
———. *Cinéma 2: L'image-temps*. Paris: Les Éditions de Minuit, 1985. *Cinema 2: The Time Image*. Translated by Hugh Tomlinson and Robert Galeta. Minneapolis: University of Minnesota Press, 1989.
———. *Différence et repetition*. Paris: Presses universitaires de France, 1968. *Difference and Repetition*. Translated by Paul Patton. New York: Columbia University Press, 1994.
———. *Expressionism in Philosophy: Spinoza* (1968). Translated by Martin Joughin. New York: Zone, 1992.
———. *The Fold: Leibniz and the Baroque* (1988). Translated by Tom Conley. Minneapolis: University of Minnesota Press, 1993.
———. *Francis Bacon: Logique de la sensation*. Paris: Éditions de la Différence, 1981. *Francis Bacon: The Logic of Sensation*. Translated by Daniel W. Smith. Minneapolis: University of Minnesota Press, 2003.
———. *Kant's Critical Philosophy* (1963). Translated by Hugh Tomlinson and Barbara Habberjam. Minneapolis: University of Minnesota Press, 1984.
———. *Nietzsche et la philosophie*. Paris: Presses universitaires de France, 1962. *Nietzsche and Philosophy*. Translated by Hugh Tomlinson. New York: Columbia University Press, 1983.
———. *Spinoza: Practical Philosophy* (1970, revised 1981). Translated by Robert Hurley. San Francisco: City Lights, 1988.
Deleuze, Gilles, and Félix Guattari. *Anti-Oedipus: Capitalism and Schizophrenia* (1972). Translated by Robert Hurley, Mark Seem, and Helen R. Lane. Minneapolis: University of Minnesota Press, 1983.
———. *Qu'est-ce que la philosophie?* Paris: Les Éditions de Minuit, 1991. *What Is Philosophy?* Translated by Hugh Tomlinson and Graham Burchell. New York: Columbia University Press, 1994.
———. *A Thousand Plateaus*. Translated by Brian Massumi. Minneapolis: University of Minnesota Press, 1987.
Demiéville, Paul. "The Mirror of the Mind." In *Sudden and Gradual: Approaches to Enlightenment in Chinese Thought*. Edited by Peter N. Gregory, 13–40. Honolulu: University Press of Hawai'i, 1987.
Derrida, Jacques. *The Beast and the Sovereign*, vol. 1. Translated by Geoffrey Bennington. Chicago: University of Chicago Press, 2009.
The Diamond Sūtra. Translated by Red Pine [Bill Porter]. Washington, DC: Counterpoint, 2001.
Dōgen Eihei. *Dōgen's Extensive Record: A Translation of Eihei Kōroku*. Translated by Dan Leighton and Shōhaku Okumura. Boston: Wisdom, 2004.
———. *Dōgen's Manuals of Zen Meditation*. Translated by Carl Bielefeldt. Berkeley: University of California Press, 1988.
———. *Dōgen's* Pure Standards for the Zen Community: *A Translation of* Eihei Shingi. Translated by Taigen Daniel Leighton and Shōhaku Okumura. Edited by Taigen Daniel Leighton. Albany: State University of New York Press, 1996.
———. *The Heart of Dōgen's Shōbōgenzō*. Translated by Norman Waddell and Masao Abe. Albany: State University of New York Press, 2002.
———. *Master Dōgen's Shōbōgenzō*. 4 vols. Translated by Gudō Wafu Nishijima and Mike Chodo Cross. London: Windbell, 1994.

---. *Moon in a Dewdrop: Writings of Zen Master Dōgen*. Edited by Tanahashi Kazuaki. San Francisco: North Point, 1985.

---. *A Primer of Sōtō Zen [Shōbōgenzō Zuimonki]*. Translated by Reihō Masunaga. Honolulu: University Press of Hawai'i, 1971.

---. *Shōbōgenzō: La réserve visuelle des événements dans leur justesse*. Edited and translated by Nakamura Ryōji and René de Ceccatty. Paris: Éditions de la Différence, 1980.

---. *Treasury of the True Dharma Eye [Shōbōgenzō]*. 2 vols. Edited by Kazuaki Tanahashi. Boston: Shambhala, 2010.

---. *The Wholehearted Way: A Translation of Eihei Dōgen's* Bendōwa *with Commentary by Kōshō Uchiyama Rōshi*. Translated by Shōhaku Okumura and Taigen Daniel Leighton. North Clarendon, VT: Tuttle, 1997.

---. *The Zen Poetry of Dōgen: Verses from the Mountain of Eternal Peace*. Translated by Steven Heine. North Clarendon, VT: Tuttle, 1997.

Dörrie, Doris, director. *How to Cook Your Life*. Documentary, DVD, 2007.

Droit, Roger-Pol. *The Cult of Nothingness: The Philosophers and the Buddha*. Translated by David Streight and Pamela Vohnson. Chapel Hill: University of North Carolina Press, 2003.

Dumoulin, Heinrich. *Zen Buddhism: A History*. Vol. 1: *India and China*. Translated by James W. Heisig and Paul Knitter. New York: Macmillan, 1988.

Edelglass, William, and Jay L. Garfield, editors. *Buddhist Philosophy: Essential Readings*. Oxford: Oxford University Press, 2009.

Elberfeld, Rolf. *Kitarō Nishida (1870–1945): Moderne japanische Philosophie und die Frage nach der Interkulturalität*. Amsterdam: Rodopi, 1999.

Elberfeld, Rolf, and Arisaka Yōko, editors. *Kitarō Nishida in der Philosophie des 20. Jahrhunderts: Mit Texten Nishidas in deutscher Übersetzung*. Freiburg: Karl Alber, 2014.

Elman, Benjamin A. "Nietzsche and Buddhism." *Journal of the History of Ideas* 44.4 (October–December 1983), 671–686.

Faure, Bernard. "The Kyoto School and Reverse Orientalism." In *Japan in Traditional and Postmodern Perspectives*. Edited by Charles Wei-Hsun Fu and Steven Heine, 245–281. Albany: State University of New York Press, 1995.

---. *The Rhetoric of Immediacy: A Cultural Critique of Chan/Zen Buddhism*. Princeton, NJ: Princeton University Press, 1994.

Figl, Johann. *Nietzsche und die Religionen: Transkulturelle Perspektiven seines Bildungs- und Denkweges*. Berlin: Walter de Gruyter, 2007.

Flavel, Sarah. "Nishitani's Nietzsche: Will to Power and the Moment." *Journal of Nietzsche Studies* 46.1 (Spring 2015), 12–24.

The Flower Ornament Scripture: A Translation of the Avataṃsaka Sūtra. Translated by Thomas Cleary. Boston: Shambhala, 1993.

Foucault, Michel. "Nietzsche, Genealogy, History." In *Language, Counter-Memory, Practice: Selected Essays and Interviews*. Translated by Donald Bouchard and Sherry Simon. Ithaca, NY: Cornell University Press, 1977.

Freeman, Timothy. "The Shimmering Shining: The Promise of Art in Heidegger and Nietzsche." *Comparative and Continental Philosophy* 5.1 (May 2013), 49–66.

---. "Zarathustra, Zhuangzi, and Zen: The Challenge of Remaining Loyal to the Earth in the Time of Climate Change," *The Wandering Dance*, ed. David Jones, forthcoming.

Froese, Katrin. *Nietzsche, Heidegger, and Daoist Thought*. Albany: State University of New York Press, 2004.

Gadamer, Hans-Georg. "On the Enigmatic Character of Health." In *The Enigma of Health*. Translated by Jason Gaiger and Nicholas Walker. Stanford, CA: Stanford University Press, 1996.

Garfield, Jay L. *Empty Words: Buddhist Philosophy and Cross-Cultural Interpretation*. Oxford: Oxford University Press, 2002.

_____. *The Fundamental Wisdom of the Middle Way*. Oxford: Oxford University Press, 1995.

Gasché, Rodolphe. *Geophilosophy: On Gilles Deleuze and Félix Guattari's What Is Philosophy?* Evanston, IL: Northwestern University Press, 2014.

Geist, Kathe. "Buddhism in *Tokyo Story*." In *Ozu's Tokyo Story*. Edited by David Desser, 101–117. Cambridge: Cambridge University Press, 1997.

Gillespie, Michael Allen. *Nihilism before Nietzsche*. Chicago: University of Chicago Press, 1995.

Hakamaya Noriaki. "Critical Philosophy versus Topical Philosophy." Translated by Jamie Hubbard. In *Pruning the Bodhi Tree: The Storm over Critical Buddhism*. Edited by Jamie Hubbard and Paul L. Swanson, 56–80. Honolulu: University Press of Hawai'i, '1997.

_____. "Thoughts on the Ideological Background of Social Discrimination." Translated by Jamie Hubbard. In *Pruning the Bodhi Tree: The Storm over Critical Buddhism*. Edited by Jamie Hubbard and Paul L. Swanson, 339–355. Honolulu: University Press of Hawai'i, 1997.

Hakuin Ekaku. *Beating the Cloth Drum: Letters of Zen Master Hakuin*. Translated by Norman Waddell. Boston: Shambhala, 2012.

_____. *The Embossed Tea Kettle and Other Stories*. Translated by R. D. M. Shaw. London: Allen & Unwin, 1963.

_____. *The Essential Teachings of Zen Master Hakuin: A Translation of the* Sokkō-roku Kaien-fusetsu. Translated by Norman Waddell. Boston: Shambhala, 2010.

_____. *Hakuin on Kenshō*. Edited with commentary by Albert Low. Boston: Shambhala, 2006.

_____. *Hakuin's Precious Mirror Cave: A Zen Miscellany*. Translated by Norman Waddell. Berkeley, CA: Counterpoint, 2009.

_____. *Poison Blossoms from a Thicket of Thorn*. Translated by Norman Waddell. Berkeley, CA: Counterpoint, 2015.

_____. *Wild Ivy: The Spiritual Autobiography of Zen Master Hakuin*. Translated by Norman Waddell. Boston: Shambhala, 1999.

_____. *The Zen Master Hakuin: Selected Writings*. Translated by Philip B. Yampolsky. New York: Columbia University Press, 1971.

_____. *Zen Words for the Heart: Hakuin's Commentary on the Heart Sūtra*. Translated by Norman Waddell. Boston: Shambhala, 1996.

Hanaoka Eiko. *Zen and Christianity: From the Standpoint of Absolute Nothingness*. Kyoto: Maruzen, 2009.

Hatab, Lawrence. *A Nietzschean Defense of Democracy: An Experiment in Postmodern Politics*. La Salle, IL: Open Court, 1995.

_____. *Nietzsche's Life Sentence: Coming to Terms with Eternal Recurrence*. London: Routledge, 2005.

Heidegger, Martin. *Being and Time: A Translation of* Sein und Zeit (1927). Translated by Joan Stambaugh. Albany: State University of New York Press, 1996.

_____. *Country Path Conversations*. Translated by Bret W. Davis. Bloomington: Indiana University Press, 2010.

_____. *Nietzsche*, vol. 3, *The Will to Power as Knowledge and as Metaphysics*. Translated by Joan Stambaugh, David Farrell Krell, and Frank A. Capuzzi. San Francisco: Harper, 1987.

Heine, Steven. *Zen Skin, Zen Marrow: Will the Real Zen Buddhism Please Stand Up?* Oxford: Oxford University Press, 2008.
Heisig, James W. *Nothingness and Desire: An East-West Philosophical Antiphony.* Honolulu: University Press of Hawai'i, 2013.
_____. *Philosophers of Nothingness: An Essay on the Kyoto School.* Honolulu: University Press of Hawai'i, 2002.
_____. "Tanabe Hajime's God." *Nanzan Institute for Religion and Culture Bulletin* 38 (2014), 21–42.
Heisig, James W., Thomas P. Kasulis, and John C. Maraldo, editors. *Japanese Philosophy: A Sourcebook.* Honolulu: University Press of Hawai'i, 2011.
Holder, John J., editor. *Early Buddhist Discourses.* Translated by John J. Holder. Indianapolis, IN: Hackett, 2006.
Hubbard, Jaimie, and Paul L. Swanson. *Pruning the Bodhi Tree: The Storm over Critical Buddhism.* Honolulu: University Press of Hawai'i, 1997.
James, William. *The Varieties of Religious Experience* (1902). New York: Modern Library, 2002.
Janaway, Christopher, editor. *Willing and Nothingness: Schopenhauer as Nietzsche's Educator.* Wotton-under-Edge, UK: Clarendon Press, 1998.
Jorgensen, John. *Inventing Hui-neng, the Sixth Patriarch: Hagiography and Biography in Early Ch'an.* Leiden: Brill, 2005.
Kadowaki Kakichi. *Zen and the Bible.* Translated by Joan Rieck. Maryknoll, NY: Orbis, 2002.
Kalmanson, Leah, Frank Garrett, and Sarah Mattice, editors. *Levinas and Asian Thought.* Pittsburgh, PA: Duquesne University Press, 2013.
Kierkegaard, Søren. "A Glance at Danish Literature." In *Concluding Postscript*, Part 2: *Concluding Unscientific Postscript to* Philosophical Fragments, vol. 1. Translated by Howard V. Hong and Edna H. Hong. Princeton, NJ: Princeton University Press, 1992.
Kikumura Norihiko. *Shinran: His Life and Thought.* Los Angles: Nembutsu, 1972.
Kim, Hee-Jin. *Dōgen Kigen: Mystical Realist.* Tucson: University of Arizona Press, 1987.
_____. *Dōgen on Meditation and Thinking: A Reflection on His View of Zen.* Albany: State University of New York Press, 2007.
Klossowski, Pierre. *Nietzsche and the Vicious Circle.* Translated by Daniel Smith. Chicago: University of Chicago Press, 1997.
Kodera, Takashi James. *Dōgen's Formative Years in China: An Historical Study and Annotated Translation of the 'Hōkyō-ki'.* Boulder, CO: Prajñā, 1980.
Kofman, Sarah. *Nietzsche and Metaphor.* Translated by Duncan Large. Stanford, CA: Stanford University Press, 1993.
Kopf, Gereon. *Beyond Personal Identity: Dōgen, Nishida, and a Phenomenology of No-Self.* Richmond, UK: Curzon, 2001.
Krummel, John. *Nishida Kitarō's Chiasmatic Chorology: Place of Dialectic, Dialectic of Place.* Bloomington: Indiana University Press, 2015.
Kundera, Milan. *Testaments Betrayed: An Essay in Nine Parts.* Translated by Linda Asher. New York: HarperCollins, 1995.
Lambert, Gregg. *In Search of a New Image of Thought: Gilles Deleuze and Philosophical Expressionism.* Minneapolis: University of Minnesota Press, 2012.
Lampert, Laurence. *Nietzsche's Teaching: An Interpretation of* Thus Spoke Zarathustra. New Haven, CT: Yale University Press, 1986.

Leighton, Taigen Dan. *Visions of Awakening Space and Time: Dōgen and the Lotus Sūtra.* Oxford: Oxford University Press, 2007.
Lemm, Vanessa, editor. *Nietzsche and the Becoming of Life.* New York: Fordham University Press, 2015.
Linji Yixuan. *The Record of Linji.* Translated by Ruth Fuller Sasaki. Edited by Thomas Yūhō Kirchner. Honolulu: University Press of Hawai'i, 2009.
———. *The Zen Teachings of Master Lin-Chi.* Translated by Burton Watson. New York: Columbia University Press, 1999.
Lippit, John, and Jim Urpeth, editors. *Nietzsche and the Divine.* Manchester, UK: Clinamen, 2000.
Loori, John Daido. *Teachings of the Earth.* Boston: Shambhala, 2007.
Löwith, Karl. *Nietzsches Philosophie der ewigen Wiederkehr des Gleichen* (1935), 4th proofed ed. based on the corrected 3rd ed. Hamburg: Felix Meiner, 1986.
Loy, David. *Lack and Transcendence.* Amherst, NY: Prometheus, 1996.
Ma Lin, and Jaap van Brakel. *Fundamentals of Comparative and Intercultural Philosophy.* Albany: State University of New York Press, 2016.
Magee, Bryan. *The Philosophy of Schopenhauer*, rev. ed. Clarendon: Oxford University Press, 1998.
Marcuse, Herbert. *One-Dimensional Man.* Boston: Beacon, 1964.
McRae, John R. *Seeing through Zen: Encounter, Transformation, and Genealogy in Chinese Chan Buddhism.* Berkeley: University of California Press, 2003.
McWeeny, Jennifer, and Ashby Butnor, editors. *Asian and Feminist Philosophies in Dialogue: Liberating Traditions.* New York: Columbia University Press, 2014.
Mills, Charles W. *The Racial Contract.* Ithaca, NY: Cornell University Press, 1997.
Mistry, Freny. *Nietzsche and Buddhism: Prolegomenon to a Comparative Study.* Berlin: Walter de Gruyter, 1981.
Mohr, Michel. "Emerging from Nonduality: Kōan Practice in the Rinzai Tradition since Hakuin." In *The Kōan: Texts and Contexts in Zen Buddhism.* Edited by Steven Heine and Dale S. Wright, 244–279. Oxford: Oxford University Press, 2000.
Moore, Gregory. *Nietzsche, Biology and Metaphor.* New York: Cambridge University Press, 2002.
Moore, Gregory, and Thomas H. Brobjer, editors. *Nietzsche and Science.* Burlington, VT: Ashgate, 2004.
Morrison, Robert G. *Nietzsche and Buddhism: A Study in Nihilism and Ironic Affinities.* Oxford: Oxford University Press, 1997.
———. "Nietzsche and Nirvana." In *"Nietzsche and the Gods.* Edited by Weaver Santaniello, 87–113. Albany: State University of New York Press, 2001.
Nāgārjuna. *Nāgārjuna's Middle Way [Mūlamadhyamakakārikā].* Translated and edited by Mark Siderits and Shōryū Katsura. Boston: Wisdom, 2013.
Nagatomo Shigenori. "The Logic of the *Diamond Sutra*: A is not A, Therefore A." *Asian Philosophy: An International Journal of the Philosophical Traditions of the East* 10.3 (2000), 213–244.
Nancy, Jean-Luc. *Being Singular Plural.* Translated by Robert D. Richardson and Anne E. O'Byrne. Stanford, CA: Stanford University Press, 2000.
Nelson, Eric S. *Chinese and Buddhist Philosophy in Early Twentieth-Century German Thought.* London: Bloomsbury, 2017.

Nichols, Moira. "The Influences of Eastern Thought on Schopenhauer's Doctrine of the Thing-in-Itself." In *The Cambridge Companion to Schopenhauer*. Edited by Christopher Janaway, 171–212. Cambridge: Cambridge University Press, 1999.

Nietzsche, Friedrich, *Kritische Gesamtausgabe*. Edited by Giorgio Colli and Mazzino Montinari. Berlin: Walter de Gruyter, 1967–.

———. *On the Genealogy of Morality* (1887). Translated by Maudemarie Clark and Alan J. Swensen. Indianapolis, IN: Hackett, 1998.

———. *Sämtliche Briefe: Kritische Studienausgabe in 8 Bänden*. Edited by Giorgio Colli and Mazzino Montinari. Munich: Deutscher Taschenbuch, 1986.

———. *Sämtliche Werke: Kritische Studienausgabe in 15 Einzelbänden*. Edited by Giorgio Colli and Mazzino Montinari. Munich: Deutscher Taschenbuch, 1988.

———. *Thus Spoke Zarathustra: A Book for Everyone and Nobody*. Translated by Graham Parkes. Oxford: Oxford University Press, 2005.

———. *Werke in drei Bänden* (the so-called *Schlechta-Ausgabe*). Edited by Karl Schlechta. Munich: Hanser, 1959.

Nishida, Kitarō. *Art and Morality* (1923). Translated by David Dilworth and Valdo Viglielmo. Honolulu: University Press of Hawai'i, 1973.

———. *An Inquiry into the Good* (1911). Translated by Masao Abe and Christopher Ives. New Haven, CT: Yale University Press, 1990.

———. *Intelligibility and the Philosophy of Nothingness: Three Philosophical Essays*. Translated by Robert Schinzinger. Honolulu: East-West Center, 1966.

———. *Last Writings: Nothingness and the Religious Worldview* (1945). Translated by David Dilworth. Honolulu: University Press of Hawai'i, 1987.

Nishitani Keiji. "Emptiness and Sameness." In *Modern Japanese Aesthetics: A Reader*. Translated and edited by Michele Marra. Honolulu: University Press of Hawai'i, 1999.

———. "The I-Thou Relation in Zen Buddhism." Translated by N. A. Waddell. In *The Buddha Eye: An Anthology of the Kyoto School*. New York: Crossroad, 1982.

———. *Nishida Kitarō*. Translated by Yamamoto Seisaku and James W. Heisig. Berkeley: University of California Press, 1991.

———. *On Buddhism* (1982). Translated by Yamamoto Seisaku and Robert E. Carter. Albany: State University of New York Press, 2006.

———. *Religion and Nothingness*. Translated by Jan van Bragt. Berkeley: University of California Press, 1982.

———. *The Self-Overcoming of Nihilism*. Translated by Graham Parkes and Aihara Setsuko. Albany: State University of New York Press, 1990.

———. "The Standpoint of Zen." Translated by John C. Maraldo. *Eastern Buddhist* 18.1 (1984), 1–26.

Ōhashi Ryōsuke. *Japan im interkulturellen Dialog*. Munich: Iudicium, 1999.

Ōkōchi Ryōgi. "Nietzsches *Amor Fati* im Lichte von Karma des Buddhismus." *Nietzsche-Studien* 1 (1972), 36–94.

Okumura Shōhaku. *Realizing Genjōkōan: The Key to Dōgen's Shōbōgenzō*. Boston: Wisdom, 2010.

Oldenberg, Hermann. *Buddha: His Life, His Doctrine, His Order*. Translated by William Hoey. London: Williams and Norgate, 1882.

Ozaki Makoto. *Individuum, Society, Humankind: The Triadic Logic of Species according to Hajime Tanabe*. Leiden: Brill, 2001.

———. *Introduction to the Philosophy of Tanabe: According to the English Translation of the Seventh Chapter of the* Demonstratio of Christianity. Amsterdam: Rodopi, 1990.

Panagopoulos, Nic. *The Fiction of Joseph Conrad: The Influence of Schopenhauer and Nietzsche*. Frankfurt am Main: Peter Lang, 1998.

Panaïoti, Antoine. *Nietzsche and Buddhist Philosophy*. Cambridge: Cambridge University Press, 2013.

Park, Jin Y. *Buddhism and Postmodernity: Zen, Huayan, and the Possibility of Buddhist Postmodern Ethics*. Lanham, MD: Lexington Books, 2010.

Parkes, Graham. "Body-Mind and Buddha-Nature: Dōgen's Deeper Ecology." In *Frontiers of Japanese Philosophy 7: Classical Japanese Philosophy*. Edited by James W. Heisig and Rein Raud, 122–147. Nagoya, Japan: Nanzan Institute for Religion and Culture, 2010.

———. *Composing the Soul: Reaches of Nietzsche's Psychology*. Chicago: University of Chicago Press, 1994.

———. "The Early Reception of Nietzsche's Philosophy in Japan." In *Nietzsche and Asian Thought*. Edited by Graham Parkes, 177-199. Chicago: University of Chicago Press, 1991.

———. "Kukai and Dōgen as Exemplars of Ecological Engagement." *Journal of Japanese Philosophy* 1 (2013), 85–110.

———. "Mountain Brushes, Ink of Oceans: Nature as Sacred in Japanese Buddhism." In *Wandel zwischen den Welten*. Edited by H. Eisenhofer-Salim, 557–574. Frankfurt: Peter Lang, 2003.

———. "Nature and the Human 'Redivinized': Mahāyāna Buddhist Themes in *Thus Spoke Zarathustra*." In *Nietzsche and the Divine*. Edited by John Lippitt and Jim Urpeth, 181–199. Manchester, UK: Clinamen, 2000.

———. "Nietzsche and East Asian Thought: Influences, Impacts, and Resonances." In *The Cambridge Companion to Nietzsche*. Edited by Bernd Magnus and Kathleen M. Higgens, 356–383. Cambridge: Cambridge University Press, 1996.

———. "Nietzsche and Zen Master Hakuin on the Roles of Emotion and Passion." In *Nietzsche and the Gods*. Edited by Weaver Santaniello, 115–134. Albany: State University of New York Press, 2001.

———. "Nietzsche, Panpsychism and Pure Experience: An East-Asian Contemplative Perspective." In *Nietzsche and Phenomenology*. Edited by Andrea Rehberg, 87–100. Newcastle upon Tyne: Cambridge Scholars, 2011.

———. "Open Letter to Bret Davis: Letter on Egoism: Will to Power as Interpretation." *Journal of Nietzsche Studies* 46.1 (Spring 2015), 42–61.

———. "Reply to Bret Davis: Zarathustra and Asian Thought: A Few Final Words." *Journal of Nietzsche Studies* 46.1 (Spring 2015), 82–88.

———. "Savoring Tastes: Appreciating Food in Japan." In *New Essays in Japanese Aesthetics*. Edited by A. Minh Nguyen, 109–119. Lanham, MD: Lexington, 2018.

———, editor. *Nietzsche and Asian Thought*. Chicago: University of Chicago Press, 1991.

Pawelski, James O. *The Dynamic Individualism of William James*. Albany: State University of New York Press, 2007.

Pendell, Dale. *Pharmako/Dynamis: Stimulating Plants, Potions and Herbcraft*. Berkeley, CA: North Atlantic, 2009.

———. *Pharmako/Gnosis: Plant Teachers and the Poison Path*. Berkeley, CA: North Atlantic Books, 2009.

———. *Pharmako/Poeia: Power Plants, Poisons and Herbcraft*, updated ed. Berkeley, CA: North Atlantic, 2010.

Perry, R. B. *The Thought and Character of William James*, 2 vols. Boston: Little, Brown, 1935.

Pippin, Robert B. *Nietzsche, Psychology, and First Philosophy*. Chicago: University of Chicago Press, 2010.
Pollan, Michael. *The Omnivore's Dilemma: A Natural History of Four Meals*. New York: Penguin, 2006.
Pollard, David. *Nietzsche's Footfalls: A Triptych*. East Sussex, UK: Geraldson, 2001.
Regehly, Thomas. "Schopenhauer, Buddha and Kamadamana: The Problem of Suffering and Redemption in Thomas Mann's Novel 'The Transposed Heads.'" In *Schopenhauer and Indian Philosophy: A Dialogue between India and Germany*. Edited by Arati Barua. New Delhi, India: Northern Book Centre, 2008.
Richie, Donald. *Ozu: His Life and Films*. Berkeley: University of California Press, 1974.
Roberts, Tyler T. *Contesting Spirit: Nietzsche, Affirmation, Religion*. Princeton, NJ: Princeton University Press, 1998.
Ryōkan (Yamamoto Eizō). "Reading the *Record of Eihei Dōgen*." Translated by Taigen Daniel Leighton and Kazuaki Tanahashi, *Moon in a Dewdrop: Writings of Zen Master Dōgen*. Edited by Kazuaki Tanahashi. Berkeley, CA: North Point, 1985.
Safranski, Rüdiger. *Schopenhauer and the Wild Years of Philosophy*. Translated by Ewald Osers. Cambridge, MA: Harvard University Press, 1989.
Sallis, John. *Chorology: On Beginning in Plato's Timaeus*. Bloomington: Indiana University Press, 1999.
_____. *Force of Imagination: The Sense of the Elemental*. Bloomington: Indiana University Press, 2000.
_____. *Logic of Imagination: The Expanse of the Elemental*. Bloomington: Indiana University Press, 2012.
_____. *Transfigurements: On the True Sense of Art*. Chicago: University of Chicago Press, 2008.
Schelling, F. W. J. *Clara: Or on the Relationship between Nature and the Spirit World*. Translated by Fiona Steinkamp. Albany: State University of New York Press, 2002.
_____. *The Grounding of Positive Philosophy*. Translated by Bruce Matthews. Albany: State University of New York Press, 2007.
_____. *Philosophische Untersuchungen über das Wesen der menschlichen Freiheit und die damit zusammenhängenden Gegenstände* (1809). Edited by Thomas Buchheim. Hamburg: Felix Meiner Verlag, 1997. *Philosophical Investigations into the Essence of Human Freedom* (1809). Translated by Jeff Love and Johannes Schmidt. Albany: State University of New York Press, 2006.
Schirmacher, Wolfgang. "Living Disaster: Schopenhauer for the Twenty-first Century." In *The Essential Schopenhauer*. Edited by Wolfgang Schirmacher. New York: Harper, 2010.
Schmidt, Isaac Jacob. *Über das Mahâjâna und Pradschnâ-Pâramita der Bauddhen*, vol. 4. Saint Petersburg: Mémoires de l'Académie impériale des sciences de St. Pétersbourg, 1836,
Schopenhauer, Arthur. *Arthur Schopenhauers Sämmtliche Werke*, 2nd ed. Edited by Julius Frauenstädt. Leipzig: Brockhaus, 1891.
_____. *Grundlage der Moral*. In *Arthur Schopenhauers Sämmtliche Werke*, 2nd ed. Edited by Julius Frauenstädt. Leipzig: Brockhaus, 1891, vol. 4. "On the Basis of Morals." In *The Two Fundamental Problems of Ethics*. Translated by David E. Cartwright and Edward E. Erdmann. Oxford: Oxford University Press, 2010.
_____. *The Two Fundamental Problems of Ethics*. Translated by David E. Cartwright and Edward E. Erdmann. Oxford: Oxford University Press, 2010.

———. *The World as Will and Representation*, 2 vols. Translated by E. F. J. Payne. Indian Hills, CO: Falcon's Wing, 1958.
Schrader, Paul. *Transcendental Style in Film: Ozu, Bresson, Dreyer*. New York: Da Capo, 1988.
Schrift, Alan D. *Nietzsche's French Legacy: A Genealogy of Poststructuralism*. New York: Routledge, 1995.
Schroeder, Brian. "Dancing through Nothing: Nietzsche, the Kyoto School, and Transcendence." *Journal of Nietzsche Studies* 37 (Spring 2009), 44–65.
———. "The Dilemma of Dōgen." In *Asian Texts–Asian Contexts: Encounters with Asian Philosophies and Religions*. Edited by David Jones and E. R. Klein, 133–143. Albany: State University of New York Press, 2010.
Schroeder, John W. *Skillful Means: The Heart of Buddhist Compassion*. Honolulu: University Press of Hawai'i, 2001.
Scott, Jacqueline, and A. Todd Franklin, editors. *Critical Affinities: Nietzsche and African American Thought*. Albany: State University of New York Press, 2006.
Scripture of the Lotus Blossom of the Fine Dharma [*Saddharmapuṇḍarīka Sūtra*]. Translated by Leon Hurvitz. New York: Columbia University Press, 1976.
Sharf, Robert H. "The Rhetoric of Experience and the Study of Religion." *Journal of Consciousness Studies* 7.11–12 (2000), 267–287.
Shinran. *Tannishō (A Record in Lament of Divergences)*. In *The Collected Works of Shinran*. Translated by Dennis Hirota, Hisao Inagaki, Michio Tokunaga, and Ryushin Uryuzu. Kyoto: Jōdo Shinshū Hongwanji-ha, 1997.
Singer, Peter, and Jim Mason. *The Way We Eat: Why Our Food Choices Matter*. Emmaus, PA: Rodale, 2006.
Skowron, Michael. *Nietzsche, Buddha, Zarathustra: Eine West-Ost Konfiguration*. Daegu, South Korea: Kyungpook National University Press, 2006.
Snyder, Gary. *Earth House Hold: Technical Notes and Queries to Fellow Dharma Revolutionaries*. New York: New Directions, 1969.
———. "Mountains Hidden in Mountains: Dōgen-zenji and the Mind of Ecology." In *Dōgen Zen and Its Relevance for Our Time*. Edited by Shōhaku Okumura. San Francisco: Sōtō Zen Buddhism International Center, 2003.
Stambaugh, Joan. *Impermanence Is Buddha-Nature: Dōgen's Understanding of Temporality*. Honolulu: University Press of Hawai'i, 1990.
———. *The Other Nietzsche*. Albany: State University of New York Press, 1994.
Suzuki, Daisetz T. "The Role of Nature in Zen Buddhism" (1953). In *Studies in Zen*. London: Rider, 1955.
Tan, Joan Qionglin. *Han Shan, Chan Buddhism and Gary Snyder's Ecopoetic Way*. Eastbourne, UK: Sussex Academic, 2009.
Tanabe Hajime. "Kant's Theory of Freedom." Translated by Takeshi Morisato with Cody Staton. In Takeshi Morisato and Cody Staton. "An Essay on Kant's Theory of Freedom from the Early Works of Tanabe Hajime." *Comparative and Continental Philosophy* 5.2 (November 2013), 150–156.
———. "The Logic of the Species as Dialectics." Translated by David Dilworth and Taira Sato. *Monumenta Nipponica* 24.3 (1969), 273–288.
———. "On the Universal." Translated by Takeshi Morisato with Timothy Burns. In Takeshi Morisato and Timothy Burns. "Groundwork for the Metaphysics of Deductive Reasoning: The Relation of the Universal and the Particular in Early Works of Tanabe Hajime." *Comparative and Continental Philosophy* 5.2 (November 2013), 124–149.

———. *Philosophy as Metanoetics*. Translated by Takeuchi Yoshinori, Valdo Viglielmo, and James W. Heisig. Berkeley: University of California Press, 1987.

Thompson, Evan. *Waking, Dreaming, Being: Self and Consciousness in Neuroscience, Meditation, and Philosophy*. New York: Columbia University Press, 2015.

Tuck, Andrew. *Comparative Philosophy and the Philosophy of Scholarship*. Oxford: Oxford University Press, 1990.

Ueda Shizuteru. *Die Gottesgeburt in der Seele und der Durchbruch zu Gott. Die mystische Anthropologie Meister Eckharts und ihre Konfrontation mit der Mystik des Zen Buddhismus*. Gütersloh: Gütersloher Verlagshaus Gerd Mohn, 1965.

———. *Wer und Was bin ich: Zur Phänomenologie des Selbst im Zen-Buddhismus*. Freiburg: Karl Alber, 2011.

Unno Taitetsu. *River of Fire, River of Water: An Introduction to the Pure Land Tradition of Shin Buddhism*. New York: Doubleday, 1998.

Unno Taitetsu, and James W. Heisig, editors. *The Religious Philosophy of Tanabe Hajime: The Metanoetic Imperative*. Berkeley, CA: Asian Humanities, 1990.

Valgenti, Robert T. "Nietzsche and Food." In *Encyclopedia of Food and Agricultural Ethics*. Edited by P. B. Thompson and D. M. Kaplan, 1440–1446. Dordrecht: Springer, 2014.

Van der Braak, André. "Nietzsche and Japanese Buddhism on the Cultivation of the Body: To What Extent Does Truth Bear Incorporation?" *Comparative and Continental Philosophy* 1.2 (Autumn 2009), 223–251.

———. *Nietzsche and Zen: Self-Overcoming without a Self*. Lanham, MD: Lexington, 2011.

———. "Zen and Zarathustra: Self-Overcoming without a Self." *Journal of Nietzsche Studies* 46.1 (Spring 2015), 2–11.

Verrecchia, Anacleto. *La catastrofe di Nietzsche a Torino*. Turin, Italy: G. Einaudi, 1978.

Victoria, Brian Daizen. *Zen at War*. New York: Weatherhill, 1997.

———. *Zen War Stories*. London: Routledge Curzon, 2003.

The Vimalakīrti Sūtra. Translated by Burton Watson. New York: Columbia University Press, 1997.

Wang, Robin. *Yinyang: The Way of Heaven and Earth in Chinese Thought and Culture*. Cambridge: Cambridge University Press, 2012.

Wargo, Robert. *The Logic of Nothingness: An Essay on Nishida Kitarō*. Honolulu: University Press of Hawai'i, 2005.

Warner, Jisho, Shōhaku Okumura, John McRae, and Taigen Daniel Leighton, editors. *Nothing Is Hidden: Essays on Zen Master Dōgen's Instructions for the Cook*. New York: Weatherhill, 2001.

Weineck, Silke-Maria. "Digesting the Nineteenth Century: Nietzsche and the Stomach of Modernity." *Romanticism* 12.1 (2006), 35–43.

Wirth, Jason M. *Commiserating with Devastated Things: Milan Kundera and the Entitlements of Thinking*. New York: Fordham University Press, 2016.

———. *The Conspiracy of Life: Meditations on Schelling and His Time*. Albany: State University of New York Press, 2003.

———. "Dōgen and the Unknown Knowns: The Practice of the Wild after the End of Nature." *Environmental Philosophy* 10.1 (Spring 2013), 39–62.

———. *Mountains, Rivers, and the Great Earth: Reading Gary Snyder and Dōgen in an Age of Ecological Crisis*. Albany: State University of New York Press, 2017.

———. "Never Paint What Cannot Be Painted: Master Dōgen and the Zen of the Brush." *Diaphany: A Journal and Nocturne*, vol. 1, edited by Aaron Cheak, Sabrina dalla Valle, and Jennifer Zahrt, 38–65. Auckland: Rubedo, 2015.
———. "On Not Disturbing Still Water: Ozu Yasujirō and the Technical-Aesthetic Product." In *New Essays in Japanese Aesthetics*. Edited by A. Minh Nguyen, 353–365. Lanham, MD: Lexington, 2018.
———. "One Bright Pearl: On Japanese Aesthetic Expressivity." In *The Movement of Nothingness: Trust in the Emptiness of Time*. Edited by Daniel Price and Ryan Johnson, 21–36. Aurora, CO: Davies Group, 2013.
———. "Painting Mountains and Rivers: Gary Snyder, Dōgen, and the Elemental Sūtra of the Wild." *Research in Phenomenology* 44 (2014), 240–261.
———. *Schelling's Practice of the Wild: Time, Art, Imagination*. Albany: State University of New York Press, 2015.
———. "When Washing Rice, Know that the Water Is Your Own Life: An Essay on Dōgen in the Age of Fast Food." In *Ontologies of Nature: Continental Perspectives and Environmental Reorientations*. Edited by Gerard Kuperus and Marjolein Oele, 235–244. Cham, Switzerland: Springer, 2017.
Wirth, Jason M., with Patrick Burke, editors. *Merleau-Ponty, Schelling, and the Question of Nature*. Albany: State University of New York Press, 2013.
Wirth, Jason M., Brian Schroeder, and Bret Davis, editors. *Engaging Dōgen's Zen: The Philosophy of Practice as Awakening (Commentaries on Dōgen's "Shushōgi" and "Fukanzazengi")*. Boston: Wisdom, 2016.
Wright, Dale S. *Philosophical Meditations on Zen Buddhism*. Cambridge: Cambridge University Press, 1998.
Yamada Shōji. *Shots in the Dark: Japan, Zen, and the West*. Chicago: University of Chicago Press, 2009.
Yampolsky, Philip B. "Introduction." In *The Zen Master Hakuin: Selected Writings*, 1–21. New York: Columbia University Press, 1971.
Yoshida Kiju, *Ozu's Anti-Cinema*. Translated by Daisuke Miyao and Kyoko Hirano. Ann Arbor: University of Michigan Press, 2003.
Yoshizawa Katsuhiro. *The Religious Art of Zen Master Hakuin*. Berkeley, CA: Counterpoint, 2010.
Young, Julian. *Friedrich Nietzsche: A Philosophical Biography*. Cambridge: Cambridge University Press, 2010.
Yusa Michiko. *Zen and Philosophy: An Intellectual Biography of Nishida Kitarō*. Honolulu: University Press of Hawai'i, 2002.
Zhuangzi. *The Essential Chuang Tzu*. Translated by Sam Hamill and J. P. Seaton. Boston: Shambhala, 1998.
Ziporyn, Brook. "Omnidesire as the Ending of Desire: *Zarathustra*, Mahāyāna Buddhism, Tiantai." *Journal of Nietzsche Studies* 46.1 (Spring 2015), 25–41.

INDEX

Ahaṃkāra, 40, 45
anātman, see no-self
Anesaki Masaharu, 29
Anaximander, 7
Aristotle, xxvii

Bataille, Georges, 28, 41
Bazzano, Manu, xxii, xxxin12, 11n3, 22, 29
Bhagavad Gītā, 39–40, 45. See also *ahaṃkāra*
Bhūmisparśa mudrā, 7–8
Blake, William, 66–67, 100; *Jerusalem*, 66–67
Buddha Dharma, xv, xvii, xix–xxii, xxiv–xxvi, xviii, xxxn2, 2, 5–8, 10, 15–16, 30–31, 33–34n19, 50, 52, 72n4, 76–78, 80, 86–88, 90, 92–93, 95, 103–110
Burik, Steven, xxv
Bush, George W., 37

Canguilhem, Georges, 45–46; *The Normal and the Pathological*, 45–46
Christianity, xxiv, 7, 15–16, 20, 23–27, 33n19, 83, 109; *agapē*, 20; Nietzsche's critique of, 23–27, 83, 109. See also religion
Comparative philosophy, *see* philosophy after comparative philosophy
Compassion, 16, 20–22, 24–27, 49, 67, 71, 109–110
Confucius, xvii–xviii
Conrad, Joseph, 16; *The Heart of Darkness*, 16
convalescence, 35, 41–42, 51, 97
Cornaro, Luigi, 81, 91
Critical Buddhism, xx–xxi, 108–109. See also Hakamaya Noriaki

Danto, Arthur, 14
Darwin, Charles, 28
Davis, Bret W., 3–5, 12n8, 29, 73n16
Death of God, The, 25, 27, 29, 35, 39, 82–83
Décadence, 23, 25, 27–28. See also Nietzsche, Friedrich

Deleuze, Gilles, xxiiii–xxiv, xxvi, xxix, 7, 9–10, 47–48, 69–70, 72, 74n18, 78–79, 87, 91–97, 98n18, 98n21, 99n27, 100; *Cinema 1: The Movement-Image*, 98n18; *Cinema 2: The Time-Image*, 92–97; dark precursor, 70; *Difference and Repetition*, xxix, 70, 74n18, 100; *Nietzsche and Philosophy*, 7, 9–10, 47–48, 69. See also Deleuze, Gilles, and Félix Guattari; image of thought; planomenal
Deleuze, Gilles, and Félix Guattari, xxiii, xxvi, 77–78, 87, 91–92, 99n27; *A Thousand Plateaus*, 78, 92; *What is Philosophy?*, xxiii, xxvi, 77–78, 87, 91–92, 99n27. See also Deleuze, Gilles; image of thought; plane of immanence; planomenal
Deshan Xuanjian (Jp. Tokusan Senkan), xx
Dharma eye, xvi, xviii, xxi–xxiii, 77–79, 84, 88, 90–93, 95, 101. See also Dōgen
Diamond Sūtra, xx, 10, 21, 72–73n4
digestion, xxv, xxx, 9, 32, 42, 75, 82–83, 91–92. See also dyspepsia, food; Nietzsche, Friedrich; nutrition; rumination
Dionysus, 28
Dōgen Eihei, xvi, xviii–xxii, xxiv–xxvi, 5–6, 8–9, 12n15, 13, 18, 29–30, 60, 65, 73n5, 75–80, 85–92, 95–96, 98–99n26, 103, 105–106, 110; *Bendōwa*, xviii, 12n15, 86; *dōtoku* (communication), 6; *Eihei Kōroku*, 76; *Eihei Shingi* (*The Record of Zen Pure Monastic Standards*), 80, 87, 91; *Ikka Myōju* (*One Bright Pearl*), 5–6; *Fukanzazengi*, 60, 86; *Fushukuhanpō* (*The Dharma for Taking Food*), 91; *Genjō Kōan*, 18; *Kankin* (*Reading a Sūtra*), xxii; *Keisei Sanshoku* (*Valley Sounds, Mountains Colors*), xix–xx; the oneness of practice-realization (*shushō-ittō*), xx, 29; *Sansuikyō* (*Mountains and Waters Sūtra*), 79; 98n25; Senika Heresy, The, 9, 12n15;

127

Dōgen Eihei (*cont.*)
  shikantaza (just sitting), 86–87, 90–91;
  Shin Fukatoku (*Ungraspable Mind*, first
  version), xx; *shinjin datsuraku* (falling and
  casting away of body and mind), 8, 30, 78;
  Shōbōgenzō (*Treasury of the True Dharma
  Eye*), xvi, xviii–xx, xxv, 5–6, 65, 77, 92, 95,
  98n24; *Shōji* (*Birth and Death*), 65; *Tenzo
  Kyōkun* (*Instructions to the Tenzo*), 80,
  87–91, 98n14; 98–99n26; *Uji* (*Time Being*),
  xxv, 79
Dostoyevsky, Fyodor, 63–64; *The Brothers
  Karamazov*, 63–64
duḥkha, *see* Four Noble Truths
dyspepsia, xxx, 32, 82–83, 97n9. *See also*
  digestion, food; Nietzsche, Friedrich;
  nutrition; rumination

egoism, 4–10, 20, 29, 38–40, 49–50, 60–63,
  65, 68, 71, 88, 106. *See also ahaṃkāra*;
  egolessness
egolessness, 24–25, 72. *See also ahaṃkāra*;
  egoism
Ekayāna, 105–106, 108
Elman, Benjamin A., 33n19
emptiness (*śūnyatā*), xviii, xxvi, 4, 14, 26,
  29–32, 48–49, 67, 73n12, 79, 96, 109–110;
  emptiness sickness (Jp. *kūbyō*), xxvi, 14,
  26, 29–32, 109–110; field of emptiness
  (Jp. *kū no ba*), 4, 96
eternal return, the, *see* Nietzsche, Friedrich
European Buddhism, *see* Nietzsche
experience, xvi–xvii, xx, xxvi–xxvii, 7,
  30, 35–41,44, 47, 49, 55, 71–72, 81–82; 92,
  100–110; experience of awakening, 30;
  experience of nihilism, 55; experience
  of philosophy as metanoetics, 71–72;
  experience of *śūnyatā*, 49; experience of
  value, 81–82; experience of philosophy
  after comparative philosophy, 92;
  experience of what matters as philosophy,
  xvi; pure experience, xvii, 100–110;
  religious experience, 35–41, 44, 47; Zen
  experience, xx, xxvi, 7, 49

Faure, Bernard, 105
Figl, Johann, 33–34n19

food, xxvi, xxx, 49, 72, 75, 79–92, 96. *See
  also* digestion; dyspepsia; nutrition;
  rumination
Four Noble Truths, The, 17–19, 60, 81;
  duḥkha (suffering; first noble truth) 17–18,
  103; *nirodha* (extinction; third noble
  truth), 19; noble eightfold path (fourth
  noble truth), 19; *tṛṣṇā* (thirst, *Sehnsucht*;
  second noble truth), 18–19. *See also*
  Schopenhauer, Arthur; *Sehnsucht, die*.

Gadamer, Hans-Georg, 46
Gramsci, Antionio, 101–102; *The Prison
  Notebooks*, 101–102
Great Death, The (Jp. *daishi*), 3–4, 30, 64–65,
  67–68, 70, 105. *See also* Hakuin Ekaku
Great Health, The, xxvi, 9–10, 32, 35–36,
  42–48, 51–52, 54n28, 58, 82. *See also*
  Nietzsche, Friedrich

Hakamaya Noriaki, 108
Hakuin Ekaku, xvi, xxi–xxii, xxiv–xxvi,
  13–14, 26, 28–31, 35, 48–52, 53n21, 68,
  73n5, 88, 109–110; *Dokugo shingyō* (*Poison
  Words for the Heartpiece*), 48–50; Great
  Death, The, 3–4, 30, 64–65, 67–68, 70, 105;
  "Letter to a Sick Monk Living Far Away,"
  51–52; on emptiness sickness (Jp. *kūbyō*),
  xxvi, 14, 26, 29–32, 109–110; on poison,
  48–52, 53n21; solid frozen all sameness
  of the *Tathātā*, 88; *Tale of How I Spurred
  Myself on in My Childhood, The*, 30–31;
  Wild Ivy, 31, 50; *Yasenkanna* (*Idle Talk on
  a Night Boat*), 31
health, xxv–xxvi, 9–10, 12n14, 32, 35–38,
  41–54, 54n28, 58, 80–83, 85; healthy
  mindedness, 35–37, 41. *See also* Great
  Health, The; sickness
Heart of Darkness, The, *see* Conrad, Joseph
Heart Sūtra, 19, 48–50
Hegel, GWF, 58, 62–63, 66, 70, 92, 102
Heidegger, Martin, xxv, 2–4, 6, 25, 56, 72n2,
  95
Heine, Stephen, xx–xxi, 107
honganbokori (arrogance of the primal vow),
  59–62, 65, 68–70. *See also* Shinran; Tanabe
  Hajime

How to Cook Your Life, 85, 98n14
Huineng, 2, 5, 10–11

image of thought, the, 77–78. See also Deleuze, Gilles; Deleuze, Gilles, and Félix Guattari

James, William, xxiv, xxvi, 36–41 43–48, 56; once-born, 37–38; religion, 38–41, 43–44; sick soul, 35, 39–41, 43–45; twice-born, 37–38, 41, 56; *The Varieties of Religious Experience*, 36–41, 43–48. See also health; religion; sickness
jiriki (self-power), 59–60, 62, 67–68, 70, 72n4. See also *tariki* (other-power)
justice, 7, 20, 22

Kadowaki Kakichi, 64
Kant, Immanuel, 19–20, 83, 102
karma, 59–60, 69, 106–107
Kaufmann, Walter, 13–14
Kenshō, 29–30, 50
Kierkegaard, Søren, 39–40, 62; *Concluding Unscientific Postscript to Philosophical Fragments*, 49; despair, 39; *Fear and Trembling*, 40; knight of faith, the, 40
Kleśas, the, 18, 50, 59–60
Knight of faith, the, *see* Kierkegaard, Søren
Kurosawa, Akira, 92–93; *Ikiru*, 92–93; *Seven Samurai, The*, 92

Lalitavistara Sūtra, 8
Linji Yixuan (Jp. Rinzai Gigen), xxviii–xxix
loneliness, 22, 38–39. See also solitude
Lotus Sūtra, The, 65–66, 104–105, 110
Löwith, Karl, 44–45

medicine, 9, 17 31, 43–48, 51, 53n11, 80, 106, 109; Āyurvedic medicine, 17; philosophy as medicine, 43–48
Meister Eckhart, xxiv, 32n3
metanoēsis (*zangedō*), xxvi, 62–65, 67–69; as the eternal return, 68–69; as the solution to the problem of passage, 68–69, *soku* circulation of *metanoēsis*, 67. See also Tanabe Hajime
mettā (loving-kindness), 20, 110

Mills, Charles, 102–103
The Racial Contract, 102–103
mu, 93

Nāgārjuna, xxviii, 31–32, 65–66, 109
Nembutsu, 59–60. See also Shinran
Nichols, Moira, 32–33n6
Nietzsche, Friedrich, xv–xviii, xxii, xxiv–xxvi, xxx, 1–11, 11–12n7, 12n14, 13–14, 20–29, 32, 33–34n19, 35, 38–39, 41–48, 51–52, 55–59, 61–63, 68–72, 73n9, 73n16, 75, 79–83, 86, 96–97, 107, 109–110; affirmation, 3–4, 23, 44, 68–70, 83; *Antichrist, The*, 24–26, 28; *Beyond Good and Evil*, 4, 8; critique of Christianity, 23–27, 83, 109; critique of Schopenhauer, xxvi, 9–10, 21–29, 33–34n19, 39, 83, 109–110; *Ecce Homo*, 8–9, 80–83; eternal return, the, 8, 43, 68–70; European Buddhism, xv, xxvi, 25, 27, 83, 109; food, 79–83; *Gay Science, The*, 1, 24, 42–43, 75, 80, 107; *Genealogy of Morality, The*, 9, 25, 27, 43; *Human, All Too Human*, 97n9; laughter, 1–2, 107; *Nachlaß*, 4, 46–47, 72n3, 83; Nishitani on, 55–57; *ressentiment*, 7, 14, 20, 24, 69; *Schopenhauer as Educator*, 22–23; Tanabe on, xxvi, 57–59, 62–63, 68–71, 73n16; *Thus Spoke Zarathustra*, 2–4, 8–11, 12n14, 14, 26–27, 32, 57–58, 62, 68–70, 73n9, 109–110; truth, 1, 11, 82; *Twilight of the Idols*, 23–28, 81; Wagner, 80–81; will to power, the, 3–7, 9–11, 23–24, 28, 43, 73n16, 83
nihilism, xxvi, 3, 9, 14–16, 25, 27–29, 31–32, 33–34n 19, 36, 39, 49, 55–57, 72n3, 82, 91, 109; active nihilism, 47, 57, 72n3, 82; nihilism in Zen practice, 14, 29, 31–32; nihilism of *kūbyō*, 29, 31–32, 109; passive nihilism, xxvi, 16, 47, 72n3; reactive nihilism, 14, 16, 39; will to nihilism, 9, 16
Nishida Kitarō, xvii, 52n6, 56–58, 66, 72n4, 78, 100–101, 106, 108; pure experience (*junsui keiken*), xvii, 52n6, 100–101, 108
Nishitani Keiji, xv, 3–4, 11n3, 12n8, 14, 55–57, 73n12, 88, 96, 108, 111n12; field of emptiness (Jp. *kū no ba*), 4, 96; problem of nihilism, 55–57; *Religion and Nothingness*, 73n12; *Self-Overcoming of Nihilism*, 55–57

no-self (*anātman*), 3–4, 29
nutrition, xxv, xxx, 80–82. *See also* digestion; dyspepsia; food; rumination

Oldenberg, Hermann, 26–27
omnivore's dilemma, the, 85. *See also* Pollan, Michael
optimism, 19, 36–37, 42; George W. Bush as optimist, 37
original face, xix, 29, 70–71
Ox Herding Poems, 11
Ozu Yasujirō, 92–96; *Tokyo Story*, 92–96

Panaïoti, Antoine, 33n19
Parkes, Graham, 4–5, 11n3, 14, 29, 51, 73n16, 90
Pendell, Dale, 53n21
philosophy after comparative philosophy, xxii, xxv–xxx, 52, 59, 71–72, 83–84, 92, 100–111
plane of immanence, 77–79, 87, 91–92, 96, 99n27. *See also* Deleuze, Gilles, and Félix Guattari; planomenon
planomenon, xxvi, 77, 87, 92, 94, 96. *See also*: Deleuze, Gilles, and Félix Guattari; plane of immanence
Plato's Cave, 85, 102
poison, xxv, xxx, 9–10, 23, 47–52, 61, 82–83, 91, 109; Poison Path, The, 53n21, 58; Three Poisons, The, 4, 59–60
Pollan, Michael, 85. *See also* omnivore's dilemma, the
prapañca (hypostatization or reification), 31–32, 109. *See also* Nāgārjuna
principium comparationis, xxix
principium individuationis, 21, 24, 109
pure experience (*junsui keiken*), *see* Nishida Kitarō
Pure Land, 50, 58–61, 63, 65, 67–68, 70. *See also* True Pure Land sect (*Jōdo Shinshū*), Shinran

racism, 102–103
religion, 15–16, 23–24, 28, 38–41, 43–44, 72n4, 87, 108; Dionysian religion versus other worldly religion, 28, 87; James on religion, 38–41, 43–44; relationship to nihilism, 23–24; religion without transcendence, 87; Schopenhauer on religion, 15–16, 23, 33n19
ressentiment, *see* Nietzsche, Friedrich
rumination, xxv, xxix–xxx, 9–10, 32, 47, 52, 58, 71, 75, 82–83; metanoetics as rumination, 71. *See also* digestion; dyspepsia; food; Nietzsche, Friedrich; nutrition
Ryōkan Taigu, 75–76, 78–79

Saigyō Hōshi, 78
saṃsāra, 18, 27
satori, 29, 50, 60–61
Schelling, FWJ, 25, 44–46, 64, 66, 70, 73–74n17, 100–101; barbarian principle, 66; intellectual intuition, 100–101; *Philosophical Investigations into the Essence of Human Freedom*, 45, 73–74n4
Schirmacher, Wolfgang, 16
Schmidt, Isaac Jacob, 19
Schopenhauer, Arthur, xxii, xxv–xxvi, 7, 9–10, 14–29, 33–34n19, 39, 49, 80, 83, 109–110; Anaximander as forerunner, 7; and the Four Noble Truths, 17–19; Buddha of Frankfurt, The, xxvi, 15–21, 109–110; compassion (*Mitleidsgefuhl*), 15–16, 20–22, 24–27, 109; could not chew the cud of nothingness, 32; ethics, 19–21, 83; *Grundlage der Moral* (*On the Basis of Morals*), 20–21; *Nachlaß*, 15; "Nachträge zur Lehre vom Leiden der Welt," 17–18; Nietzsche on, xxvi, 9–10, 21–29, 33–34n19, 39, 83, 109–110; *principium individuationis*, 21; religion, 15–16, 23, 33n19; versus Leibniz's theodicy, 18; *Welt als Wille und Vorstellung, Die* (*The World as Will and Representation*), 15–19, 109; will to life, the, 7, 9–10, 16, 18–19, 21, 23–27, 43, 83, 109
Schopenhauerei, die, 23, 25, 28–29, 49
Schrader, Paul, 95, 98–99n26
Schroeder, Brian, 11n3, 29
Schroeder, John, xxii
Sehnsucht, die, 16, 18, 22–23

self-overcoming, 54n28, 57–58, 61–62, 68, 82; *honganbokori* solved by Nietzschean self-overcoming, 68. *See also* Nietzsche, Friedrich; Nishitani Keiji
Sengcan Jianzhi (Jp. Sōzan Kanchi), xvii–xviii
Sharf, Robert, 101, 106–107
shinjin datsuraku, see Dōgen
Shinran, xxiv, xxvi, 58–60, 62, 67, 72n4; *Tannishō*, 59–60. *See also* Pure Land; True Pure Land sect (*Jōdo Shinshū*)
sick soul, *see* James, William
sickness, xxvi, 14, 25–27, 29–32, 37–39, 42–52, 109–110; and ascetic priests, 25; Canguilhem on, 45–46; emptiness sickness (Jp. *kūbyō*), xxvi, 14, 26, 29–32, 109–110; Gadamer on, 46; inability to affirm the death of God, 35; nihilistic sickness, 14, 39, 42; Schelling on, 45–46. See also *décadence*
skillful means, see *upāya*
Snyder, Gary, 8, 89, 108
soku, 66–70, 72n4, 73n12
solitude, 17, 22, 38–41, 44, 56; solitude of singularity, 56. *See also* loneliness
suchness (*tathātā*), 8, 88, 91
Suzuki, Daisetz Teitarō, 72n4, 98–99n26, 106–107
svabhāva ("own-being"), xxiv, xxviii

talking cure, the, 36. *See also* James, William
Tanabe Hajime, xxvi, 52, 57–71, 72n4, 73n16; *gensō*, 67, 70; *ōsō*, 67, 70; on Nietzsche, xxvi, 57–59, 62–63, 68–71, 73n16; *Philosophy as Metanoetics*, 57–71. See also *honganbokori*; *jiriki*; *metanoēsis* (*zangedō*); *tariki*
tariki (Other-power), 59–60, 62, 67–68, 70. See also *jiriki*

True Pure Land sect (*Jōdo Shinshū*), xxiv, xxvi, 52, 58. *See also* Pure Land; Shinran
Trump, Donald, 37

Uchiyama Kōshō, 87–88
upāya (skillful means, J. *hōben*), xxii, 6, 8, 10–11, 65–69, 83, 103–107

Van der Braak, André, 29, 54n28
Vimalakīrti Sūtra (*Vimalakīrti Nirdeśa Sūtra*), 6, 10–11
Varieties of Religious Experience, The, see James, William

Watsuji Tetsurō, 14
wei wu wei (doing without doing), 67,72
Whitman, Walt, 36
will to life, the, *see* Schopenhauer, Arthur
will to power, the, *see* Nietzsche, Friedrich

Xiangyan Zhixian (Jp. Kyōgen Chikan), xix

Yoshida Kiju, 96
Yunmen Wenyan (J. Ummon Bun'en), 94

Zen, xv–xxvi, 1–6, 7, 10–11, 12n9, 14, 16, 26, 28–32, 35, 44, 48–52, 57–60, 64, 73n5, 73n16, 78–81, 85–95, 98–99n26, 100, 103, 105–110; academic or Brain Zen, 49; and the experience of philosophy, xviii–xxi; and the problem of experience, 100–111; and skillful means, xxii; communication, 6; funerary Zen, 5, 12n9; infinite fragrance, 103; *kūbyō*, xxvi, 14, 26, 29–32, 109–110; meaning of, 1–2; rhetoric of immediacy, xxi, 105, 107–108, 110; ruminates the ego, 10; Zen arrow, 78; Zen practice of the *tenzo*, 80, 87–91, 98n14; 98–99n26. *See also* Dōgen Eihei; Hakuin Ekaku
Zhuangzi, 68, 108

JASON M. WIRTH is Professor of Philosophy at Seattle University. His recent books include *Mountains, Rivers and the Great Earth: Reading Gary Snyder and Dōgen in an Age of Ecological Crisis*; *Commiserating with Devastated Things: Milan Kundera and the Entitlements of Thinking*; and *Schelling's Practice of the Wild: Time, Art, Imagination*. With Bret Davis and Brian Schroeder, he edited *Continental and Japanese Philosophy: Comparative Approaches to the Kyoto School* (Indiana University Press).

www.ingramcontent.com/pod-product-compliance
Lightning Source LLC
Chambersburg PA
CBHW030656230426
43665CB00011B/1122